Designer's Guide
to the Internet

DESIGNER'S GUIDE
TO THE INTERNET

by

Rick Albertson,
Jeffrey Fine,
Mike Zender,
et al.

Hayden
Books

ABE 569

Designer's Guide to the Internet

Library of Congress Catalog Number: 95-77731
ISBN: 1-56830-229-0

97 96 95   4 3 2 1

Interpretation of the printing code: the rightmost double-digit number is the year of the book's printing; the rightmost single-digit number is the number of the book's printing. For example, a printing code of 95-1 shows that the first printing of the book occurred in 1995.

The Hayden Books Team

Publisher	David Rogelberg
Editor-in-Chief, Design	Michael Nolan
Development/Copy Editor	Steve Mulder
Technical Reviewer	Stella Gassaway
Marketing Manager	Andy Roth
Publishing Coordinator	Rosemary Lewis
Interior and Cover Design	Zender + Associates
Production	Kim Cofer, Dave Eason, Terri Edwards, Joe Millay, Erika Millen, Beth Rago, Christine Tyner
Indexers	Bront Davis
Composed in	Meta Plus, Bodoni, Univers, and Copperplate Gothic

To Our Readers

Dear Designer,

Thank you on behalf of everyone at Hayden Books for choosing *Designer's Guide to the Internet* to enable you to explore this exciting new online world. As an entirely new medium, the Net brings with it new opportunities for both personal and financial success in design. This book will help you discover the best ways to use the power of the Internet.

We'd love to hear how this book helps you in your design work. Please write and let us know. What you think of this book is important to our ability to better serve you in the future. If you have any comments, no matter how great or small, we'd appreciate you taking the time to send us email or a note by snail mail. Of course, we'd love to hear your book ideas.

Sincerely yours,

Michael J. Nolan
Editor-in-chief, design,
Hayden Books and Adobe Press
You can reach Hayden Books at the following address:

Hayden Books
201 West 103rd Street
Indianapolis, IN 46290
(800) 428-5331 voice
(800) 448-3804 fax

Email addresses:

America Online: Hayden Bks
AppleLink: hayden.books
CompuServe: 76350,3014
Internet: hayden@hayden.com

About the Authors

Rick Albertson

Rick's education includes an undergraduate degree in Radio & Television Production and a Master's Degree in Education, specializing in Instructional Systems Technology. Rick's career in marketing communications began as the Director of Graphics of an advertising agency followed by 15 years with Bell Promotions, a successful sales promotion business. Prior to joining Zender + Associates, Rick sold Bell Promotions and formed Upper Room Communications which for two years provided communications and organizational development consulting to major missionary organizations. Rick's primary role as Interactive Producer at Zender + Associates is in driving entry into the development of new media presentations for its varied clientele.

Rick currently resides in Cincinnati, Ohio, with his wife, Nancy, and their two active, high school-aged sons, David and Andy.

Jeffrey M. Fine

After receiving a B.A. in Economics from the University of Cincinnati, Jeff began his design career in 1978, cofounded a design firm three years later, only to leave in 1984 and join Zender + Associates assuming responsibility for business management and account development. As Managing Partner he instituted many of the operational systems that serve the company yet today.

Jeff's strong foundation in business and strategic marketing has benefited many clients as well as Zender + Associates. These skills helped alert the company early on to the potential of interactive multimedia, electronic publishing, and Internet marketing.

Jeff serves as director on several boards and spends much of his time praising the merits of the Internet. Together with his lovely wife Dana, he lives on top of one of Cincinnati's picturesque hillsides, taking pleasure from their wonderful young daughter Katie.

Mike Zender

Mike is a third-generation designer/typesetter, following in the steps of his father and grandfather. Mike has been the beneficiary of an excellent education, first attending the University of Cincinnati, then completing graduate studies at Yale University under many of this century's best designers. He founded Zender + Associates, Inc., one month after completing school and began part-time teaching one year later. Mike's work and that of the associates in his firm have been published regularly since 1980.

Mike lives in southwestern Ohio with his high school sweetheart and three amazing children. Designing, writing, and teaching are outward expressions of his introspective and thoughtful personality.

John Blair

John is completing his Bachelor of Philosophy from the School of Interdisciplinary Studies at Miami University. His work on multimedia projects for the university eventually led to an interest in the World Wide Web. Before long, he had convinced the right people to let him administrate a cluster of NeXT Workstations, learning the ropes of Unix System Administration and Web programming. He plans to buck the trend of Unix hacks and finish his degree on time, then pursue a Ph.D. in Computer Science.

When he isn't sitting in front of a computer, you can find him riding his mountain bike or juggling.

Table of Contents

Introduction   Change History x

Part I   Getting Started with the Net 2

1   The Internet: What It Is and Why It Matters 6

2   How to Get Connected 16

3   How to Find Information 40

Part II   Getting the Most from the Net 86

4   Connecting to Peers 90

5   Connecting to Clients 114

6   Connecting to Suppliers and Vendors 134

Part III   Helping Clients Use the Net 156

7   Sharing Online: Collaboration 160

8   Telling Online: Public Relations 176

9   Selling Online: Electronic Commerce 194

Part IV   Designing for the Net 218

10   Shifting Paradigms for a New Medium 222

11   Learning New Tools 234

12   Developing New Skills 260

13   Refining Design Methods 294

14   Web Page Design Case Studies 318

Appendix A   Essential Internet Resources 384

Appendix B   HTML for Yoyo 400

Appendix C   Bibliography 408

INTRODUCTION

CHANGE HISTORY

This Internet stuff is amazing! We begrudgingly let technology slip into our offices a few years ago with the desktop publishing revolution, and now it won't stop growing. It's taking over. Since when did any-one ever prove that higher tech, more complex, more sophisticated is better per se? What's wrong with low tech?!

Take paper, for example, the substance computers are supposed to replace. Paper is inexpensive; you can make it in your kitchen; it's inherently beautiful and recyclable. It requires only a little light in order to function effectively. There should be a compelling reason to replace paper with a computer. Computers require a constant flow of electricity, a highly evolved technological infrastructure for their manufacture, and limited environmental parame-ters to even function. You can't make a computer from scratch by yourself, certainly not in your kitchen, and they're not biodegradable. You can't use it without electricity. Further, the Internet, which connects so many computers, is totally dependent upon a complex international network of telecom-munications, microwave towers, satellites, light years of wire and fiber, modems, servers, software and people. If we follow the Internet, where will it take us? Is it really just a lot of wires and silicon, or is it something more?

The Internet is more than new technology—it is a new *medium*. Hypertext dynamics and the enabling abilities of telecommunication are impacting the world in ways that are hard to envision. The sheer collaborative capacity of the Internet, originally designed to help the military and scientific communities form virtual teams to conquer overwhelming problems, is enabling scores of *communities* to interact and attack creative, political, scientific, theoretical and analytical processes.

This new medium is already generating whole new industries to serve it and those who use its goods and services. The information developers, providers, and packagers are becoming crucial cogs that help drive the new world economy, the new culture. What will this kind of communication technology do for us. What will it do *to* us?

We need to design our future.

Any plan for the future begins with getting the past in perspective. When the electronic computer was first invented, it was a crude machine that could do a few simple equations using a "binary" method of computation. It was somewhat interesting, but inauspicious. It was strange and slow. At the time, few people, if any, understood what impact this ugly electrical box that could distinguish between os and 1s might have on their lives.

Computer technology evolved. Not many years passed before computers were able to distinguish larger bodies of os and 1s and do more complex computations. Computers became valuable assets. Large companies, the only ones able to afford a computer, could take vast amounts of data and input, store, organize, sort, broadly index, execute intricate mathematical equations, and generate reports. In short, they reaped benefits.

These mainframe machines were so large and costly that in order to amortize them, companies would normally schedule access so that they could be utilized 24 hours a day. The technology was forbidding and only those specialists with enough training were qualified to work on them. The cost of hardware was daunting, and software programmers were needed to write all the software since software applications were not prevalent—custom programming was the norm, and full-time operators were required to keep them operational. This made computers the exclusive property of big business, government, and academia.

As technology advanced further, computer prices fell and off-the-shelf software applications became available to do almost any task one could imagine. Now employees had a computer in their *own workspace*, even in small companies. This was an amazing revolution. Computers became so prevalent that it was common to see them sit unused much of the day. Yet they kept getting more powerful, faster, and able to handle extremely complex operations by people with little or no computer training.

Computers became, in effect, *brain-extensions*. When you had one in your workspace, you had more data at your fingertips, better recall, and were more organized, more productive, and more effective. Not unexpectedly, computer use continued to grow.

Today, technology has gained a momentum of its own. It continues to evolve and change. Now, not only is your efficiency increased in your workspace because you have a computer, but three even more extraordinary innovations are revolutionizing our lives

The first is CONNECTIVITY. Now, you are not limited by the amount of information in your computer, but have access to all the computers in your organization, because they are all on the same network and "talk" to each other.

The second is PORTABILITY. Transportable laptops, now as powerful as the mainframe behemoths of the past, give us increased effectiveness wherever we want to go.

The third innovation is a network outside your organization, a sprawling international network of computers called THE INTERNET. Our world is evolving toward one complete and total computer network. Your computer, that ugly box counting the os and 1s, now has access to information on computer servers all around the world.

These brain-extensions now have not only the speed and power of the old mainframe systems, the composite of all the information on all the servers, and the portability to be used anywhere, but also the decreased pricing and ease of use so that even children, perhaps especially children, can operate them. So, where are we going? What do more, better, and faster os and 1s mean for our children? Our future?

Where indeed.

Information technology, this brain-extension, has changed our past. It will certainly mold our future. Graphic designers are information gatekeepers. Through our professional activity we use and promote information technology, and through its use enhance its impact on our society, for better or worse. We are the willing accomplices of the Information Age. We will share responsibility for whatever changes the Internet brings.

We need to cast off assumptions and choose technology intelligently. Designers, of all people, cannot let media, advertising, and purveyors of hype, including the authors of books like this one, to control rationality. We need to know not just what the Internet is, but why it matters. We need to ask hard questions.

Computers are the most excellent devices yet imagined for sorting, indexing, and analyzing information content. So what? Information can flow at the speed of light. Is that always good? We can press vast volumes into a microscopic spot but need a month's pay to pack and unpack it. Is that what we want? Is that what is important?

This book attempts to balance these issues: What is the Internet and why does it matter. Without being promotional, this book tries to envision the Internet's potential. Without being negative, it tries to describe the Net's limits. While making ample reference to rapidly changing material, it attempts to give timeless advice.

Part I of the book gives an overview of what the Internet is, why it matters, and generally how to get connected and find information. Part II describes how to use the Internet to better manage your design work and get the most from the Net by connecting to your peers, your clients, and your suppliers and vendors. Part III shows how to impact your clients' businesses by helping them use the Internet for collaboration, public relations, and online sales. And Part IV explores the issues, tools, and techniques necessary for designing Internet documents. Above all, this book tries to give you, as a designer, a sense of the power and the responsibility the Internet grants you. *Designer's Guide to the Internet* will succeed if it does a fraction of all of these. We hope it helps you.

A book on this topic is impossible to do alone. The authors are indebted to uncounted individual contributions to this book. John Blair wrote substantial portions of chapter 12 and provided technical background as only a 21-year-old computer science major and juggler can. The editor, Steve Mulder, and editor-in-chief, Michael Nolan, offered excellent criticism, advice, and information at every turn. Stella

Gassaway, our technical editor, kept us accurate. And information providers all over the world on the Internet contributed knowledge, experience, and raw information that is sprinkled throughout these pages.

We want to also thank our families and coworkers for their patience. The world did not pause in its path while we worked all hours. Thanks everyone!

Rick Albertson

Jeffrey Fine

Mike Zender

PART I

GETTING STARTED WITH THE NET

Part I

PART I OF *DESIGNER'S GUIDE TO THE INTERNET*
FIRST PROVIDES A BASIC OVERVIEW OF THIS
RATHER AMORPHOUS THING WE CALL THE
INTERNET, AND THEN BEGINS TO ANSWER THE
QUESTION OF WHY IT MATTERS TO US AS DE-
SIGNERS. THE RAMIFICATIONS RAISED IN THIS
SECTION AND THROUGHOUT THE BOOK HAVE
MUCH TO SAY TO PROFESSIONAL DESIGNERS
AND COMMUNICATORS PEERING INTO THE
BRIGHT FUTURE, OUR EYES SQUINTING, TRYING
TO DISCERN JUST WHAT ALL OF THIS MEANS—TO
US, TO OUR TRADE, AND TO OUR FUTURE AS
COMMUNICATORS.

Chapter 1

CHAPTER 1 EXPLAINS WHAT THE INTERNET IS
ALL ABOUT AND WHY IT MATTERS TO US
DESIGNERS.

Chapter 2

CHAPTER 2 PROVIDES AN OVERVIEW OF THE
WAYS IN WHICH YOU CAN CONNECT, AND HELP
YOUR CLIENTS CONNECT, TO THE INTERNET.

Chapter 3

CHAPTER 3 DESCRIBES THE MANY WAYS TO
SEARCH FOR INFORMATION ON THE INTERNET.

Act I

Scene 1

In a hip downtown restaurant and hangout for designers, Steven and Kit meet for lunch. Though working in very different environments, they have been friends since high school. Kit is a junior de-signer at SOS Design, a large consultancy. Steven is partner of dEdge, a hot, new, two-person design shop.

Steven: "Hey Kit, how are things at the design factory!?"

Kit: "Ya know, I think SOS stands for 'same ole stuff.' I feel like I'm in a major rut."

Steven: "Well, you can circle this date on your calendar. You're going to look back at this day as the beginning of your electronic design career. From now on you'll be communicating important time-based information to people all over the world."

Kit: "Whoa, you're pumped today. Communicating with people around the world? I can't communicate with my cat! You talkin' about the Internet again?"

Steven: "You bet."

Kit: "You guys are so small, I mean, how's a two-person design firm going like you to help me con-vince SOS big wigs to change?"

Steven: "What would they say if you told them that in addition to the regular commu-nications you do for BigCorp, like their magazine and direct mail, you could show them how to reach millions of people, and even more, a lot more, for much less than the client is currently spending on media?"

Kit: "What're we gonna do, get millions of volunteers to knock on every door in the world?!"

Steven: "Well...yeah. Well...no. Kind of. You see, I'll show you how you can develop a World Wide Web site. You can put up a home page for BigCorp on the Internet....People all over the world can FTP to their site to download anything they've ever published....You really can reach millions!"

Kit: "Internet, Internet, Internet! I'm getting sick of hearing about the Internet. It's just a big computer network, right? What's the big deal?"

Steven: "Right, a worldwide network of computers that's creating global business opportunities never before possible. Kit, listen, more people will hit your client's site in one day than they currently communicate with all year!"

Kit: " Whoa, hold on. Slow down. What's a Web site? Visit our home page? More in one day than all year? Global opportunities? Every time you talk like this it's like... it's like a foreign language. What are you talking about?"

Kit isn't alone in her confusion and limited understanding of the Internet. Lots of people are talking about it, but few understand it—and even fewer people realize the immense changes it will bring to the ways in which we communicate. Brad, the techno-savvy young designer, was right. The Internet will bring about unprecedented global opportunities, the likes of which Susan—and most of us—have never before considered possible.

Designer's Guide to the Internet includes thirteen chapters organized into four major sections, enabling you to find the information that will best equip you to adapt to this exciting new communication medium. Throughout the book, we have used a hypertext-like model to highlight sections of the text into which you may wish to delve deeper. And, once you're connected to the Internet, be sure to check out the book's accompanying home page on Zender + Associates' Web site, which you'll find at this URL address: http://www.zender.com/designers-guide-net. The *Designer's Guide to the Internet* site contains information more dynamic and up-to-date than is possible in the book, as well as a lot of links to other Web sites you'll want to explore.

hypertext

A term used to describe the linking of one text block to another associated text block located within the same document or within a different document.

Chapter 1

The Internet: What It Is and Why It Matters

This chapter explains what the Internet is all about

and why it matters to us designers.

Act I

Scene 2

Thursday after work. Kit is at Steven's office to go for her first ride on the Internet.

Steven: "I bet your new programmer, John, can write the HTML you'll need. And, you can show him how to use clickable maps and tables in Netscape."

Kit: "Wait a minute, Steven, you're talking a foreign language again. Are you sure this'll really work at SOS? And, hey, just what is this Internet, anyway?

The Internet seems a bit bewildering, having entered so suddenly into our lives, bringing about what may be unprecedented changes. In this chapter, we'll put aside the technobabble, at least as much as possible, and present a basic introduction to the Internet and why it matters to us as designers.

technobabble

Here's a word I like, which unfortunately just missed the closing date of the latest *Oxford English Dictionary*. *Technobabble* refers to the seemingly incessant, often unintelligible, and usually inconsequential language often used by computer scientists to describe how our newfound electronic tools operate. (Put your fears aside: We've tried to avoid technobabble throughout this book.)

What Is the Internet?

The Internet is often referred to as the computer network of all computer networks. In essence, that's really what it is, or at least what is has become — an incredible cyber-based spider web connecting computers, their users, and vast amounts of information all over the world.

cyber

This lingo is derived from the words "cybernetics," referring to the theoretical study of communications, and "cyberspace," coined by the science fiction author William Gibson in his seminal book *Neuromancer. Cyber,* when used as a prefix, indicates the virtual space created through which computers communicate.

It's this connection to other computers all over the world that really makes the Internet so great. Want to send a quick message to your designer friend in Seattle? No problem. Just type a note, attach that new Illustrator file, and click on the Send button. A few seconds later your friend will be reading the note and critiquing your work. Heard about some new software? Search a few shareware sites and you can download it for your immediate use. Or, maybe you need quick answers to a technical question. Chances are you'll find just what you're looking for in a newsgroup.

Well, more about all of this in the chapters that follow. Suffice it to say that the Internet and its connections can take you just about anywhere to just about anything, all in a very short time. We're talking some major productivity here!

But first...

A Little History

What we think of today as the Internet was first created by the U.S. Department of Defense in the 1960s as a means to connect a number of smaller government networks supporting military research. With the Cold War threatening on so many fronts, this super-network, originally called ARPAnet, was intentionally designed without any central locations to withstand possible damage inflicted upon it during a nuclear war and yet survive, enabling continued communications. As a result, the Internet today is extremely resilient, flexible, and adaptable, facts that make it that much more interesting to professional communicators as a new medium.

By the early 1980s, ARPAnet was split in half to serve military needs on the one hand and those of research and business on the other. About this same time, several other smaller networks came into existence, including BITNET (the "Because It's Time" network), with the majority of its sites located at universities, colleges, and research centers, and Usenet (the "User's" network). These smaller networks, along with many like them, soon became important components of the ever-expanding Internet.

In 1986, the National Science Foundation Network (NSFN) was created to connect five supercomputer research centers in the U.S. It soon became apparent, however, that many researchers still had no means with which to connect to the NSFN. The network was then expanded to include a number of existing regional networks and connected many universities, colleges, and schools in the process. This resulted in a tremendous increase in network traffic, as a large number of students and staff suddenly took advantage of their newfound access. As the Internet grew and grew, it also became more sophisticated, demanding constant updating with much faster telephone lines and faster computers to control its traffic.

Today, the Internet is a vast, continually expanding global network connecting more than five million host computers used by approximately 30 million people inside and outside of government and educational institutions. Interested in more stats about the Internet and its growth? Check out Mark Lottor's Network Wizards World Wide Web site—you'll learn more about the World Wide Web and other parts of the Internet in chapter 3.

host computers
Large computers providing access to the Internet for smaller computers, such as my trusty Mac.

Network Wizards
http://www.nw.com

NVN

Welcome to Network Wizards

Network Wizards creates unique hardware and software solutions for the computer and communications industry.

- Our Products
- Catalog.Com Internet Services
- Internet Domain Survey
- About Network Wizards

Okay, so the Internet is a gigantic, ever-expanding network. It spans the globe. It uses TCP/IP protocols (more on this in the next chapter) to enable computers to "speak" to one another. So what?! Just what is the big deal?

Let's back away for a few minutes and take a look at the big picture.

Why Does the Internet Matter?

When we're contemplating a headline event like the Internet, it's a good idea to step back from the hype and see if the banner has any importance to life's significant issues. In this light, does the Internet really matter? Does it have any significance at all beyond the hype and its commercial promise? Yes, the Internet matters! There's no question it holds forth significant commercial promise, and it is already having a major impact on society, both on the people using it and on those who aren't.

What about designers? Does the Internet really matter to us? Will it impact our professional lives? You bet! We are communication professionals trained and skilled in the means and tools that give us access to, and control over, a variety of powerful communication media. Society is handing us its keys. We are the gatekeepers of the information age, and nothing is more symbolic of the information age than the Internet. The Internet matters to designers if for no other reason than because it matters to communication. And communication, this foundational element of society that determines meaning and increases understanding between ourselves and others, is being redefined at its very core by the Internet.

One of the most ancient of all recorded texts, the Torah (the first five books of the Jewish Law), deals squarely with the impact that technology and communication have on society. Remember the story? Early settlers of the plain of Shinar, later known as Babylon and Baghdad today, all spoke one language, as did everyone at that time. Common communication among these people enabled them to advance technology to the point that they were able to establish secure and permanent homes. In fact, so advanced and so secure did they become that the people built a tower reaching to the heavens.

Seeing the tower and explicitly recognizing that this advanced communication ability gave the people too much power, God confused their speech and called their technological marvel "Babel," hence the reference to the Tower of Babel. The impending loss of communication dissolved social unity, halted so-

Tower of Babel

ciety's technical progress, and scattered the people abroad, far removed from their once-secure homes. This tale, whether fable or history, indicates just how ancient is the understanding of the role of communication and its close relationship with the home, human society, and technology.

Communication continues to play a pivotal role in society. Life is enriched or impoverished by our relationships, and our relationships are based squarely upon communication. Today, the Internet, perhaps more than any other communication medium, is stimulating never-before-seen levels of technological progress.

The Internet, after all, is a communication medium of unparalleled scope. Its speed, geographic size, and information volume are all greater than anything comparable in human history—at least since Babel. And there is little doubt that the Internet will have—is having—an impact on society, perhaps a huge impact. Daily, the Internet is quietly yet pervasively reaching into the most sacred aspects of our lives, challenging long-held beliefs about "home" and what home means, literally redefining even this most basic building block of society—where we live, where we're rooted, from whence we come in contact with the rest of the world.

A New Place to Call "Home"

But what is *home* in the cyberage? It's certainly taking on new dimensions, even new locations. An electronic bulletin board called Army Brats of America started recently. *Army brat* is a slang term for a child who grows up with a suitcase packed, ready to move anywhere in the world on a moment's notice because mom or dad is a member of the armed services. These kids don't get a chance to establish deep family roots in any one place, but have lived all over the world, with no one place to call home. Many Army brats have learned a significant lesson through their travels: Home is not about place; it's about relationships.

electronic bulletin board

Bulletin boards are computer systems often referred to as BBSs (bulletin board systems) that are usually private, providing files of all types—text, photos, video, audio—for downloading to connected members. Many bulletin boards are now also accessible via the Internet, and some even provide Internet access to members. More on this in the next chapter.

Cyberspace to the rescue! It seems the Army Brats of America bulletin board is a popular site for these transients because it gives them a virtual place where they can, like ET, "phone home" and share their lives with others who have experienced the same "home"lessness. The Brats bulletin board now serves as their home town. They can "go back home" and talk with people they haven't seen for years, pick up news from the Army neighborhood, and see what's changed.

Home, as you can see, is a good metaphor for the Internet. In this sense, the Internet <u>home page</u> takes on an expanded meaning. It is a home. It is a home based on information, not place, whose roots are in shared ideas and experiences. Call it a virtual community. The connection is a digital one, but the relationships formed can be quite substantial.

home page

The first page of a given World Wide Web site, an Internet "location" featuring access to formatted text, photos, graphics, and audio. See chapter 3.

In this technological age, a lot of designers have paused in their rush toward success to ask if what they are doing is making a positive contribution to their lives and to the lives of those near them, a process causing us to refocus on the issues of home and family. Today it's as common for a seasoned designer to retire "so I can spend time with my family" as it is for a designer fresh out of school to quit for the same reason. On the organizational level, a parallel activity has occurred. Organizations large and small have put at the bottom of their letterhead some variation of the statement "We Value Diversity."

These examples suggest that both individuals and organizations are evaluating their actions against core concepts that give life meaning. It is these core life issues—human relationships, home and family, communication—that are the key concepts against which the Internet should be evaluated. If the Internet matters in any profound way, it matters at this basic level, or it matters not at all.

The Brave New World of Design

Okay, we know a bit more about what the Internet is, and it's not hard to see that it's having an impact upon society. It's also having an impact on the world of design and how we practice our trade: how we organize content, how we design under the constraints of this new medium, and how we use it to collaborate with our clients. It raises so many new questions for us: What's the new language of the

Internet? What does the Internet enable and inhibit in our societal conversation? Does the Internet, in fact, potentially represent the next Tower of Babel?

And then there's the bottom line…. It's a drag, but the thing never seems to go away. The Internet matters here, too. By enabling instant global communication, it's a new medium for commerce and expression, and for you greedy designers reading this book, a new way for you to make money and be successful! Read on. If you're concerned about the bottom line, you'll be especially interested in parts II and III of this book.

In the meantime, the Internet really does matter to us as designers because of its impact on the business of design: the structure of our firms, the skills required by our employees, the changes it brings to our firm's culture, the way we find clients, and the way we communicate with them, our vendors, and one another. Its impact is growing. Our clients are certainly aware of it. You will be, too, if you aren't already.

New Medium, New Messages

Because of the Internet's growing impact on society, its character is worth studying. Neil Postman says that the tools a society uses to carry on its conversations dictate what kind of <u>content</u> can issue forth. As Marshall McLuhan said, "The medium *is* the message." The medium used to communicate not only flavors messages, but to a great degree actually determines what can be said. In this sense, the Internet is changing not only how we speak to each other, but also what we can say—though at this stage it is still too early to determine the extent of these differences.

Home, the family, the way we design, the nature of our business… the Internet matters to all of this and more, and in very significant ways. Significant in the

content

"To take a simple example of what this means, consider the primitive technology of smoke signals. While I do not know exactly what content was carried in the smoke signals of American Indians, I can safely guess that it did not include philosophical argument. Puffs of smoke are insufficiently complex to express ideas on the nature of existence, and even if they were not, a Cherokee philosopher would run short of either wood or blankets long

continued on next page

before he reached his second axiom. You cannot use smoke to do philosophy. Its form excludes the content."

Amusing Ourselves to Death, p. 6

"big picture" sense to our society, and significant to us as designers as well. These are the issues that part IV of this book attempts to address more completely.

Chapter 2

How to Get Connected

This chapter provides an overview of the ways

in which you can connect, and help your

clients connect, to the Internet.

Act I

Scene 3

Still at Steven's office, now well past midnight.

Steven: "Kit, you'll be distributing more information than you ever felt possible. The Internet will forever change the way you do business."

Kit: "Okay, okay, Steven. Now that I finally understand what the Internet is, I can see that it is going to have a really big impact on our work. But first, just how do we connect our computers to the Internet?"

The bad news is that because the Internet was designed without any central location, there is unfortunately no tech support line for this global network to guide you in connecting to it. Most people find this intimidating.

The good news is that getting on the Internet is becoming easier and easier—just ask the 20-30 million users around the globe who rely on the thousands of businesses and educational institutions offering varying degrees of access to it.

Good news or bad, intimidating or not, *now* is the time to make the connection. This chapter provides a brief overview of the different ways in which you and your clients can get connected, but first a quick detour....

Detour: Connection Speeds

For those of you—excuse me, *us*—needing it, let's take a quick look at connection speeds, something that you might know very little about today, but will certainly need to know more and more about tomorrow.

Several factors influence the speed of your connection to the Internet, most notably the speed of your modem and the "directness" of your connection to the backbone of the Internet, both of which involve the issue of bandwidth.

Modem Speeds

In the last few years, modem speeds have increased dramatically from 300 bps (bits per second) to 9,600 bps to 14,400 bps (which is perhaps the most common speed today) to 28,800 bps. Modems of this latter speed are known as 28.8 modems.

Modem speeds are increasing, yet you'll find even 14.4 modems to often be painstakingly slow for serious Net surfing. Don't fret, though: Modem manufacturers are doing their best to speed up their modems, and at the same time reach deep into your pockets to get you to buy a new, *faster* model. At the writing of this book, 28.8 modems are currently the fastest available to consumers, and some of the major commercial online services have just announced that their services are now available at these speeds.

(If you feel you need a more complete consideration of technical matters such as the ones you'll encounter in this chapter, you'd be well served to reach over to your bookshelf and pull down Adam Engst's classic, *Internet Starter Kit*, available from Hayden Books in both Mac and Windows versions.)

bandwidth

Information theory uses this term to describe the quantity of information that can flow through a given communication medium at any one time. You can think of this in terms of an information pipeline. There's only so much data you can squeeze through a certain size pipe. The larger the information pipeline, or the greater its bandwidth, the more data you can transmit.

backbone

The backbone of the Net is the high-speed (45 Mbps) network superstructure connecting the ten computer centers in the U.S. that comprise the National Science Foundation Network.

modem speeds

The following illustration is meant to give you some idea of just how quickly, or, perhaps more accurately, how slowly modems transmit data. Keep in mind that a standard 3.5" floppy disk stores 1,440,000 bytes of data (or 11,520,000 bits, since there are 8 bits in each byte). Assuming you're as old as me and also possess a partially atrophied brain that refuses to do math—or then again maybe you're quite a bit younger and you've seen how your children do it.... Well, grab the calculator, and you too can figure out that a 14.4 modem would transmit the information from one full floppy over a phone line in about 13 minutes—not very fast! Double the modem speed and you can theoretically transmit twice the data in the same amount of time. That's still not too quick, considering that even a typical local area network transmits data at a rate of about 230,400 bytes per second, which would require only 6 brief seconds for the transmission of the same floppy's data.

"Directness" of Connection

What I referred to as "directness"—how direct your connection to the Internet is—also plays a role in determining the speed with which you can transmit and receive data. Actually, "connecting" to the Internet via a modem doesn't really put you directly on the Internet, because using a modem usually enables you to connect your computer, as a terminal, only to a given host computer, which is in turn connected to the Internet. Using the PPP or SLIP protocols (more on these protocols coming up) in conjunction with your modem, however, makes it possible for your computer to network with the host computer on the Internet, thereby increasing your connection speed and giving you more interface options than a text-only terminal.

A real increase in connection speed can be realized by connecting your computer directly to the Internet, with no need for PPP/SLIP protocols and/or a modem. Doing this requires what are, at least today, rather expensive leased lines and terminal adapters (a kind of digital modem). Digital connections often bypass local host computers along the way, enabling you to connect your computer directly to a major backbone of the Internet.

Direct connections such as these, though still uncommon today, offer the very fastest connection speeds, and to a large extent are slowed down only by limits to the bandwidth of the network cable connecting your machine to the Internet. Connection speeds of 64,000 bps to 128,000 bps can be obtained using ISDN lines available from your local phone company. Leased T1 and T3 lines, though quite expensive, are the fastest lines widely available today and offer significantly greater speeds of data transmission—up to over 1,000,000 bps, ten times the speed of ISDN lines. A good place to learn more about such lines is from your local phone company.

Tired of all this technical stuff? Me too... Throw the calculator at the wall! Better hope it still works when you pick it up, though. Unfortunately, as designers we deal with major-league file sizes that force us to consider bandwidth and connection speed issues. Just keep this in the back of your mind as you read the remainder of this chapter. It may help you decide how you should connect to the Internet. As you read on, however, you'll see that connection speed alone is by no means the only criteria with which you should determine how to connect.

Don't you just hate detours!? Back to the subject at hand: how to connect to the Internet. Keep in mind as you read through this that there are many ways to connect. Try to envision the best alternative for the way you work, always asking yourself, "How can connecting to the Internet help me as a designer?"

Connecting via Commercial Online Services

Perhaps the easiest, though not particularly the most direct, connection to the Internet can now be made through one of the well-known commercial online services. In the face of heightened interest in the Internet, online services including CompuServe, America Online, Prodigy, Apple Computer's eWorld, and the new Microsoft Network have all realized that full Internet access is perhaps the most enticing service they can offer in luring subscribers.

In addition to the Internet email services that online services have made available for some time now, each of them now also offers its own gateway to Internet services to the millions of subscribers. It's important to note, however, that at this time the Internet access offered by most online services is somewhat limited. For example, some don't offer access to the Web, and most don't allow you to use traditional TCP/IP programs such as Netscape,

CU-SeeMe, and so on (more about these limitations later). As the pitched battle for subscribers continues, however, we're the winners, because access costs are being driven further and further downward and Internet services are increasing.

Today, there are many questions regarding just what role commercial online services will play in offering Internet connections in the future. Most importantly, will they even survive? Some industry pundits, including Don Crabb of *Macweek*, contend that commercial online services, at least as we know them today, will cease to exist in the near future. Crabb makes the following comparison: "Just as the transcontinental telegraph killed the pony express, the Internet and the World Wide Web will kill online services by making them unnecessary." He continues, "The Web can do the information superhighway thing better than any online service" ("The Mac Manager," p. 23—see appendix C for more complete bibliographical listings).

In contrast, other experts believe that commercial online services hold great promise, citing the fact that they do an excellent job packaging content and organizing groups of people with similar interests. As Chuck Martin, publisher of *Interactive Age*, pointed out in his March 27, 1995, editorial, "[Commercial online services] are relatively easy to get on. They have distribution. They have marketing. They are actual companies, while the Internet is amorphous, with no one really in charge" (p. 16). Martin refers to a report from Forrester Research Inc., of Cambridge, Massachusetts, that projects an estimated ten million people connected to the Internet through commercial online services by the year 2000.

In the meantime, commercial online services are alive and well, signing up thousands of subscribers to their services each week and now providing some access to the Internet as well. It's all for a price, granted, and perhaps not the fastest or most useful connection, but it's a connection to the Internet that many would otherwise be unable to achieve. Interested? Check out the following brief descriptions of the five major commercial online services. Each service offers many of the same features, yet each has its own distinct personality as well.

In reality, however, the lack of full Internet access and the slow connection speeds of the online services probably mean accessing the Internet in this fashion is somewhat impractical for designers. Your needs may be much better served by connecting through a national access provider and/or using ISDN or T1 lines (see the sections that follow).

CompuServe

Perhaps CompuServe's interface is the reason for its reputation as the most computer- and business-oriented online service. Or maybe it's the extensive

CompuServe

http://www.compuserve.com*

financial, business, and government databases this online service makes available. CompuServe is also known for the thousands of special-interest forums it provides where subscribers can leave messages, ask questions, and take part in live discussions. For Internet services, CompuServe offers email, Usenet newsgroups, FTP, and Telnet (for descriptions of these and other Internet services, see chapter 3). (800/848-8199)

* By the way, I'll explain what these URLs (Internet addresses of these sites) are and how to interpret and use them in chapter 3.

America Online

America Online, with its well-conceived, colorful interface, leads the way in providing easy online access to information. And, it's easy to use, beckoning

America Online

http://www.aol.com

America Online

America Online, a leading provider of communication, information, and entertainment services to consumers, serves a growing number of people who want to communicate, conference, receive news, financial information, mail and use other value-added services via digital technologies. With more than 2.5 million subscribers, America Online is the fastest growing provider of consumer online services in the United States.

America Online is an innovate developer of the technologies that expand the appeal of interactive services. Recognized as an early leader in offering a graphical interface (GUI), America Online now offers its subscribers an advanced multimedia user interface, seamlessly integrating video, graphics, text and sound. This interface is accessible through The Company's nationwide dialup network, and now via the Internet.

America Online has established strategic alliances with leading content providers, media companies and technology companies, such as Time Warner, CNN, ABC, NBC, MTV, Tribune Company, IBM, Apple, Viacom, Comcast Intel and General Instrument.

More information

You can obtain information about America Online from the following sources.

- For recent press releases, see the press release archive.
- For the latest on America Online's Internet activities, see this list of its Internet partners.
- To download a copy of the latest America Online software for Mac or Windows, including the Web browser for Windows, see the AOL ftp site.
- To subscribe to America Online, download the appropriate copy of the software, and follow the directions contained in that software. For more information, call 800-827-6364.

subscribers to simply click on icons to accomplish online tasks. No wonder it's the fastest-growing commercial online service, with over three million subscribers. On the other hand, AOL falls short of other online services in its range of available information sources, and it focuses more on personal rather than professional interests. America Online offers access to Internet email, Usenet newsgroups, Gopher, WAIS, and the World Wide Web. (800/827-6364)

Prodigy

Prodigy, though presenting a rather poorly de-signed interface, provides a full range of services to its subscribers and strikes a good balance between personal and business interests. It is known

Prodigy

http://www.prodigy.com

For optimal viewing, adjust your browser to the width of this banner.

⊛prodigy

Welcome to Prodigy on the Web!

If you're into reading without pictures, here's our text-only home page.

For those of you who prefer visual aids, we have a couple of alternatives. Each delivers the same content, but with a different cover page. (We decided to let you choose.)

Surfin' with some speed?

 Get the big picture. (115K)

Actually like to read?

 Use our word menu.

If you have a question, or you're interested in Employment Opportunities, contact us.

What's up at Prodigy?

particularly for its strong financial and sports infor-mation services. Prodigy's online shopping was the first such service enabling vendors of just about anything you can imagine to hawk their products online. Prodigy offers Internet email, Usenet news-groups, and Web access. (800/776-3449)

eWorld

Late to the commercial online scene, Apple has brought a new level of playfulness to its eWorld on-line service interface (available for Macs only at this time). Subscribers navigate through a visual home-town metaphor to select from what is at best a

eWorld

http://www.eworld.com

continued on next page

Welcome to eWorld on the Web!

We've been waiting for you. The World Wide Web presents a universe of information & ideas. Let us show you a few of the places that we think you'll find interesting and useful. The Learning Community presents resources for both school and home-based learning. WebCity takes you on a tour of information that you can use for work or play. Take a look around & let us know what you think!

Topics

WebCity - Covers topics like Lifestyles, Technology, Business, and more.

Learning Community - Educator and student resources from around the Web.

Web Gazettes - News, information & fun from eWorld on the Web.

Toolbar

Apple - Connect to the Apple Computer, Inc. corporate Home Page.

standard offering of online services, plus Internet services including email, Usenet, FTP, and the Web. (800/775-4556)

Microsoft Network

Microsoft

http://www.msn.net

Like Apple, Microsoft too is a latecomer to the on-line party. But then size does bring with it a certain inevitable impact. Ever wonder what an 800 lb.

 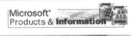

Microsoft Announces Availability of The Microsoft Network
Microsoft Windows 95 Is Available Today at Retail Outlets Worldwide

For Text Only Users
[New to the Web | About MSN | Explore the Internet | Windows 95 Launch Event | Microsoft]

[Help | Index | Search Microsoft | Feedback | @ Internet Explorer]

gorilla looks like coming late to a party? Hard not to take notice. MSN will no doubt become an impor-tant online service to the zillions of Windows users around the world. From what we can tell at this early

date, it seems intent on offering creative new services to subscribers, including serialized comics —
but it's hard to predict what Internet services it will
offer. (800/426-9400)

As you'll see if you try out the commercial online
services, they each offer the same basic services at
similar prices, differing mostly in how their content
is packaged and the ways in which they organize
groups of people with similar interests. Of course all
of this is changing daily. You'll definitely want to fa-
miliarize yourself with the commercial online services, but connecting to the Internet through access
providers via a PPP or SLIP account offers designers
a far higher level of Internet services, though at
comparable (i.e., not extremely fast) speeds.

Connecting via PPP or SLIP

Using a PPP or SLIP account affords you several relatively fast and affordable options to connect to the
Internet via modem through several national and regional companies, as well as through local
providers and BBSs, now offering such access.
(Check your local yellow pages under "Computers —
software and services.")

The fundamental service provided by any Internet
access provider is nothing more than the establish-
ment of a communication link between your computer and any one of millions of others all around
the globe also connected to the Internet. The PPP or
SLIP protocols speak the language needed to tell
your computer how to establish a temporary connection via modem to the provider's host computer,
and thus from there to the Internet. Thankfully,
these protocols and TCP/IP, the protocol that makes
it possible to ship packets of information between
computers, have been widely adopted by Internet
access providers.

speak the language

"When information is sent over the Internet, it
is divided into smaller pieces in transit and re-
assembled at a final destination. PPP allows
computers to exchange these data 'packets'
with the Internet. To make PPP work with a
modem, users need software known as a
TCP/IP stack to handle the packing and

continued on next page

Whoa! What's all this about TCP/IP and PPP and protocols?! To more fully understand and use the Internet, you need at least a working knowledge of the protocols upon which the Internet was actually founded. Please understand, however, that my oversimplified explanation below is meant only as a primer.

TCP/IP: The Language

For networks to form, as computers are connected one to another, the computers must first "speak the same language." That's what TCP/IP does. This collection of protocols is the instruction set enabling computers connected to any point of a network to send messages back and forth to one another inside what are called Internet Protocol (IP) <u>packets</u>. Once packets are addressed correctly, these protocols ensure that the packets sent from your computer can reach a <u>gateway</u> connecting you to another machine on the Internet. The end result: Messages can be sent anywhere in the world, between any two computers connected to the Internet.

Macintosh users may be familiar with Apple's MacTCP control panel, the software that actually executes TCP functions. You'll find MacTCP built into the System 7.5 operating system. (Have an older version of the Macintosh operating system? You can purchase MacTCP from Apple.) OS/2 Warp has TCP/IP support already built into its operating system as well. Under Windows (including Windows 95), the TCP/IP stack does the same thing as MacTCP. Windows users can use shareware programs such as Trumpet Winsock. A good starting place to learn more is on the Web at http://www.yahoo.com/Computers_and_Internet/Software/Protocols/Winsock.

unpacking of internet data on their computer."

Paul A. Gilster, "The Internet Made Easy," *CompuServe Magazine*, p. 14

packets

The smallest unit of information transferred over a network, a packet contains a piece of data and the address to which it is being sent. Packet sizes normally vary from a few kilobytes to 32 kilobytes in size.

gateway

A gateway is a computer existing on more than one network that controls the transfer of information between itself and other computers, and between two computers on different networks.

PPP/SLIP: The Translators

If TCP/IP is the language of the Internet, then PPP and SLIP are translators that enable your Mac or PC to speak that language via modem. PPP is a protocol that fools your computer into thinking that it's a host computer with full access to the Internet. (That's the thing about these computers: They are so darn anthropomorphic!) SLIP does the same thing, although those in the know say it's somewhat less flexible than PPP. As you connect to the Internet, you'll likely use either PPP or SLIP, because they're essential for connecting your computer to the Internet via a modem.

A more technical explanation of these matters is beyond the scope of this book. If you're interested in learning more about TCP/IP, PPP, and SLIP, or if you have to set up the corresponding software on your Mac or PC, turn to one of Adam Engst's *Internet Starter Kits*.

modem

This electronic device enables computers to communicate over standard phone lines.

SLIP

Serial Line Internet Protocol is similar to but older than PPP. SLIP and PPP are not interoperable: Machines wishing to communicate must both be using either PPP or SLIP.

PPP

Point to Point Protocol enables computers connected via TCP/IP to communicate using standard modems.

National and Regional Access Providers

The mid-90s finds the world in the midst of the great Internet shakeout, with no one Internet access provider currently claiming more than a ten percent share of the market. And in the meantime, explosive demand is driving Internet access toward a billion-dollar business, creating a few dominant national access providers and thousands of smaller local access providers that make the Internet accessible from nearly every city in the country.

Unlike their cousins, the commercial online services, companies providing true nationwide Internet access are more numerous. And to a large extent, as the user you select whatever services you need in choosing a particular national or regional access provider. You're not limited to which Internet services you can use or which software you can use to access them. Each service provider has a slightly different offer directed by a somewhat different business strategy, but overall it's a better deal than a commercial online service can provide. See some recommendations for what to look for in a provider in the Evaluation Criteria section that's coming up.

An Example: PSI

If you're new to the Net, you may be especially interested in connecting to it through a company such as Performance Systems International (PSI), with its preconfigured, low-cost InterRamp service. PSI has built a nationwide high-speed network currently

Performance Systems International

http://www.psi.com/indivservices/interramp

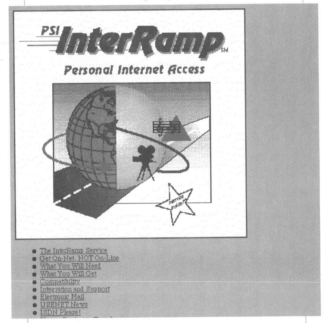

serving about 200 points of presence (POPs) and offers a wide range of services designed for individuals and businesses.

According to PSI, users of its InterRamp package get PPP dial-up access to the Internet, an electronic mailbox, and a Usenet news account with unlimited access. And with PSI's nationwide network connections, you can use your InterRamp account from your home or the office, or while you're traveling. As

points of presence

Cities are points of presence if a given Internet provider offers access to its services there, usually via either a local phone call or 800 number connection.

of the summer of 1995, PSI's published InterRamp pricing was listed as follows (as with everything in life, it's subject to change):

InterRamp, including PC/Windows or Macintosh software . . . $99 U.S.*

* (Also includes first month of unlimited service. You must call 800/827-8472 and speak to PSI's sales consultant to qualify.)

InterRamp rates after the first month of service:

First 29 hrs of usage .... $29 U.S.

ISDN usage over initial 29 hrs $1.50/hr

V.32bis and V.34 usage over initial 29 hrs ... $1.50/hr

PSI's InterRamp Service is but one of many options available from national and regional Internet access providers (see the list of providers coming up). Before signing up, however, you may want to undertake a more thorough evaluation of Internet access providers. To get started, you can log on to the Internet and check out http://web.cnam.fr/Network/Internet-access/how_to_select.html. You may also find the following information helpful in completing your evaluation. It is important to judge each national access provider on the basis of not only its connection speed, but also its rates, services, visitation privileges, reliability, and technical support.

> **V.32bis and V.34**
>
> These are the fastest current modem protocols that also support most other modem features, including error correction and data compression. Check out your modem's handbook to learn what it offers.

Evaluation Criteria

Rates

Prices vary greatly and in most cases directly correlate to the speed of connection desired. You'll run into two types of billing systems: flat-rate accounts and per-hour accounts. Flat-rate accounts are often the better deal, since you pay a set fee every month, regardless of how much time you're actually online. With a per-hour account, you get charged based on your time online—and in my opinion this can be more stressful, since you're constantly thinking about how much money is ticking away with every second. Also be careful of flat-rate accounts or per-hour accounts with specific restrictions, such as a limit of how much time you can spend online in a given session.

Other costs include startup fees, which are common and which cover the costs of the provider setting up your account. Sometimes you'll run into providers that also charge you on a per-service basis. You could pay $1 per megabyte to store email, for instance, or an additional monthly fee for setting up a Web page on their host machine.

And then there are phone charges. Local calls are always ideal, since they're effectively free—so try to find a service provider within your area code (also see the next sections, Local Access Providers and BBSs)! Some national providers have set up their own phone network, so you can dial a local phone number, but the provider may still charge you extra per hour for using the network. The other option, calling long-distance to a provider, will obviously cost you, but if it's the better overall package (particularly if you use a long-distance plan such as MCI's Friends and Family), go for it. A final note about 800 numbers: Even though they may *seem* free, chances are that Internet providers will end up billing you extra per hour for the call. Be sure to check these details with any provider you choose.

Services
While all services, including email, World Wide Web access, file transfer protocol (FTP), Usenet newsgroups, Gopher, Internet Relay Chat (IRC), and more (all these services are explained in chapter 3) are available if you take the time to learn to use them, some providers offer simplified packages (for example, PSI's InterRamp). Some providers also offer

special services such as custom domain names (i.e., a customized email address such as rick@zender.com for Zender + Associates instead of rick@psi.com), storage of Web pages, a personal FTP directory, and other business services. Be sure to ask about other offerings.

Speed

Speed is an important issue to us designers, considering the multimegabyte graphics files we deal with so often. The speed at which you can access the Internet is dependent upon a given Internet access provider's modems' capabilities as well as your own. At this time, most providers offer a maximum call-in speed of 14,400 bps, while some are now converting to faster 28,800 bps modems. In the future, more and more providers will support ISDN lines and who knows what else.

Reliability

Redundancy—the repeating of a message in order to circumvent transmission errors—is the name of the game in ensuring reliability. Some providers have it, some don't. Ask what happens when a service goes down; you may also want to ask about the number of times the service was down during the last few months and how long it usually takes to get it back up again. Hey, it wouldn't hurt to dialogue a bit with other users, too. Ask them about their experience in using the service.

Visitation

Most Internet providers make it possible to try out their service before joining. Take some time to check out their interface, access to the services you need, and everything else.

Tech Support

Your Internet access provider should have local access and easy-to-reach support personnel who are around when you need them.

List of Providers

This listing of PPP/SLIP Internet Access Providers was published in *MacUser* Magazine, May 1995. You'll also find a great many providers listed at http://www.yahoo.com/Business_and_Economy/ Companies/Internet_Access_Providers.

Nationwide

HoloNet: 510/704-0160

Internet Express: 800/592-1240

John von Neumann Computer Network: 800/358-4437

Netcom Online Communications Services: 800/501-8649

Performance Systems International (PSI): 800/827-7482

East

Agate Internet Services: 207/947-8248

BBN Internet Services: 617/873-8730

Capcon Library Networks: 202/331-5771

Clark Internet Services: 410/995-0691

Digital Express Group: 301/220-2020

Echo Communications: 212/255-3839

FishNet: 610/337-9994

MV Communications: 603/429-2223

PSI Net Pipeline: 212/267-3636

South

The Black Box: 713/480-2685

CyberGate: 305/428-4283

Global Access VNet: 704/334-3282

Internet Atlanta: 404/410-9000

Nuance Network Services: 205/533-4296

RealTime Communications: 512/451-0046

Telelink: 615/321-9100

Texas Metronet: 214/705-2900

Midwest
CICNet BBB: 313/998-6703

InterAccess: 800/967-1580

Macro Computer Solutions: 312/248-8649

Msen: 313/998-4562

Prairienet Freenet of East Central Illinois:
217/244-1962

StarNet Communications: 612/941-9177

XNet Information Services: 708/983-6064

West
Colorado SuperNet: 303/273-3471

Cooperative Library Agency for Systems and
Services: 800/488-4559

CTS Network Services: 619/637-3637

Eskimo North: 206/367-7457

Hawaii OnLine: 808/533-6981

Internet Direct: 602/274-0100

Portal Communications: 408/973-9111

Teleport: 503/223-4245

West Coast Online: 707/586-3060

Canada
HookUp Communications: 905/847-8000

UUNET Canada: 416/68-6621

UUNorth: 416/225-8649

Okay, have you completed your evaluation and are
now ready to sign up with a national or regional
Internet access provider? You may want to hold off a

few days and first do a little research into local Internet access providers in your area, too.

Local Access Providers

In addition to commercial online services and national and regional Internet access providers, there also exist a large number of community-based services providing access to the Internet. Local access providers offer the same full Internet services as national or regional providers, yet provide packaged information in a somewhat more targeted fashion to better meet the needs of their community. Local providers usually offer services only within their local area code.

One such local Internet access provider is Productivity OnLine (POL) located in our community, Cincinnati, Ohio. POL, with its easy-to-use graphical interface, features local electronic mail, discussion

Productivity OnLine

http://www.pol.com

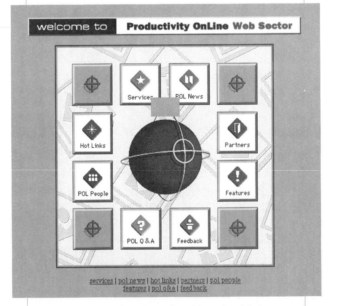

areas, and files for downloading. Its high-speed Internet gateway also gives subscribers the ability to send and receive Internet email, participate in newsgroups and mailing lists, and surf the World Wide Web all over the world. As a community-based service, POL even allows residents of the Greater Cincinnati area, whether or not dues-paying members of POL, to access information from participating local governments for up to ten minutes each day for free.

Check out the local Internet access providers in your area, but be careful. Before you sign up, be sure to ask lots of questions similar to those mentioned previously for evaluating other Internet access providers. Local access providers may, in fact, offer the features you need. Just make certain they can also provide the speed and support you need. It's hard for local concerns to keep up with the big boys in these ways (*caveat Emptor* in the electronic age!).

BBSs

Still another way to access the Internet is through private access providers known as <u>bulletin board systems</u>. While such providers typically offer fewer Internet services than other access providers (some don't provide Web access, and many don't support using TCP/IP programs such as Netscape—instead you're stuck with their own interface), they are often quite inexpensive and continue to play an important role as more and more private systems provide their users with access to the Internet.

Today there are literally tens of thousands of BBSs around the world, and as they grow in number and services, they will provide real competition for other online services. Although you will undoubtedly visit a number of design-oriented private servers and bulletin board systems (such as <u>designOnline</u> at 708/328-8723), you'll probably opt to make your actual connection to the Internet via a true Internet access provider, or even, perhaps, directly to the Net (see Connecting Directly coming up). To really explore the world of BBSs, check out Tim

bulletin board systems

These computer systems are usually established by an individual to provide users with files for downloading and a forum for electronic discussions regarding topics of interest to the system's administrator. A BBS is often a smaller system run out of a home, with only a couple of incoming phone lines. Larger bulletin board systems may be comprised of several networked computers, thereby forming a sophisticated data-rich environment.

designOnline

While you're visiting designOnline, check out AIGAlink. It's currently the only graphic design organization with its own conference area. You can check out designOnline's home page on the Web at http://www.dol.com.

continued on next page

Gerchmez's <u>BBS Page</u> on the Web or Dan

BBS Page

http://mail.eskimo.com/~future/bbs.htm

The BBS Page

What is a BBS?

A BBS (or Bulletin Board System) is simply a small online service, typically with 100 incoming lines or less. It can be hooked to the outside world via the Internet or another network, or can be completely self-contained (limited to one computer system or a local network). BBS's have been around a long time, and started out in the late 70's/early 80's as single-line systems with 300 baud or below access speed. Many BBS's are run by hobbyists who don't charge a fee for access, although more and more seem to be going to pay access. Most are a bargain compared to the "major" online services like Compuserve, AOL and Prodigy. If you enjoy being online, I suggest you find a BBS list local to your area and give them a try! You'll need a good terminal program (Windows terminal will work if you use Windows, but you should find a better one as soon as possible). BBS's are growing ever more user-friendly, and most can be navigated easily by beginners. Normally you can page the Sysop (System Operator) for help if you need it once you're online.

Area (206) BBS's

One of my favorite computer activities (other than surfing the internet) is calling local bulletin board systems. The area code 206 (Seattle and vicinity) contains a number of excellent local BBS's. Click on the link above to see a list. You can also see an OLD list of Seattle-area BBS's (from 1988) by clicking here. Please do not call any of the numbers in this old list, as most will be defunct by now. It's interesting to compare the two lists and see how the area code 206 scene has changed over the years. There were a lot fewer boards then (naturally), and the fastest modem speed available was 2400 baud. There were almost no multi-line boards around. Today, multi-line boards have become the predominant type.

Vishnesky's <u>Vicious Book of BBSs</u>, an incredibly expansive online travel guide to the vast and exciting world of bulletin board services.

Vicious Book of BBSs

http://www.dsv.su.se/~mats-bjo/bbslist.html

Just a brief warning if you consider using a BBS for access to the Internet: Many BBSs provide free access to users, but most can't monitor their systems 24 hours a day. If the system goes down, you may know about it way before operators of the BBS do.

continued on next page

The Vicious Book Of BBS's

By EverClear, alias Dan Vishnesky
08.11.94
Version 1.01
        Version note: Edited out a bbs and some typos.

WHAT THE HELL IS THIS?
        You may be wondering what this monstrous file which you
have just discovered is. Well, this is the Vicious Book of BBS's,
an online travel guide to the vast and exciting world of internet
bulliten board services. Think of this as your personal map to
the internet: A tool you use to decide where to go and what to
do when you get there. Inside you will find a sort of "highlights
guide" that can help you get to what you want fast. If you are
looking for a certain bbs, look under the BBS Lists section. If
you are looking for a certain type of bbs or certain feature, look
under the Services heading. If you just want to do a little sight-
seeing, look under the Highlights section. Also included is a
brief introduction to the different types of bbs's and how they work.
        Use this file however you want. You can print it, distribute
it, burn it, or toss it in the trash, I dont care. Just dont try
to get money for the damn thing or try to say you wrote it. Dont
go adding your own stuff in and passing it off as an original   This
is my idea, and my work. I hope everyone enjoys it.

LOGGING IN ON A NEW BBS

Think about this before depending totally on a BBS for all your Internet communications.

Connecting Directly

Ultimately, how you work as a designer and how you choose to use the Internet will determine your choice of an Internet access provider. Many designers, having adapted themselves to using the Net, have soon realized that only a direct, digital connection to the Internet provides their firm with anywhere near the real day-to-day capabilities their work requires. As I mentioned earlier in this chapter, significant gains in connection speed can be realized by connecting a computer digitally, directly to the Internet, without the need to make the analog-to-digital conversion necessary with a modem.

The problem with this no-modem-required option is that it is still pretty expensive, requiring special leased phone lines and terminal adapters (a kind of digital modem). And, even after you make the decision to spend the money and install a leased line, data transmission speeds are still far below ideal when considering the large files we so casually zip across our internal Ethernet networks. "Fast Ethernet" is capable of transmitting data at a rate of at least 10 MB/second, about ten times faster than today's fastest T1 leased line. Even with these present limitations, however, connecting to the Internet in this way may be the only realistic solution for designers to consider, *if* they expect to fully integrate the Internet into the ebb and tide of their firm and its work.

Unfortunately, there are no easy ways to do this, either. If you're interested in making a direct, digital connection to the Internet, you'll want to first look into whatever services your local telephone company can supply. Don't be surprised if it has made some kind of alliance with one of the local Internet access providers in your area, who can often install and maintain the line for you. Remember, these providers already have direct, digital connections to the Net. You can simply tap into their connections and go along for the ride, with their permission, that is...and with their full access, in turn, to a healthy portion of your firm's disposable cash!

I told you there were a lot of different ways to connect to the Internet! Have you been asking yourself which method might best serve your needs and those of your firm? Great—go, therefore, and get connected!

The next chapter introduces various ways you can use your newly made connection to find information on the Internet—there are trillions of bits of information out there waiting to be found! And, as you'll see after even the very shortest surf session, there are a lot, I mean a *whole lot*, of companies publishing this information who need your help with design, content development, and conceptualization.

Chapter 3

How to Find Information

This chapter provides an overview of the many ways you can find information on the Internet.

Act I

Scene 4

Steven, having made significant progress in introducing Kit to the Net, has but one hurdle left to clear—convincing her that people will be able to find her information.

Steven: "All right, Kit, you're finally connected to the Internet with its millions of documents worldwide."

Kit: "Millions of documents? Hold on! How in the world are people going to find our documents?"

It is indeed incredible to consider the vastness of the Internet as it connects computers all over the world, with their massive archives of digitized information. There are millions and millions of electronic files. Finding what you're looking for can be like searching for an electronic "needle in a haystack." Thankfully, searching through this vast array of information is becoming easier and easier, in large part because of the various Internet services now available, as well as new search engines and catalogs and easier-to-use software tools called browsers.

search engines
Sometimes known as search agents, these software tools enable you to conduct online searches of Internet documents and sites by keyword or subject area.

browsers
Browsers refer to software applications enabling users to "browse" through multimedia, multidocument World Wide Web sites on the Internet.

catalogs
Similar to search engines, catalogs or indexes act more like Internet yellow pages and are very useful for finding sites of interest to explore.

Another Detour: URL and File Formats

But before we get to all these information resources, we should take a detour into the world of Internet addresses and file formats.

The Uniform Resource Locator

URL stands for Uniform Resource Locator, and is the Internet equivalent of a U.S. Postal address. The URL is a consistent way to describe the location of any resource on the Internet. Currently, the resource described is usually a static file, but a URL can describe access to a database, dynamically updated information such as real-time weather data, an email address, a Usenet newsgroup, and more. In short, a URL can describe practically any piece of information that is available on any computer anywhere on the Internet.

The importance of URLs to the Web cannot be overstated. URLs, by creating a consistent syntax for describing the location of any information on the Internet, make the World Wide Web possible. Whenever you reference an image file or a link to another file inside of an HTML file, you describe the location of the other file using a URL. The best way to become comfortable with URLs is to turn on the option to display your current URL within your Web browser, and pay attention to the names of each of the pages that you load. Experiment with the URL by modifying it or typing in your own. To make this easier, a short overview of URL syntax follows.

URL Syntax

The basic form of a URL is a string of characters with two main parts. The first part, before the first colon, is a scheme descriptor, which describes the method for retrieving this particular kind of information. The string appearing after the colon follows a syntax determined by the particular scheme. Symbolically, this can be described as:

<-----scheme-----<: <-----scheme-specific-part-----<

Most common URL schemes, such as HTTP, Gopher,

and FTP, describe the location of a particular file. For
these schemes, the "scheme-specific-part" will describe the name of the host that the information is
to be requested from, and the location of the information on that host. This can be described symbolically as:

⟨····scheme····⟩://⟨····hostname····⟩/(⟨····url-path····⟩)

The parentheses mark a part of the URL that is considered optional. Some examples of URLs like this
are http://www.zender.com/designers-guide-net,
http://home.mcom.com/, and ftp://sumex-
aim.stanford.edu/pub/info-mac. In the first example, the scheme is "http," the hostname is
"www.zender.com" and the url-path is "designers-
guide-net." The second example demonstrates
leaving off the url-path part of the URL. In this case,
a default document (often named index.html) will
be returned by the server. The last example, the location of the Info-Mac software archive, demonstrates a URL for a document on an FTP server rather
than a Web server.

Other common URLs that follow different naming
schemes are mailto:designboy@zender.com, or
news:rec.backcountry. The first example allows you
to send email to the address designboy@zender.
com. The second example will load an index of articles posted to the newsgroup rec.backcountry.
There are other similar URLs, such as URLs for WAIS
and Telnet. New URLs are always being added. As
the Web evolves, the number of URL schemes will
continue to grow.

Technically, URLs are just a subset of a larger set of
descriptors called URIs, for Universal Resource
Identifiers. Other examples of URIs are URNs, for
Uniform Resource Name, and URCs, for Uniform
Resource Citation. The system of URIs is still under
development, but its designers hope to make
searching for and locating specific documents on

the Internet easier and easier. The most up-to-date information on the system is available at http://www.w3.org/hypertext/WWW/Addressing. The official specifications of the URL can be viewed from this address. The Beginner's Guide to URLs, which is short and sweet, although not completely technically up-to-date, is located at http://www.ncsa.uiuc.edu/demoweb/url-primer.html.

File Formats

No doubt you're already used to seeing a zillion different file formats cross your desktop. Well, the Internet adds a few more complexities to how we send and receive files. One important thing you need to know about is <u>ASCII encoding</u>. When you send programs or binary data files (such as a Photoshop image or Word document) via electronic mail over the Net, you have to convert them to a text-only format that all computers can understand. That's what ASCII encoding does—it converts files to straight ASCII text. Then, when the file gets to its destination, the person there can reverse the process, or decode the file, and end up with the same file you started with. You will often encounter ASCII encoding, in the form of BinHex files, on Macintosh archives as well.

What makes it more complicated is that there are different ASCII encoding formats that are used, so you have to figure out which one to use when sending a file and which one to decode when you receive a file. One of the most common is the <u>uucode</u> (or uuencode) format, which comes from the Unix world. Uucode is the most common on non-Macintosh machines. The Macintosh standard format, which you'll also find on the Internet, is <u>BinHex</u>. BinHex (.hqx) is basically used only on Macs, because it deals easily with the two "forks" of

---

ASCII encoding

Most files on a computer aren't simple ASCII text. Files like GIF and JPEG images, software, and illustration or desktop publishing files are stored as binary data. Unfortunately, the current electronic mail standard can only handle straight ASCII text. In order to send these other files over the Internet as part of an email message, they must be encoded as ASCII text. If you look at an encoded file, you will see a stream of random-looking characters. However, when the recipient of the message decodes the file, the text is converted back to binary, and the original file will be stored on the recipient's hard drive.

---

uucode

Some email programs (such as Microsoft Mail) use this format by default (and may in fact do the work of encoding and decoding for you). This format is also used when posting image files to Usenet newsgroups. Uuencoded files (.uu or .uue) can be created and decoded on the Mac with StuffIt Deluxe (which I'm sure you

continued on next page

BinHex

To binhex and debinhex files, Mac users can use the StuffIt products—StuffIt Expander is

continued on next page

already know about), UULite, or uuUndo (you can get these on the Web at http://wwwhost. ots.utexas.edu/mac/pub-mac-compression. html). Windows users should get Wincode (ftp://bitsy.mit.edu/pub/dos/utils).

---

btoa

You probably won't need to worry about btoa files, but if you do, StuffIt Deluxe can decode them for the Mac, and I honestly don't know about a program for Windows.

Mac files, the data fork and the resource fork. Those are the big two. You may also run into btoa ASCII-encoded files.

Fortunately, some Internet programs (such as Eudora, which I'll look at later) do this ASCII encoding and decoding automatically, so you don't have to worry about doing it manually. If you want to send a Photoshop file along with an email message, for example, you just "attach" it to the email message using Eudora, and Eudora takes care of encoding it properly (and it also decodes most files you receive). Fetch, an FTP client for the Macintosh, will recognize and automatically decode many forms of ASCII encoding, including BinHex.

Beyond ASCII encoding, the only other thing you'll want to do to your files is compress them. Obviously, you want to make your files as small as possible, so they transmit over the Net faster. As designers, we're already used to compressing and decompressing. But remember, there are other platforms out there, and other compression schemes than the ones we're used to.

If you're a Mac user, you know all about StuffIt's .sea and .sit, and Compact Pro's .cpt (or .cmp). But on the Internet, you may run into other formats, and you'll need software to decompress these files. For files with the .Z (uppercase Z) extension (compressed using UNIX Compress), use StuffIt or MacCompress (http://wwwhost.ots.utexas.edu/ mac/pub-mac-compression.html). For .z (lowercase z) or .gz files (the Unix gzip format), use MacGzip (ftp://ftp.tidbits.com/pub/tidbits/tisk/util). Then there's the often-encountered .zip format (from the DOS world) — use ZipIt (http://www.awa.com/ softlock/zipit/zipit.html).

If you're a Windows user, here's the quick run-down: For .zip files, use PKZIP and PKUNZIP (ftp://ftp. pkware.com/pkware). For .Z files, use uncompress

particularly useful for decoding and decompressing files all in one easy step. (Go to http://wwwhost.ots.utexas.edu/pub-mac-compression.html for these programs.) Windows users need a PC version of BinHex (ftp://boombox.micro.umn.edu/pub/binhex /MSDOS). As a side note, another encoding scheme, MacBinary (or BinHex 5) also encodes the two "forks" of a Mac file so that other computers can deal with them. MacBinary, however, is not a form of text encoding and cannot be used to encode messages to be sent via email. It is most often used for storing Mac files on FTP archives.

---

software

By the way, if the URLs I give throughout this chapter don't work (the Internet is changing constantly, after all), there are some great general resources on the Net for finding software. Software archives contain thousands of programs under every category imaginable. The Info-Mac archive (ftp://sumex-aim.stanford. edu/info-mac) is a great example (you can search it from a Web page at http://www.msc. wku.edu/Dept/Support/Tech/MSC/Macintosh/ search_infomac.html). For Windows programs,

continued on next page

Search Info-Mac

About All Files Recent Uploads This Week

The index in this service has not been updated since July 30, 1995 and soon will be moved to a new server. Please bear with us.

NOTE: THIS URL HAS MOVED, YOU ARE MOST LIKELY VIEWING A REDIRECTION. ITS NEW HOME IS http://www.msc.vku.edu/Dept/Support/Tech/MSC/... as it was. Please make a note of it...

This is a searchable index of all files in the info-mac Macintosh archive area at the sumex-aim.stanford.edu. Please fill in the form below with the appropriate information and click the button labeled "Search the Archives". You will receive a list of files matching your search criteria, which you can then subsequently retrieve by clicking the retrieve button.

You can also search the Umich archives.

Search Criteria

I'm looking for a Macintosh program with the following characteristics:

● Its name contains [_____]

☐ Recent files only.

---

try the CICA Windows Archive (ftp://ftp.cica.indiana.edu/pub/cica/pc). Another good source for all platforms is the Virtual Shareware Library (http://www.acs.oakland.edu/cgi-bin/shase).

---

archives

Is the main FTP site too busy to access? Popular FTP archives, such as the Info-Mac archive, are often so busy they are difficult to log in to. Luckily, FTP sites this popular have *mirror* sites—other FTP archives at different locations which are carbon copies of the original. If you are denied access, be sure to pay attention to the message you receive back. The mirrors of an archive will usually be listed in this text.

My favorite mirror archive is ftp://mirrors.aol.com, run as a free service by America Online. It contains mirrors of the Info-Mac archive at Stanford, the University of Michigan Mac archive, rtfm.mit.edu (home of the Usenet archive), the Windows archive at ftp://winftp.cica.indiana.edu, the PC Games Archive, the On-Line Guitar Archive, and the music archive at ftp://ftp.uwp.edu. And I've never had problems logging in.

(ftp://ftp.eecs.umich.edu/people/telfeyan/tools/dos/compression). For .z or .gz files, try gzip and gunzip (at the same URL). Finally, for StuffIt .sit or .sea files, use UNSTUFF (ftp://ftp.netcom.com/pub/leonardr/Aladdin).

Congratulations! You made it through all that less-than-exciting information!

Other file formats are much easier to deal with, and I'll simply list them below. For the graphics, audio, and movie formats listed here, see chapter 11 for how to view or play them on your specific computer.

.au	Ulaw audio file
.avi	AVI movie
.bin	MacBinary (BinHex 5) ASCII-encoded file
.bmp	Windows Bitmap graphics file
.cmp, .cpt	Compact Pro compressed archive
.exe	DOS/Windows executable program
.gif	GIF image file
.gz	GNU Zip or gzip compressed file
.hqx	BinHex 4 ASCII-encoded file
.html, .htm	HTML Web page document

.jpeg, .jpg	JPEG image file
.mov	QuickTime movie
.mpg	MPEG movie
.pict	Macintosh picture file
.ps	PostScript file
.qt	QuickTime movie
.ra, .ram	RealAudio file
.rtf	Rich Text Format
.sea	Compressed Self-Extracting Archive
.sit	StuffIt compressed archive
.tar	Unix Tape Archive
.tiff	TIFF image file
.txt	text-only file
.uu, .uue	Uuencoded
.wav	WAV audio file
.xbm	x-bitmap image file
.Z	Unix Compress file
.z	GNU Zip (gzip) compressed file
.zip	PKZIP compressed file

Internet Services

Glad to see you made it through those detours! Let's begin now with a look at the Internet services available to assist you in finding information. We'll introduce email, newsgroups and mailing lists, the World Wide Web, FTP, Gopher, WAIS, Internet videoconferencing and telephone, Internet Relay Chat, and MOOs, MUDs, and MUSHs. Got all that? For each service, we'll briefly explain how you can use it and what software you'll need.

Email

Email, though looked upon by some <u>webheads</u> as an underutilization of the power of the Internet, is actually an incredibly efficient communication tool. Electronic mail is the modern equivalent of a traditional letter or memo—only it's much, much faster. In fact, instant global communication is pretty hard to beat. Sure beats the "snail mail" of the post office!

No, it's not design-intensive. To the contrary, it's almost antidesign, with no emphasis placed on beauty and appearance. Email is "engineer speak"—just raw content delivered at what seems like the speed of light. Messages are composed quickly, addressed even more quickly, and sent with just the click of a mouse, reaching their destination just about the time your finger releases the mouse button. At that speed, who cares about beauty? Nonetheless, email is a very efficient and a very effective communication service.

It's just one of those things you've got to try to believe. A half-hour later, and you'll see just how flexible a tool email is. You'll also wonder how you ever worked without it. Need to dash off a quick note? Just type it and send it. Need to attach a file, perhaps a layout or the text for a sample book chapter? Do it. Just type your message, click the file to attach it, and send both of them together. Need to respond to, redirect, or forward <u>a message</u> you just received? Type and click. Wow, and we used to settle for snail mail, FedEx, and business trips!

Email is fast and efficient, but be forewarned: It's not exactly private. Once email messages leave your machine, they are potentially readable by a lot of geeks out there who just happen to know how to steam open your files. Passwords and encryption algorithms can help, but it's best to be mindful of the

---

webheads

This is an endearing term describing 1) those among us who have found that the line between our avocation and vocation has been blurred due to an excessive amount of Net surfing; and 2) those whose behavior exhibits the early symptoms of a modern, electronic pathological illness. Beware.

---

a message

Date: Tue, 20 Jun 95 16:56 EST

To: mzender@zender.com

From: michaeln@iquest.net (Michael J. Nolan)

Subject: Designer's Guide to the Internet

Hi Mike, Jeff, and Rick.

Just wanted to let you know that last night I stayed up past my bedtime to read over the first chapters you sent along with your email yesterday. I made copious notes on them,

continued on next page

which Steve will be incorporating into his

first pass back to you. Well done!

I like the tone of the book a lot, and there

are many provocative ideas that are just

little gems tucked away in there. Things

such as how the designer yields control to

the reader in hypertext. These things will

make great pull-quotes.

I felt that chapter 11 particularly is a great

opportunity for a heavily graphical, visual

treatment, and wonder to what extent

you'll be able to add some good graphics?

Keep up the good work. I look forward to

receiving the chapters as they come in,

and really look forward to the celebration

at publication in September!

Kind regards,

Michael J. Nolan

  -in-Chief, Design

To: mzender@zender.com
From: michaeln@iquest.net (Michael J. Nolan)
Subject: Designer's Guide to the Internet
Cc:
Bcc:
Attachments:

Hi Mike, Jeff, and Rick.
Just wanted to let you know that last night I stayed
up past my bedtime to read over the first chapters you
sent along with your email yesterday. I made copious
notes on them, which Steve will be incorporating into
his first pass back to you. Well done!

I like the tone of the book a lot, and there are many
provocative ideas that are just little gems tucked away
in there. Things such as how the designer yields
control to the reader in hypertext. These things will
make great pull-quotes.

I felt that chapter 11 particularly is a great
opportunity for a heavily graphical, visual treatment,
and wonder to what extent you'll be able to add some
good graphics?

Keep up the good work. I look forward to receiving the
chapters as they come in, and really look forward to
the celebration at publication in September!

Kind regards,

Michael J. Nolan
Editor-in-Chief, Design

Editor

A rare yet helpful breed of humans capable of pushing lowly writers to extremes.

Email Address-Finding Tools

http://twod.med.harvard.edu/labgc/roth/Emailsearch.html

fact that your email—both what you send and what you receive—is vulnerable.

Another problem with email is that it can be quite difficult to locate people's email addresses. There is no central directory to turn to, and there really aren't any special services that have been established for this purpose. Well, that's not quite true—it's just difficult. There is a great FAQ on this whole subject that describes several techniques for locating email addresses. Check out Email Address-Finding Tools.

FAQ

FAQ is the abbreviation for Frequently Asked Questions (and their responses) that appear within various Internet services, most often Usenet newsgroups. It's wise to read the FAQ on a particular topic or group before asking a lot of frequently posed questions.

FAQ: How to find people's E-mail addresses

Archive-name: finding-addresses
Version: $Id: finding.n,v 2.2 1995/07/04 15:15:09 dalamb Exp $

Copyright 1991,1992,1993,1994 Jonathan I. Kamens
Copyright 1994, 1995 David Alex Lamb
See end of file for copying permissions.

This FAQ is available on the World-Wide Web (via browsers such as Mosaic or lynx) at
 <URL:http://www.qucis.queensu.ca/FAQs/email/finding.html>

****
*   Introduction   *
****

   A question which appears frequently on the Usenet is, "I know someone's name, and I think they might have an electronic mail address somewhere. How can I find it?"

   There are many different techniques for doing this. Several of them are discussed below. Your best bet is to try the pertinent methods in this posting in the order in which they are listed (well, sort of; at the very least, please try all the pertinent methods which do not involve posting queries to soc.net-people before resorting to that).

   I've listed "Direct contact" near the end of this list because, for some reason, people seem to be reluctant to call people on the telephone or write them a paper-mail letter asking what their E-mail address is, as long as there is even a remote chance that it might be found without asking. This attitude is somewhat counterproductive, since in most cases, it is much easier to get someone's E-mail address by asking them than it is by following the other

One of the most popular Internet email applications for Mac and Windows is Qualcomm's Eudora. Several versions of this software are currently available, including a freeware version called Eudora Light. Eudora's popularity is due in large part to its ease of use (for example, it automatically ASCII encodes files you send) and its support of Internet standards such as MIME for multimedia email. The commercial version, Eudora Pro, also includes TCP/IP access software, as well as a built-in spell

checker. You can contact Qualcomm for more information. Want my recommendation? Download it today. Use it tomorrow. No, make that today. It's that great!

Other email applications include SoftArc's First Class, Banyan Systems' BeyondMail, Lotus Corporation's Notes, Microsoft's cc:Mail, and CE Software's QuickMail.

Privacy issues aside, email is indeed a powerful, nonintrusive, quick, efficient, inexpensive, and precise communication service. These attributes make email ideal for communicating with your peers, your clients, and your suppliers. Try it...you'll like it...you won't live a day longer without it! Our firm did...we

---

MIME

The Multipurpose Internet Mail Extensions provide a standard format for describing the format of an electronic mail message. MIME makes multimedia email possible by describing the file type of a mail message so it can be properly decoded by a mail reader.

---

multimedia email

Multimedia email makes it possible to easily transmit documents more complex than simple ASCII, or to include more complex documents along with a simple text message. These documents can, theoretically, include images, sound, and video. Bandwidth places limitations on what is practical.

---

freeware

Freeware refers to software available, often over the Internet, for your free use and distribution, though not modification. (See public domain and shareware).

---

public domain

Public domain software, like freeware, is available for free use and distribution. Unlike freeware, public domain software can be modified in any way you wish.

---

shareware

Shareware refers to software that is freely distributed for trial purposes. Should you decide to keep shareware, you are expected to send payment to its author.

Qualcomm

http://www.qualcomm.com

do...we won't...and we just wish everyone with whom we communicate would get it, too!

Usenet Newsgroups

Got a question or an opinion? Post it to a newsgroup over Usenet. Usenet is one of the Internet's most popular features, providing a news space where you can post messages on just about any topic you like, to which other people on the Internet can reply. It's kind of like sending email, but it's sent to anyone who may be interested in reading it. Or, it's like posting messages on a public bulletin board that's organized by subject. You go to the bulletin board and read only the messages you're interested in.

You name it and you'll find it discussed on Usenet: politics, religion, computers, sports, recreation, earthworm agriculture—even design. As of this writing, there are at least 10,000 newsgroups, though you'll currently find relatively few on design-related topics.

Here are the names of some newsgroups of interest for designers:

- alt.aldus.pagemaker

- alt.aldus.freehand

- alt.aldus.misc

- alt.corel.graphics

- alt.soft-sys.corel.draw

- alt.soft-sys.corel.misc

- alt.binaries.clip-art

- alt.binaries.fonts

- comp.fonts

- comp.graphics

- comp.text.desktop

newsgroups

An extensive list of useful Usenet newsgroups (and mailing lists—see the next section), maintained by Geof Peters, can be found at the DTP Internet Jumplist (http://www.cs.purdue.edu/homes/gwp/dtp/groups.html).

- comp.text.pdf

- comp.sys.mac.graphics

- comp.sources.postscript

- comp.publish.prepress

As you can see, newsgroups are named strangely. But actually it's not hard to translate this techno-babble. The first group of letters (before the period) defines the general topic area: "comp" for computers, "rec" for recreation, "alt" for alternative (kind of a catch-all area), and so on. The next group of letters tells you the subcategory under that general topic—above, we see a few of the many categories under "alt": aldus, corel, soft-sys, binaries, etc. And the subcategorizing continues in the same way, getting more and more specific with each group of letters. So, for example, we can figure out that alt.corel.graphics is probably a newsgroup in which people talk about (and possibly exchange) graphics with CorelDRAW.

```
news.announce.newusers (17 articles)

Articles   Sort   Search

>  1241  07/27  the *.answers mode    373  In1
   1242  07/28  Brad Templeton        267  Cop
   1243  07/28  Joel K. Furr          413  DR/
   1244  07/28  Mark Moraes           112  Hir
   1245  07/28  Edward Vielmetti      471  Wha
   1246  07/28  Mark Moraes           389  Wha
   1247  07/28  Mark Moraes           532  Em:
   1248  07/28  Mark Moraes           416  A I
   1249  07/28  David.W.Wright@bnr    131  DR/
   1250  07/28  Mark Moraes           194  In1
   1251  07/28  Mark Moraes           215  Hov
   1252  07/28  Mark Moraes           962  Ans
   1253  07/28  Mark Moraes           358  Rul
   1254  07/28  Dave Taylor           284  A (
   1255  07/28  Mark Moraes           608  Use
   1256  07/27  Perry Rovers         1203  Anc
   1257  08/08  Chris Lewis          1019  Hov
```

If you're new to newsgroups and want to give them a try, you can start by subscribing to the news.an-nounce.newusers group. To do so, however, you'll

news.announce.newusers

first have to get <u>newsreader</u> software to access and read newsgroups. To begin, try <u>Nuntius</u> for the Mac and <u>WinVN</u> for Windows. Or, you can use the Netscape Navigator Web browser, which enables both Macs and Windows computers to read news. You can find other newsreaders at the utexas mac

newsreader

This kind of software enables you to read individual newsgroup articles and news threads—groups of Usenet messages on the same subject.

WinVN

ftp://ftp.cica.indiana.edu/pub/pc/win3/winsock

Nuntius

ftp://ftp.ruc.dk/pub/nuntius

Current directory is /pub/nuntius

Up to higher level directory

Nuntius1.0.sit.hqx	400 Kb	Thu Apr 21 00:00:00 1994	macintosh archive
Nuntius1.0.src.sea.	325 Kb	Thu Apr 21 00:00:00 1994	macintosh archive
Nuntius1.1.sea.hqx	404 Kb	Thu Apr 21 00:00:00 1994	macintosh archive
Nuntius1.1.src.sea.	577 Kb	Thu Apr 21 00:00:00 1994	macintosh archive
Nuntius1.2.sea.hqx	462 Kb	Thu Apr 21 00:00:00 1994	macintosh archive
Nuntius1.2.src.sea	597 Kb	Thu Apr 21 00:00:00 1994	macintosh archive
Nuntius2.0.3.src.s.	1078 Kb	Mon Feb 27 08:43:00 1995	macintosh archive
Nuntius2.0.4.sea.hqx	1083 Kb	Wed May 3 09:54:00 1995	macintosh archive
old-versions/		Wed Jul 26 09:31:00 1995	Directory

archive (http://wwwhost.ots.utexas.edu/mac/main.html) or The Consummate Winsock Apps List (http://cwsapps.texas.net)—both great resources.

WinVN: 5854 groups; 2 subscribed

Network Group Utilities Config Window Help

```
    0 alt.comp
    0 alt.comp.acad-freedom
    0 alt.comp.acad-freedom.news
  108 alt.comp.acad-freedom.talk
    0 alt.comp.compression
    1 alt.comp.databases.xbase.clipper
    0 alt.comp.fsp
    0 alt.comp.hardware
   22 alt.comp.hardware.homebuilt
   17 alt.comp.periphs.mainboard.asus
    8 alt.comp.shareware
    0 alt.comp.shareware.for-kids
    2 alt.comp.virus
    0 alt.computer
  209 alt.computer.consultants
  175 alt.config
```

Once you have a newsreader, check out its Read Me file to learn how to use it to subscribe to the news.announce.newusers group. Every newsreader works a little differently, but once you've learned how to find the newsgroup you're looking for, you can download text to your hard drive's heart's content. Unlike mailing lists (see the next section), which automatically send messages to your email in-box, you browse an index of every posting to the newsgroup, choosing to download only what you want to look at.

You can't post to the news.announce.newusers group, but you'll find it helpful just to read its postings—written questions and responses from visitors concerning how to use Usenet. Hey, with a limited number of newsgroups for designers, maybe you'd like to start your own. If so, you'll also find a document describing how to do so.

Lastly, a bit of useful newsgroup Netiquette. You should always conserve bandwidth when possible. Remember that your messages will be distributed to many, many different sites located all over the world, so avoid making posts that could have been better dealt with using email directly to a single person. Also, avoid the practice of cross-posting. Often, a message will be appropriate for more than one newsgroup. Only post it in more than one group if you feel it is absolutely necessary. Along these lines, if you wish to post an advertising message of some kind, be discreet and post your message to only specific groups—indiscriminate posting of messages to multiple groups, known as "spamming," wastes bandwidth and will often be met with hostility. Lastly, don't flame people. Flaming, the practice of unrelenting personal attacks on a poster, rather than commenting on the post itself, is all too common. Usually it has no place in a newsgroup.

Mailing Lists

The basic idea behind a mailing list is simple. Any email message sent to a particular address is distributed to everybody that subscribes to the list. Since email is virtually instantaneous, a mailing list presents a means of discussion that is very similar to a newsgroup; the postings just end up in your email in-box instead of being viewed with a newsreader. You don't actually communicate with a specific person on the list. Instead, it's more like sending a newsletter to a group of people with similar interests. Everyone on the list sees your mailing and can comment at will.

Unlike newsgroups, however, messages you send to a mailing list are targeted to a more specific audience: just the members on the list, not the wide distribution of a newsgroup. There are also mailing lists that aren't used for discussion, but for distribution of information, such as bug reports, software updates, and bulletins. For example, the java-announce mailing list is used strictly to distribute announcements of significant new releases or ports of Java or HotJava (more on Java in chapter 11). If you're interested in this or other Java-related mailing lists, read about them at http://java.sun.com/mail.html.

The fact remains that there's a lot of overlap between newsgroups and mailing lists. In fact, you'll find that just about any subject has both a newsgroup and a mailing list. I guess some people prefer newsgroups and some mailing lists. How about you? Don't know? Give them a try and find out.

Whatever your interests, subscribe to mailing lists and you'll never be out of the loop again. There are lists for anything, some with thousands of members, others with just a few. But be careful! When you sign up for a large mailing list, you can expect to receive lots of messages, maybe hundreds each day. That's right, *hundreds*. And they come right to your email in-box. Got an extra few hours to keep up with all that email?

Finding mailing lists can be difficult. Unlike Usenet newsgroups, there is no central list of available mailing lists. The lists I subscribe to I learned about via references in other information, such as FAQs, Web pages, and, not surprisingly, postings in newsgroups and mailing lists. But what if you want to know right away if there is a list on a particular topic?

There are large directories of mailing lists out there. Try sending an email message to listserv@ricevm1. rice.edu, with LIST GLOBAL somewhere in the body of your message. You will receive back a 662K file containing references to approximately 6,500 different mailing lists. Other good places to look for mailing lists are, as I mentioned before, Web pages and FAQs. Also, any good mailing list will make itself known in related forums. Desktop publishing lists are listed on good desktop publishing Web pages, such as the DTP Internet Jumplist (http://www. cs.purdue.edu/homes/gwp/dtp/groups.html) mentioned earlier. You can also try searching for a list by keyword at Inter-Links' site (http://www.nova.edu/ Inter-Links/cgi-bin/news-lists.pl). You will encounter many useful lists in your searches for other information.

For subscribing to mailings lists, you have to know about the two main kinds of mailing lists: those that are maintained manually and those maintained by a server system. A manually maintained system will have an actual person who adds and deletes people from the list. Subscribing to these lists is easy. You find the email address of the person maintaining it and send him or her a polite message asking to be subscribed.

An automated server, often referred to as a LIST-SERV, maintains many separate mailing lists. To subscribe to any of these lists, you email the proper command to the LISTSERV. These commands are simple, usually involving simply writing "subscribe" or "add" and your name, your email address, and the name of the list you wish to subscribe to somewhere in the body of the message. If you don't know how to use a particular LISTSERV, send a message to the server's address with the word "help" in the body of the email address. You will usually receive a file explaining the commands that are available.

LISTSERV

A LISTSERV is a mailing list server, which automatically maintains many separate mailing lists. In addition to allowing users to subscribe and unsubscribe, many systems offer other services, such as archive searching.

The term LISTSERV actually refers to a specific software package, called LISTSERV, that is common on IBM mainframes. Most Unix-based servers use Majordomo or Listproc instead. There is also a Macintosh-based system called ListStar. Since LISTSERV was the first kid on

continued on next page

Usually, these questions will be answered for you when you find a reference to a mailing list elsewhere. It is customary to include a brief explanation of how to subscribe when a list is described.

the block, the term has come to refer to most every automated mailing list.

And now, to get you started, here are some useful mailing lists:

- Adobe PageMaker:
  address: listserv@indycms.iupui.edu
  command: SUBSCRIBE PAGEMAKR (Your Name)

- QuarkXPress:
  address: listserv@iubvm.ucs.indiana.edu
  command: SUBSCRIBE QUARKXPR (Your Name)

- Adobe Photoshop:
  address: listserv@bgu.edu
  command: SUBSCRIBE ADOBEPS (Your Name)

- Adobe Illustrator:
  address: listserv@netcom.com
  command: SUBSCRIBE ILLSTRTR-L (Your Name)

- Macromedia FreeHand:
  address: listserv@galileo.uafadm.alaska.edu
  command: SUBSCRIBE FREEHAND-L (Your Name)

World Wide Web

Ready to find more on the Net than just plain old text? Welcome to the multimedia funhouse, the Internet of the 90s! The World Wide Web brings a fresh, new graphical user interface to the Internet, a welcome relief from the text-only Internet services mentioned above. Finally, we have full access to fonts, styles, text styles, graphics—remember those things you use in practicing your profession, which up until the Web were basically of no use on the Internet?! The Web is rapidly becoming the most popular part of the Internet, growing faster than any other service. Here's where you'll probably spend most of your time browsing the Net and searching for information.

At its heart, the Web enables you to find documents (called Web pages or home pages) on the Net that contain a variety of formats, anything from text to photos and graphics to audio and even video (though few of us today have access to enough bandwidth to take advantage of video). Whereas the Internet used to be a black-and-white land filled only with text, the Web has transformed it into a colorful, slick universe with multimedia potential. And the Web, or more accurately, Web browsers, give you the ability to jump seamlessly from one document to another on <u>servers</u> anywhere in the world.

For example, simply type the URL into your browser and check out the <u>Weather Page</u> located at Harvard. Want to see what the weather's like in Australia today? No problem. Just click on the words

servers

The kind of huge and fast computer you wish you could afford that, for the most part, is dedicated to transmitting files back and forth over a network.

Weather Page

http://acro.harvard.edu/GA/weather.html

Weather information

Last Update: Friday, 07-Jul-95 11:09:22 EDT

This document contains all the links to weather information that I could find. If anybody knows of other weather information sources, please let me know so I can include them. I have not checked out all of the references. In particular I have not checked whether there are duplications of links. Please let me know if you find anything wrong or would like to see anything changed in this document.

Latest satellite images and weather maps

Weather information sources

▶ Aviation Weather Information

This document contains links to aviation specific weather sources. There separate links to information on the same server to make it easier to find particular information (like airmets, sigmets, etc).

▶ Australia, New Zealand

Australian National University Bioinformatics server
Australian National University Bioinformatics server. Connections to many weather resources worldwide on their very nice Weather Page (weather.html). Comments to David.Green@anu.edu.au.
Victoria University Meterology
New Zealand Weather
Western Australian Weather
Forecasts for Western Australia

"Australian National University Bioinformatics server" (a <u>hypertext link</u>) further down the page, and you'll take the fast route to Australia, via cyberspace, to automatically connect to that University's <u>Weather & Global Monitoring</u> home page a few seconds later—not bad! See the beauty of this? Any Web page can contain links to any other documents, regardless of whether or not those documents

hypertext link

A visual metaphor, usually indicated by underlined and colored text, indicates an interactive connection with another file. Simply click on the link and you're transported to the Internet site or file the hypertext link refers to.

Weather & Global Monitoring

http://life.anu.edu.au/weather.html

continued on next page

Weather & global monitoring

The following information is available via <u>ANU Bioinformatics Hypermedia Service</u>

- <u>Current weather satellite images</u>, including
  - <u>Australia (most recent)</u>
  - <u>Pacific hemisphere (most recent)</u>
  - <u>Antarctica</u>
  - <u>USA (infrared)</u>
  - <u>Atlantic hemisphere</u>
  - <u>Japan, China & Korea</u>
  - Current US weather maps & movies: <u>via MSU</u>, and <u>via NIH</u>
  - <u>Current European weather images (via UK)</u>
  - <u>GMS weather satellite images (FTP to Archie)</u>
- Weather reports and forecasts
  - <u>Australia (gopher to Bureau of Meteorology)</u>
  - <u>Canada</u>
  - <u>USA & North America</u>
- Australian environment:
  - <u>Greenness Index for Australia using NDVI</u>
  - <u>Tasmanian Climate</u>
- <u>Recent earthquakes</u>
- <u>Frequently asked questions about weather services on Internet</u>
- <u>Frequently asked questions about weather services on Internet</u>
- <u>Other weather information services</u>
- <u>Environmental monitoring from space</u>

Related information

reside on the same server or on another server half-way around the world. To the user, the link is completely transparent.

Dynamically linking information in this way obviously has tremendous ramifications for us as designers. Get going on the Web and start to get some feel for how you'll be organizing content for your next interactive Web site! (You'll find more on designing for the Internet in part IV.)

Once you've got a taste of the Web, you'll want to spend more time on it. Web browsers, the software that hide a myriad of complicated commands behind simple-to-use graphical user interfaces, make navigating the Web easy and intuitive. If you can click a mouse, you can navigate the Web, jumping from one site to another just by selecting highlighted words and pictures. And everything happens in the brief time it takes those fast little electrons to fly across the Internet.

The World Wide Web, which didn't really come into being until 1993 with the development of the first Web browser, Mosaic, has been responsible to a great extent for the recent explosive growth of the

Internet. At this time, Netscape Communications Corporation's <u>Netscape Navigator</u> Web browser has practically become the de facto industry standard.

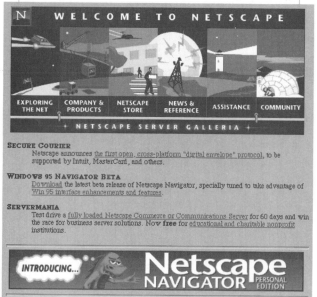

Netscape works, like other browsers, by reading documents that have been formatted with the <u>HTML</u> programming language. HTML basically defines how a Web page will look and indicates how hypertext-linked documents perform. Much of Netscape's success has come from its speed and its implementation of numerous additions to standard HTML code. (See part IV of this book for the ramifications of HTML, this somewhat limited tool, for designers.)

Unfortunately, few standards currently exist on how Web browsers interpret HTML. So a given Web page will most likely look slightly different depending on which browser you use. Because HTML is so extensible and basically without standards, however, there is tremendous competition underway in the production of new and better Web browsers, which seem to appear almost weekly.

Other Web browsers you might want to check out include NCSA Mosaic for Mac (http://www.ncsa.uiuc.edu/SDG/Software/MacMosaic) and Windows (http://www.ncsa.uiuc.edu/SDG/Software/WinMosaic),

MacWeb (http://galaxy.einet.net/EINet/MacWeb/MacWebHome.html), and WinWeb (http://galaxy.einet.net/EINet/WinWeb/WinWebHome.html).

FTP

FTP is the File Transfer Protocol that enables computers to connect to one another and transfer actual files back and forth. It's been around for quite a while, and in fact is still probably used more than any other service to transfer files over the Internet. I know I've already used the word "incredible" to describe other features of the Internet. But, *incredible* and maybe *totally amazing* are the only words that

transfer files

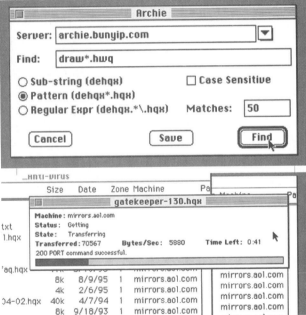

come to mind in describing the vast number of files stored on FTP sites. Terabytes upon terabytes of files are just lounging around waiting to be FTPed! Perhaps this is a slight exaggeration, but hey, feel sorry for at least a few of those poor files, and bring some home.

In recent years, the protocols embodied by FTP have been adopted by most other Internet services as well, enabling you to use this powerful tool even

Terabytes

A whole lot of bytes. A terabyte is 1,099,511,627,776 bytes of data to be exact, the equivalent of about 759,000 high-density floppies, that if stacked would reach one and a half miles high.

from a Web page using a Web browser, for example.
Once you become familiar with FTP, you can use it to
log on to a remote FTP site, locate the files you
need, download them, and then log off again. You'll
need to use a program such as the Mac-based
Anarchie (ftp://ftp.share.com/pub/peterlewis) or
the Windows-based WS_FTP to help you conduct
Archie searches and get files.

WS_FTP

http://www.csra.net/junodj/ws_ftp.htm

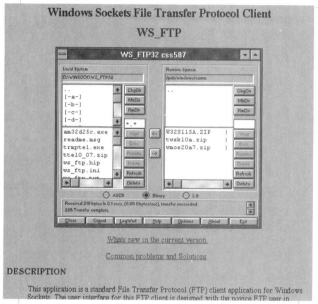

Archie

A huge electronic database listing many files available through FTP. For more info, see the last section of this chapter regarding non-Web search engines.

A common mistake when using FTP to transfer a file
relates to the difference between ASCII and binary
files. You must set your FTP client program to either
ASCII or binary mode depending on the type of file
you are transferring. If you download a GIF file from
an FTP archive but have your client set to ASCII
mode, the file will be munged. A good rule of
thumb: If your file fails to decode properly when you
download it, check your file type mode. Luckily,
Fetch on the Macintosh will automatically set the
transfer type based on the suffix of the file being
downloaded.

FTP, unlike the more visually oriented Web, is difficult to explain. Once you use FTP a few times,
though, you'll begin to see its usefulness.

difference between ASCII and binary

Standard ASCII consists of 128 different characters, which can be encoded using only 7 bits. Unfortunately, each character is stored in a single byte, which uses 8 bits. This means the eighth bit is wasted. Because of this, it seemed foolish to transmit all 8 bits over the Internet if one was copying a text file between computers, since 1/8 of the data would be an unnecessary waste of bandwidth. To deal with this situation, two modes of transmission were created: ASCII and binary. ASCII mode transmits only the first 7 of the 8 bits of each byte. Binary mode transmits all 8. You'll discover the

continued on next page

Gopher

Gopher is yet another protocol that, like FTP, is useful in finding information on the Internet. Gopher is in many ways the Web's predecessor. Unlike the multimedia hypertext links of the WWW, text-only Gopher documents are usually limited to text and are hierarchically organized. However, Gopher did a good job of organizing and publishing information, and was much easier to use than simple FTP. Since Web browsers can download files from Gopher servers, "Web space" is now said to encompass "Gopher space" within it. Technically speaking, Gopher servers are now part of the Web, since any document on a Gopher server can be described with a URL and displayed by a Web browser.

So to use Gopher to find information, you can use your Web browser. Or, you can get a Gopher-specific application such as TurboGopher for the Mac (this and other Mac Gopher clients can be downloaded

difference when you transfer a binary file, such as a GIF file, but leave the transfer mode set to ASCII. The file won't load properly, since 1/8 of the file, every eighth bit, wasn't transmitted.

TurboGopher

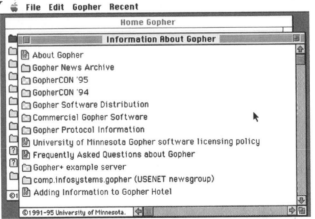

from http://wwwhost.ots.utexas.edu/mac/internet-gopher.html) or WS Gopher for Windows (http://snake.srv.net/~dlb/DaveBrooks.html).

As with other Internet services, working with Gopher renders almost meaningless the concept of physical location. As you visit one Gopher server, you'll soon discover that it's also linked with many other such servers in the world. You search Gopher space using Veronica and Jughead (which, combined with Archie, give us a regular comic book full of search tools!). Give Gopher a chance. "Go fer" that information you're trying to find.

WAIS

WAIS, pronounced "ways," stands for Wide Area Information Servers, yet another standardized Internet protocol resident on Internet servers. Though originally a stand-alone information retrieval application, WAIS servers today often function as the search engines behind Web pages. Yet, there are still considerable reasons to use WAIS on its own for finding the information you need on the Internet.

WAIS solves a major problem in finding information by helping people communicate with huge databases in something other than complex computer database languages. As powerful as it is, WAIS makes it easy to simply pose your query in pretty much plain old English. Want to learn more about how to use AIFF sound files with Macromedia Director? Just type: "Tell me about using AIFF sound files with Macromedia Director." The WAIS protocol works by searching a database using the important words

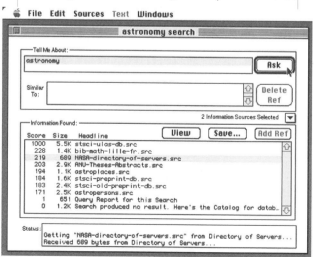

(i.e., AIFF, sound, Macromedia, Director) in your query, finding only those items that match your search—and even ranking them in order of usefulness.

WAIS will probably play an even greater role in the future, given the fact that the protocol allows for information to be sold and gives information providers complete control over who, what, how, and when information is distributed. With the help of WAIS, "pay for view" is about to become the *modus operandi* of the Internet. And guess who will become the information gatekeepers of the future? That's right: designers, at least to some extent. Better learn to use WAIS now in preparation for your future role.

Software for WAIS includes MacWAIS (http://galaxy. einet.net/EINet/MacWAIS.html) and winWAIS (http://galaxy.einet.net/EINet/winWAIS.html). You can also search <u>WAIS directly from the Web</u>.

WAIS directly from the Web

http://www.wais.com/newhomepages/

wais-dbs.html

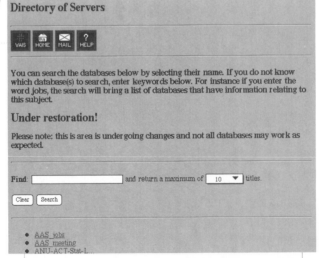

Directory of Servers

You can search the databases below by selecting their name. If you do not know which database(s) to search, enter keywords below. For instance if you enter the word jobs, the search will bring a list of databases that have information relating to this subject.

Under restoration!

Please note: this is area is under going changes and not all databases may work as expected.

Find [   ] and return a maximum of [10 ▼] titles.

[Clear] [Search]

- AAS_jobs
- AAS_meeting
- ANU-ACT-Stat-L

Internet Videoconferencing

The videoconference...the next best thing to being there. Some say it's even better. A lot of hype? There's been plenty of it, along with lots of unfulfilled promises regarding this technology. You'll have to be the judge. Stand-alone and room-based videoconferencing systems, costing hundreds of thousands of dollars, have been around since the early 1980s. Desktop videoconferencing, on the other hand, enables the use of personal computers to collaborate with an individual or groups at remote sites using voice, video, text, and graphics.

Better today than ever before, desktop videoconferencing may have finally arrived, thanks to the Internet. Again, you'll have to be the judge. There's no question that today's systems are a significant milestone for collaborative communications, and that they point the way to what may well become the standard communication tool of the near future. But what about today?

Ladies and Gentlemen, gather round for yet another great Internet bargain. You'll want to check out White Pine Software's CU-SeeMe, a freeware program originally developed by Cornell University as a videoconferencing application for use over the

White Pine Software's CU-SeeMe

http://www.wpine.com/cu-seeme.html

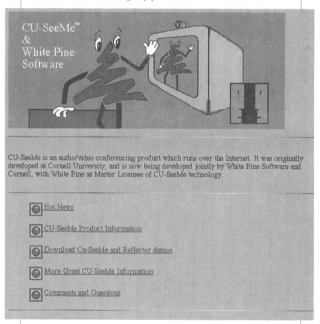

Internet and TCP/IP networks. CU-SeeMe is definitely way cool, and it's free! You probably already have plenty of hardware horsepower in-house. Why not give it a try?

CU-SeeMe

CU-SeeMe can be used over the Internet to make connections to any other desktop using

continued on next page

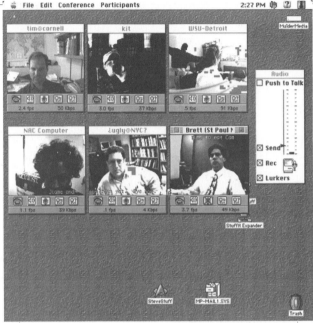

CU-SeeMe in the same fashion as email, except that with CU-SeeMe you can have a real-time meeting with video, audio, and written messages. With its unique "reflector" technology, CU-SeeMe can be used for group conferencing or TV-type broadcasting.

CU-SeeMe is targeted at low-bandwidth connections, requires no special hardware, and supports inexpensive video cameras. A software-only solution for both Windows and Macintosh, CU-SeeMe will affordably bring videoconferencing to offices, educational institutions, and homes worldwide.

Later this year, Santa Clara, California-based 3Com Corporation will release an enhanced, commercial version of CU-SeeMe featuring add-on applications

3Com Corporation

http://www.3com.com

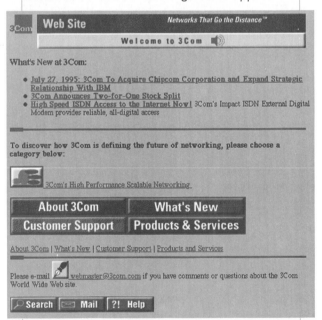

for extended functionality such as whiteboard, rolodex, and application sharing. Suffice it to say, CU-SeeMe is a tremendous tool, and hey, you can't beat the price!

On the other hand, if you want to spend some money, maybe some big money, check out Leigh Anne Rettinger's <u>Desktop Videoconferencing Product Survey</u>, a very extensive review of Internet videoconferencing products.

Desktop Videoconferencing Product Survey

http://www2.ncsu.edu/eos/service/ece/
project/succeed_info/dtvc_survey/
survey.html

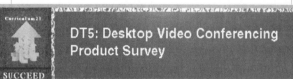

Several significant product announcements in recent months have provided the foundation for developing truly useful and cost-effective videoconferencing tools. Of course, bandwidth remains a major issue. Transmitting digital video requires an enormous <u>pipeline</u>. Recent solutions from companies such as <u>Avistar Systems</u>, and <u>Creative Labs</u>, however, enable users to conduct pretty impressive desktop videoconferences with specs in the range of 12-15 frames per second (fps), at resolutions of approximately 120 x 110 pixels over the Internet. Other important developments include Apple's new QuickTime Conferencing extension, available as part of its Media Conference Kit and System, and Microsoft's Video for Windows.

Avistar Systems

http://www.siren.com/avistar

Creative Labs

http://www.creaf.com

pipeline

Pipeline is a metaphor describing the channel or conduit (i.e., phone lines, network cabling, etc.) carrying data transmitted from one computer to another. Viewing full-motion, broadcast-quality video requires transmission of approximately 30 MB per second of digitized information—far more than the Internet can currently support. Hence, today's desktop videoconferencing applications require significant compression and the transmission of a much lower-quality image.

continued on next page

PRODUCT INFORMATION

Avistar Conference enables users on PCs, Macintosh and UNIX workstations to collaborate using high-quality video.

Avistar is a family of high-quality collaboration products that includes video conferencing, document conferencing and visual directory applications. The Avistar product family runs on Windows PCs, Macintosh, and UNIX workstations, and enables you to collaborate with others on local and remote LANs as well as conference room users and remote telecommuters.

High Quality for Natural Interaction

Avistar architecture is designed to maximize video quality and enable natural conversations that enhance the collaborative process. Local area conferences feature full-color,

CRE TIVE ™

CREATIVE LABS, INC.

Welcome to the Creative Labs

World Wide Web Server

Creative Labs, Inc., based in Milpitas, California, is the leader in PC sound, video and CD-ROM multimedia solutions, with Sound Blaster setting the industry standard for sound on PC-based platforms. Creative develops, manufactures, and markets a family of multimedia sound and video products, and a range of multimedia kits for entertainment, education and productivity markets.

Creative Product Information

- Sound Cards
- Business and Communications

Internet Relay Chat

Feeling chatty? You can use Internet Relay Chat (IRC) to talk it up with people all over the world on the Internet. "Talking" on IRC literally means talking to the world. When using IRC, anything you type is instantly communicated everywhere in the world to whomever may be using IRC at the same time—in essence, interactive communications in real time, with your audience able to respond by typing messages back to you. What everybody types scrolls by on your monitor, so it even looks like a back-and-forth conversation.

back-and-forth conversation

IRC in action

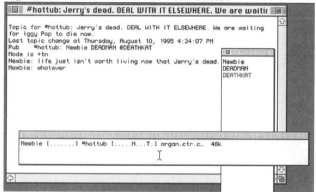

Still feeling chatty? You can take advantage of IRC to find information on just about any topic imaginable. There are always many "channels" to choose from; each channel is generally devoted to a certain topic, just like each newsgroup is. You can find out which channels currently exist through your IRC software. To learn more about IRC, check out Paul Graham's Web site, IRC-Related Resources on the Internet. While there, be sure to link to France with a quick mouse click and check out Nicolas Pioch's

IRC-Related Resources on the Internet

http://urth.acsu.buffalo.edu/irc/WWW/ ircdocs.html

IRC Related Resources on the Internet
Version 2.1.7 by pjg

from

Version 2.1.6 by ricks

Contents:

- Introduction to this document
- What's new
- Documents
  - General purpose (primer, faq, manual,....)
  - Reference material - IRC protocol
  - Policy and Administration
  - Sociology and Psychology
  - Misc documents - Look here !
- Misc resources
  - IRC Stats
  - IRC channels with WWW pages
  - Pictures of IRC users
  - Meta list of other IRC users' home pages
  - Logs from big events
- Other sources of information
  - Other good hypertext IRC pages
  - IRC related newsgroups
  - IRC related mailing lists
  - IRC related ftp sites
  - DALnet info
  - Undernet hints

IRCprimer 1.1

http://mistral.enst.fr/~pioch/IRC/IRCprimer

/IRCprimer1.1/IRCprimer1.1.html

IRCprimer 1.1 for a great introduction to the whole IRC thing.

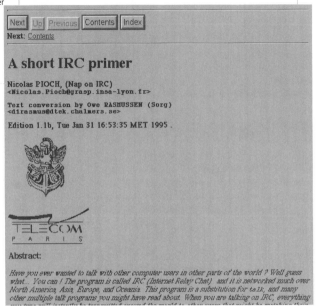

Next   Up   Previous   Contents   Index

Next: Contents

A short IRC primer

Nicolas PIOCH, (Nap on IRC)
<Nicolas.Pioch@grasp.insa-lyon.fr>

Text conversion by Owe RASMUSSEN (Sorg)
<d1rasmus@dtek.chalmers.se>

Edition 1.1b, Tue Jan 31 16:53:35 MET 1995 .

Abstract:

Have you ever wanted to talk with other computer users in other parts of the world ? Well guess what... You can ! The program is called IRC (Internet Relay Chat) and it is networked much over North America, Asia, Europe, and Oceania. This program is a substitution for talk, and many other multiple talk programs you might have read about. When you are talking on IRC, everything

Good software for IRC includes Homer for the Mac (ftp://ftp.utexas.edu/pub/mac/tcpip) and WS-IRC for Windows (ftp://ftp.clark.net/pub/csamsi).

MUDs, MOOs, and MUSHs

MUDs, MOOs, and MUSHs? You're right, I may have finally MOOs, and MUSHs (for our purposes we'll group them all together) refer to text-based virtual reality environments you can visit on the Internet. This stuff is pretty esoteric, and perhaps of limited value to busy designers looking for information on the Internet, but people tell me they're fun, so much so that they're addictive. Sorry, I don't have time for addictions. Too much work and too many responsibilities.

A MOO (which stands for MUD, Object Oriented) is the most complex of these systems. MOOs allow whole environments to be described via text. Each object in this environment gets a description and responds to commands (or "verbs"). For instance, a "baseball" on LambdaMoo can be "thrown." If you throw it, you'll see a description of, perhaps, how it flies across the room and hits your friend in the eye. Your friend, at the same time, would see a textual description explaining that a baseball just hit him in the eye. You can communicate to all the people in the room, or just whisper in one person's ear (effectively having a private conversation). There are commands used to convey gestures and emotions. If you have an active imagination, it's easy to get lost in a MOO for hours.

MUDs (Multi-User Dungeons/Dimensions) and MUSHs (Multi-User Simultaneous Hallucinations) were originally created for multiplayer role-playing adventure games to be played in textual environments. MUDs and MUSHs are still often used for this purpose, but some have outgrown their beginnings and are used for IRC-like interaction. MUDs were the predecessors of MOOs.

If you've got the time, you can visit one of these environments, where you'll first be given a special vocabulary to describe your actions as you participate. Sound confusing? It really isn't, but it's definitely a lot easier to understand once you take a visit yourself. A good place to start is at none other than MOOcentral: For Educational Uses of MOOs, MUDs,

MOOcentral

http://www.pitt.edu/~jrgst7/MOOcentral.html

Welcome to . . .

MOOcentral

Last Modified 6/24/95

MUSHs, and Other Text-Based Virtual Realities.

To visit a more interesting (and perhaps even practical!) use of a MOO, check out the MOO virtual office space for professors being created at the MIT Media Center. Telnet to purple-crayon.media.mit.edu:8888 (the 8888 refers to the port). A designer could set up a personal MOO, creating a virtual office at which to meet with clients anywhere in the world! It's an intriguing possibility.

Really, you've got to try MUDs, MOOs, and MUSHs. It's the only way you'll begin to truly understand this unique environment of interactive communication. It gets pretty interesting when you consider that literally thousands of people are continually building new information environments, and all at the same time. But be careful. Don't get addicted. We know of more than one person who has literally lost his or her job over this!

Internet Search Tools

In addition to all these Internet services, there are also plenty of great Internet search tools to assist you in finding information. Hey, maybe finding that "needle" isn't going to be so hard after all!

Connect the libraries of the world, throw in a few hundred thousand corporate databases, add in tens of thousands of new Web sites, and you've got information nirvana. It's no wonder users complain about how difficult it is to locate information on this enormous multicultural library we call the Internet.

Web Catalogs and Search Engines

Since the most popular way to publish information on the Internet is to use the Web, it makes sense to search the Web first if you are looking for something. Unfortunately, since the Web is growing so fast and is so anarchic in structure, it's difficult for

---

port

Whenever you connect to a computer on the Internet, you enter through a specific "port." You can think of a port on a computer as a doorway. Every time you access information on a machine using a Web browser, for example, your browser knocks on the "Web" door of the other machine. The Web server software sits behind that door waiting for requests. However, sometimes it makes sense to put a server behind a different door. When this happens, there will be numbers appended to a URL for an address, like 8888 is added here.

To continue the analogy, there is a specific door that is used to receive Telnet connections. MOOs and MUDs, however, wait behind a different door. If you neglect to telnet to the correct port, you will be greeted with the cold "login:" and "password:" authentication request. If you reach the correct port, you will be greeted by the welcome message of the MOO or MUD. An easy way to connect to the correct port is to use your Web browser. Ask your browser to connect to the URL representing the MOO or MUD (telnet://purple-crayon. media.mit.edu:8888), and it will start up the appropriate Telnet program automatically and connect you.

Telnet

Often made into a verb, to telnet, this term actually refers to the standard terminal emulation protocol used when logging on to other computers. When you telnet to a site, you open a "terminal session," which enables the other machine to display text in a window on your machine. You can reply in text, usually via a classic command-line environment. To telnet to a site, you need telnet software, such as NCSA Telnet for the Macintosh (http://www.ncsa.uiuc.edu/SDG/Software/Brochure/Overview/MacTelnet.overview.html) or the PC (http://www.ncsa.uiuc.edu/SDG/Software/Brochure/Overview/PCTelnet.overview.html).

automated searching to take place at all. There are two main ways to look for information on the Web: You can consult a catalog or directory organized by subject, or you can use a search engine.

The most popular catalog right now is <u>Yahoo</u> (http://www.yahoo.com). Yahoo ("Yet Another Hierarchical

Yahoo

http://www.yahoo.com

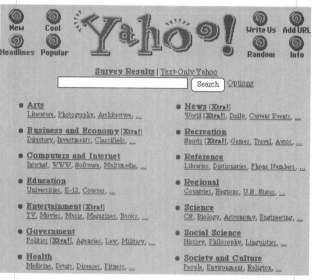

Officious Oracle") is a sort of free "Internet Yellow Pages," an <u>index</u> cataloging other Web pages that's organized by subject. Interested in design? Just click on Arts on the main Yahoo page, and then Design on the next page, and Graphic Design on the next. Yahoo lists many resources, including over a hundred design-related companies, at least ten font suppliers, Web sites with tips on using Photoshop, several institutes, and even an online type museum. Click on what you're interested in, and you're instantly transported to that site. Listings change regularly, thanks to one of the strengths of Yahoo—its daily maintenance by its creators, David Filo and Jerry Yang, originally from Stanford University and now housed at Netscape, who constantly add new sites and make further improvements.

index

This term is used interchangeably with "catalog" when referring to the organization of information by subject on a certain site on the Internet.

The advantage to using catalogs is that they, at least in theory, contain only sites that are large enough to merit listing. Since everything is organized by subject, a particular site can be found very quickly. The disadvantage is that perhaps the bit of information you want is out there, but it hasn't been cataloged, so therefore it's not in the index yet. This is becoming less and less a problem as the catalogs become larger, but is likely to always be a minor pitfall. That's why it's often wise to check for topics in numerous catalogs.

Other major indexes include:

• GNN's Whole Internet Catalog

GNN's Whole Internet Catalog

http://gnn.com/gnn/wic

• EINet Galaxy

EINet Galaxy

http://galaxy.einet.net/galaxy.html

Planet Earth's Home Page Virtual Library

http://godric.nosc.mil/planet_earth/
info.html

- **Planet Earth's Home Page Virtual Library**

PLANET EARTH HOME PAGE

- Photograph Credit
- Introductory Information

- **Planet Earth Home Page Virtual Library**

  - Comprehensive Image Map
  - Library Floorplan
  - Text Version

- World Population

- **The WWW Virtual Library.**

The WWW Virtual Library

http://www.w3.org/hypertext/DataSources
/bySubject

The WWW Virtual Library

This is a distributed subject catalogue. See Category Subtree, Library of Congress Classification (Experimental), Top Ten most popular Fields (Experimental), Statistics (Experimental), and Index. See also arrangement by service type ., and other subject catalogues of network information.

Mail to maintainers of the specified subject or www-request@mail.w3.org to add pointers to this list, or if you would like to contribute to administration of a subject area.

See also how to put your data on the web. All items starting with ! are NEW (or newly maintained). New this month: Genetics Caenorhabditis elegans (nematode) Developmental Biology Drosophila (fruit fly) Epidemiology Journalism Mycology (Fungi) Pharmacy (Medicine) Physiology and Biophysics Roadkill Yeasts

Aboriginal Studies
This document keeps track of leading information facilities in the field of Australian Aboriginal studies as well as the Indigenous Peoples studies.
Aeronautics and Aeronautical Engineering
African Studies
Agriculture
Animal health, wellbeing, and rights
Anthropology
Applied Linguistics
Archaeology
Architecture
Art
Asian Studies
Astronomy and Astrophysics
Autos
Aviation
Beer & Brewing
Bio Sciences
Biotechnology
Pharmaceutical development, genetic engineering, medical device development, and related fields.

- **TheWorld's InterList**

TheWorld's InterList

http://www.theworld.com/SUBJECTS.HTM

continued on next page

The InterList

The World's Index of Subjects

Your gateway to the Internet and the world

Presented by WorldWide Net Coporation, Information updated daily.

- You may search the InterList with a keyword.

Table of Contents

- Uncategorized Links
- Business
- .... Banking & Finance
- .... Insurance
- .... International Trade
- .... Investments
- ....Commodities
- ....Funds
- ....Stocks

- Starting Point

Starting Point ....

http://www.stpt.com

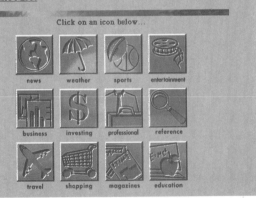

Starting Point

Starting Point is here to serve YOU. Our goal is to provide your single best starting point for World Wide Web exploration. Please add this site to your Hotlist / Bookmarks. Here's how.

Click on an icon below...

news weather sports entertainment
business investing professional reference
travel shopping magazines education

There are also a few sites that bill themselves specifically as "Yellow Pages":

- TheYellowPages.com

TheYellowPages.com

http://theyellowpages.com

continued on next page

TheYellowPages.com

Quick Finder

A B C D E F G H I J K L M N O P Q R S T U V W X Y Z

- Submit to TheYellowPages
- email Us
- The PagePoster - *Have some fun by designing your own temporary homepage*

A

Architecture
Arts
Astronomy and Astrophysics
Automobiles
Airlines/Aviation

B

Biology/Biotechnology
Books
Business and Finance

• Virtual Yellow Pages

Virtual Yellow Pages
http://www.vyp.com

• New Riders' Official World Wide Web Yellow Pages

World Wide Web Yellow Pages
http://www.mcp.com/nrp/wwwyp

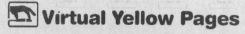

The second way to look for information on the Web is via a search engine, which can search its database of Web pages based on keywords you type. The power of search engines comes from the way in which they continually compile huge lists of URLs and their links throughout the Web. While compiling

continued on next page

NEW RIDERS' OFFICIAL

World Wide Web Yellow Pages

1995 Edition

New Riders' Official
World
Wide Web
Yellow
Pages

THE.ULTIMATE.WEB.REFERENCE!

Type keywords in the box below to search the Web!
They can be partial site names, URLs, or words from a description.
The more keywords you supply, the narrower the search results will be.

Maximum number returned: 30 ▼

[Search The Yellow Pages]   [Clear Search Box]

...or Search by Category:

```
art
business
cities
colleges and universities
commercial
computers
conferences
```

lists, a search engine also samples the textual content of each Web page, thereby allowing for keyword searches.

One of the best search engines is <u>Lycos</u>, run by Carnegie Mellon University. It continuously traverses

Lycos

http://lycos.cs.cmu.edu

Lycos™ 🕷

The Catalog of the Internet

A 1995 GNN Best of the Net Nominee.
Rated number 1 in content by Point Survey.

Enter search keywords: [   ] [Search] Search Options Formless

Lycos users: We want your feedback! You could win a CD-ROM!

- Employment Opportunities at Lycos, Inc.
- Advertising Information
- Licensing Information

- Lycos Inc. Business Partners
- Frontier Technologies licenses Lycos Internet Catalog software

- Lycos: Frequently Asked Questions

the World Wide Web looking for documents that it hasn't already cataloged. Since this search engine is able to catalog 5,000 documents a day, it is updated very rapidly. No search engine can claim to contain every document available on the Web, but the good ones (listed below) do a really good job. Visit one of them and experiment to get a feel for how they work.

Other powerful, automated World Wide Web search engines include:

• InfoSeek

InfoSeek

http://www.infoseek.com

"The best way to search on the Internet"

Free Net Search Service. The most popular way to search the Web with over 1 million queries answered daily.

● Search the Web for FREE!

InfoSeek Search. Our easy-to-use and very affordable service gives you quick access to Web pages, Usenet news, continuous newswires, and business, computer, health and entertainment publications.

Members Only
● Search
● Information about your account
● Free trial over? Sign up as a paying member

For our Guests
● How to get your free trial
● Free demo and basic information

What's **new and cool** at InfoSeek
What people are saying about InfoSeek
More information about InfoSeek

InfoSeek Corporation
2620 Augustine Drive, Suite 250
Santa Clara, CA 95054

• CUI's W3 Catalog

CUI's W3 Catalog

http://cuiwww.unige.ch/w3catalog

Please enter a search word/pattern or provide a Perl regular expression:

[Submit] [   ]

NB: Searches are case-insensitive.

Welcome to CUI's **W3 Catalog**, a searchable catalog of W3 resources.

You are strongly encouraged to mirror the W3catalog ! Please consult the **mirroring documentation**.

Please consult also the **List of W3Catalog mirrors** to look for a mirror possibly closer to your side.

For information about the contents of this catalog, see the *W3 Catalog documentation*

NB: For clients without support for forms, an alternative interface is available.

This file was generated by htmp v1.6a.

• The Open Text Web Index

The Open Text Web Index ....

http://www.opentext.com:8o8o/omw.html

Welcome to the Open Text Web Index

New! Result summaries!
Search for a word or a phrase, such as DNA or Return on Investment

Search **for**: [_____] [Search] [Clear]

This is a *Simple Search*, go here for instructions, or here if your search isn't simple.

[Searches: Simple , Compound , Ranked | Statistics | Hot Searches | Languages | Products]

Power tools for precision searching:

Compound Search
    Search only parts of web pages (Subject, Title, Hyperlink), combine searches using Boolean
    (AND, OR, NOT) and proximity (NEAR, FOLLOWED BY) operators.
Ranked search
    Weight your search terms.
Hot Searches!
    Our favorite Web Index searches.

    We are indexing **tens of thousands** of pages per day. You can contribute to the growth
and development of the Open Text Web Index:

  • Add your pages to the Web Index
  • Report problems
  • Tell us what you think – send feedback

• WebCrawler

                                                                                          WebCrawler

                                                                  http://webcrawler.com

To search the WebCrawler database, type in your search keywords here. Type as many relevant
keywords as possible; it will help to uniquely identify what you're looking for. **Last update**: July
13, 1995.

[_____]

  [Search]   ☒ AND words together

        Number of results to return: [25 ▼]

News | Home | Random Links | FAQ | Top 25 Sites | Submit URLs | Discussion | Simple Search

Recent News: Get some randomly selected links from the WebCrawler. It's a fun way to surf the net!
Also, check out the WebCrawler's idea of the number of servers on the Web.

AOL is offering free Internet access for a limited time through its MegaWeb beta program. Check it
out!

    The WebCrawler is operated by America Online as a service to the Internet.

Copyright © 1995, America Online, Inc.

info@webcrawler.com

http://www.cs.indiana.edu/aliweb/

form.html

ALIWEB Search Form

Indiana University Mirror

This form queries the ALIWEB database. You can provide multiple search terms separated by spaces, and the results will be displayed in a best-match order.

This mirror should be no more than a couple days behind the main ALIWEB site, where queries about being added to ALIWEB should be directed.

Search term(s): [   ] [Submit] [Reset]

There are several types of search: [Substring ▼] [ ] Case Sensitive

Which type records would you like to search: [Any ▼]

What fields would you like to search?
☒ Titles ☒ Descriptions ☒ Keywords ☐ URL's

What fields would you like displayed in addition to the title?
☒ Descriptions ☐ Keywords ☐ URL's ☐ Other fields

You can restrict the results to a domain (e.g. "uk"): [   ]

Stop after the first [   ] matches.

This mirror is run by Marc VanHeyningen. It should be no more than a couple days behind the main ALIWEB site, where queries about being added to ALIWEB should be directed.

• World Wide Web Worm

WWWW – WORLD WIDE WEB WORM

Best of the Web '94 - Best Navigational Aid. Oliver McBryan

Serving 3,000,000 URL's to 2,000,000 folks/month.
Instructions, Definitions, Examples, Failures, Register, WWWW Paper.
Last Run: April 15

[1. Search all URL references ▼]

[a. AND – match all keywords] [5 matches ▼]
[b. OR – match any keyword]
Keywords: [   ]
[Start Search]

World Wide Web Worm

http://www.cs.colorado.edu/home/

mcbryan/WWWW.html

The CUSI page (http://www.eecs.nwu.edu/susi/ cusi.html) and the W3 Search Engines page (http:// cuiwww.unige.ch/meta-index.html) are also good to try, because they enable you to search all the databases listed above (and more) from a single Web page.

Also note that many catalogs also contain search engines. Yahoo, for instance, is good for either browsing by subject or searching directly by keyword.

Of course there's also plenty of information available on the Internet that does not reside on Web sites. Fortunately, many of these same search engines can also search non-Web sites such as Gopher sites and FTP archives. There are also a number of excellent catalogs and search engines especially developed for non-Web sites, which I'll turn to now.

Non-Web Search Engines

Several useful search engines for conducting non-Web site searches are available, including Archie for FTP searches and Veronica and Jughead for Gopher searches. You can also search for someone's email address or a company's domain name, and more searches are becoming possible all the time.

Archie is a software agent that creates and searches its own huge database listing of the publicly known files available via FTP. As such, Archie proves to be a tremendous search tool in helping you locate specific software available on the Internet. Archie is of no use for revealing the contents of a file on an FTP site, but if you know the file's name you're looking for, agent Archie will help you find it. (If you don't know the name of the file, try using the software archives mentioned early in this chapter and search by category.)

Some software programs, such as Anarchie for the Mac, incorporate Archie, so you can search for and get files using the same application. You can also access Archie in other ways: Send an email message to archie@archie.internic.net with "help" in the body of the message. Telnet to archie.sura.net (log in as qarchie). What might be easiest is using Archie right from a Web page, such as Rutgers University's <u>Archie Request Form</u> or CUI's ArchiePlexForm.

ArchiePlexForm

http://cuiwww.unige.ch/./archieplexform.html

Archie Request Form

http://www.ns.rutgers.edu/htbin/archie

For more specific information on using Archie, check out SURANET's very helpful Guide to the Archie

continued on next page

continued on next page

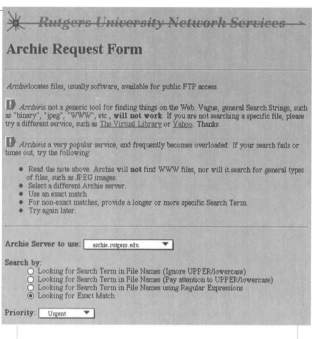

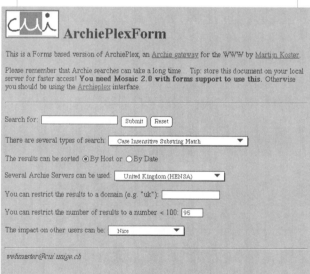

Service (http://www.sura.net/archie/Archie-Usage.html).

Veronica and Jughead are searching agents, too, and like Archie were named for the popular comic book characters. While you'll use Archie to search FTP databases, you'll use the Veronica and Jughead tools to search Gopher databases. Veronica searches through all of "Gopher space," often resulting in hundreds of search results. Jughead searches through a specific subset of Gopher and thus can be more accurate, though less comprehensive.

You access Veronica and Jughead through your Gopher program (see the section on Gopher earlier); you'll find a Veronica or Jughead menu on many Gopher sites. Some Gopher sites, which you can also visit using a Web browser, include gopher://veronica.scs.unr.edu/11/veronica and gopher://info.psi.net:2347/7. You can also go to certain Web pages, such as Inter-Links' Searching Gopherspace (http://www.nova.edu/Inter-Links/search/gophersearch.html), for more information.

If you're trying to find people or businesses on the Net, there are also ways to search for email addresses and domain names. For the former, check out the helpful Email Address-Finding Tools Web page, which uses Web sites, Gopher sites, and Telnet sites

Email Address-Finding Tools

http://twod.med.harvard.edu/labgc/roth/

Emailsearch.html

FAQ: How to find people's E-mail addresses

Archive-name: finding-addresses
Version: $Id: finding.n,v 2.2 1995/07/04 15:15:09 dalamb Exp $

Copyright 1991,1992,1993,1994 Jonathan I. Kamens.
Copyright 1994, 1995 David Alex Lamb.
See end of file for copying permissions.

This FAQ is available on the World-Wide Web (via browsers such as Mosaic or lynx) at
<URL: http://www.quois.queensu.ca/FAQs/email/finding.html>

****
*   Introduction   *
****

   A question which appears frequently on the Usenet is, "I know someone's name, and I think they might have an electronic mail address somewhere. How can I find it?"

   There are many different techniques for doing this. Several of them are discussed below. Your best bet is to try the pertinent methods in this posting in the order in which they are listed (well, sort of; at the very least, please try all the pertinent methods which do not involve posting queries to soc.net-people before resorting to that).

   I've listed "Direct contact" near the end of this list because, for some reason, people seem to be reluctant to call people on the telephone or write them a paper-mail letter asking what their E-mail address is, as long as there is even a remote chance that it might be found without asking. This attitude is somewhat counterproductive, since in most cases, it is much easier to get someone's E-mail address by asking them than it is by following the other methods outlined below. Furthermore, even if you do manage to find an E-mail address using one of the on-line methods described below, it is not guaranteed that the person at the other end of the line checks that address regularly or even that it is the correct address.

to assist you. There is also a form on the Web (http://ibc.wustl.edu/domain_form.html) to help you find domain names based on keyword searches (enter the word "zender" and you find out that our firm's domain name is zender.com—makes sense!).

Just a quick note for Mac users: The latest version of AppleSearch, Apple Computer's commercially available information-retrieval software, just happens to make a great Internet clipping service. The software's new Internet connection now extends AppleSearch's powerful search capabilities to external information resources—such as the Net! So, if your firm has AppleSearch and access to the Internet, you can easily search WAIS databases (see the section on WAIS earlier) for whatever information you may need.

If you expect to take full advantage of the Internet's research capabilities, you'll need to become friends with Archie, Veronica, Jughead, and all the rest of these tools. Once again, you can also check out *Internet Starter Kit* to get to know these folks better. (Also, see part II of this book for actual examples of how you as a designer can use these tools.)

Well, do you think you can find that "needle" now? Read on. In chapters 4, 5, and 6, I'll show you examples of practical ways you can use these Internet services and tools when communicating with your peers, clients, and suppliers and vendors.

PART II

GETTING THE MOST FROM THE NET

Part II

PART I DESCRIBED WHAT THE INTERNET'S PHYSICAL COMPOSITION IS, HOW TO GET CONNECTED, WHAT SERVICES ARE AVAILABLE, AND WHY IT ALL MATTERS. PART II OF *DESIGNER'S GUIDE TO THE INTERNET* SHOWS HOW YOU CAN USE THE INTERNET TO CONNECT TO YOUR PEERS, CLIENTS, AND SUPPLIERS AND VENDORS—TO BETTER MANAGE THE FRENETIC PACE OF YOUR FIRM.

Chapter 4

CHAPTER 4 OFFERS PRACTICAL WAYS TO USE THE NET TO WORK MORE CLOSELY WITH PEERS AND FRIENDS AND TO ENHANCE PROFESSIONAL DEVELOPMENT.

Chapter 5

CHAPTER 5 HITS CLOSER TO THE BOTTOM LINE— USING THE NET TO PROVIDE BETTER SERVICE TO OUR CLIENTS.

Chapter 6

CHAPTER 6 CONSIDERS OPPORTUNITIES FOR IMPROVING OUR WORKING COLLABORATION WITH SUPPLIERS AND VENDORS.

Act II

Scene 1

The office of dEdge. Casey and Steven, having graduated in the late 90s from leading design schools
with minors in computer science, may be up to their
eyes in debt to pay for the bevy of computerized design tools surrounding them, but their new firm
dEdge is riding a wave. Clients are flocking to their
firm for cutting-edge design and cost-effective communication solutions — in print, multimedia, and
electronic publishing. They've got the tools, they're
connected to the Internet, and they know how to
work effectively and efficiently with their peers,
their clients, and their suppliers and vendors.

Casey: "**PHENOMENAL!** Steven, check this
out. I was surfin' the Net last night and found this
conference we just have to go to."

Steven: "Really? Can we get in?"

Casey: "Yeah, while I was online I emailed our registration, got hotel reservations, and signed up for a
couple of seminars."

Steven: "That's great!"

Casey: "Yeah, **instant communication**
—no honking around making calls and being put on
hold.

Steven: "I wish Kit could go to this one. She's really in a rut. I was going to email
her, but she's not online and otherwise it's too much hassle."

Phenomenal indeed. Casey and Steven, although rather casual about its use, have come to depend upon the Internet, with its worldwide connections, for successfully managing their growing two-person firm.

The Internet is a lot more than chips and wires, protocols and databases. It's about less stress, smoother communication, or even simple conference registration. The Internet's communication facilitation is making our lives easier. On a personal level, I learned the latest surgical procedures, prognosis, and side effects of my dad's pending cancer surgery on the Net. Just knowing made the experience less fearful. The Net works just as well on a professional level. It helps us designers keep in touch with friends and peers, provide better service to our clients, and interact with suppliers and vendors.

Chapter 4

Connecting to Peers

In this chapter, you'll see just how useful the

Internet can be in helping you connect with your

friends and your peers, enhancing your profes-

sional development along the way.

Act II

Scene 2

Steven and Casey pressing to meet an annual report deadline, later that week.

Casey: "Hey, Steven, did you see how many answers we got from the comp.graphics newsgroup to our question about selectively distorting part of that scanned image for the cover?"

Steven: "Glad we got an answer, and so fast. Thanks to the help from that designer in France, now we can finish the cover illustration for the annual report."

Casey: "Yeah, and it was kind of neat to see how many other designers have had the same problem. Can you imagine what it would have been like to try to solve that one over the phone with tech support?"

Steven: "Hey, and it was free!"

The ultimate test of technology is not that it exists, but that it is useful. The invention of refrigeration was an impressive leap, but not to Eskimos. Similarly, the Internet may be an awesome tool for communication and information exchange, but only if we designers can make good use of it. Savvy designers everywhere (literally) are doing just that; they're putting the Internet to good use to gain a competitive edge for themselves. And, in the process, they're building relationships with other designers, sharing themselves and their skills. It's a classic win-win situation for everyone.

Let's take a look at how you can use the Net to get a few tips, become an active participant in the design community, find some inspiration, and collaborate with other designers.

Get Tips and Advice

I don't know about your firm, but our designers are suffering from severe information overload. Staying on the cutting edge is getting tougher and tougher; the learning curve seems to get steeper and steeper. I go home some nights thinking that I couldn't possibly squeeze one more bit of information into the hard drive in my skull. "If I have to learn just one more computer program...." I do, but not without help. All of us need help—our jobs have just become too complex managing these ever-changing techno-design tools.

Just about the time I have something figured out, I need a tip about this or some advice about that. Now where do I turn? Interrupting the office technical guru to ask him just one more technical question can be dangerous. After all, we do still keep a few X-ACTO knives around. Often, it's better to turn to the Internet for advice solving current problems and for new, creative ideas. A place to start is Goeff

DTP Jumplist

http://www.cs.purdue.edu/homes/gwp/dtp/

dtp.html

Peter's Web site, DTP Jumplist. (Also, be sure to see chapter 6 for a more thorough review of how you can get technical support on the Net, where you'll find several mailing lists and newsgroups of interest to designers).

Probably the most common format for storing tips and techniques on the Internet is the FAQ— Frequently Asked Questions. The creation of FAQs started in discussion groups such as Usenet news-groups. Old hands in the group created FAQ files to avoid answering common questions over and over again. The FAQs prevented significant bandwidth from being used up, since they answered the ques-tion in only one place. It soon became standard Netiquette to always check the FAQ file of a news-group before posting your first question.

Today, FAQs are generated by helpful individuals on virtually every computer-related subject. Time taken to read through FAQs relating to the software and hardware that you regularly use will be well spent. For example, let's say you're having trouble rotating text in PageMaker. You could call some friends, but that would take a lot of time. You could post a

Netiquette

"Even if you can't see your fellow citizens of the electronic highways, it's still a good idea to mind your manners. Some of the more com-monly preached guidelines: Make sure the ad-dress is correct. Don't be vulgar. Don't add another link to a chain letter. Don't SHOUT (send messages in ALL UPPERCASE LETTERS).

continued on next page

Don't flame (get abusive) — cool off before
send your anger out into the ether."
Tom Fahey, *net.speak: the internet dictionary*,
p.103

question in a PageMaker mailing list, and you might
get an answer within a couple hours or so. Or, you
could download the PageMaker FAQ and take a look
at it. Sure enough, while glancing through the table
of contents, you find Question 4.7: "How do I rotate
text? graphics?" Magic!

PageMaker FAQ

http://www.cs.purdue.edu/homes/gwp/pm/
pmstation.html

Welcome to the PageMaker WebStation!

Welcome to the premier Adobe PageMaker web site on the Internet. This site is
at the very earliest planning stages. Nothing is here but the barest skeletons. Be
sure to keep checking back with us, to see the site grow into its skin, so to
speak.

In the mean time, check out the precursor to the WebStation at the PageMaker
Archives.

The hypertexted PageMaker FAQ
The PageMaker Archives: FAQs and Tip lists
Other PageMaker Resources on the Internet
Search the PageMaker Mailing List Archives for Previous Discussion
Topics

FAQs are usually quite extensive. The PageMaker
FAQ alone is approximately 120K in size, and there
are other FAQ and tip files concerning more specific
aspects of the program as well. Other popular software packages, such as QuarkXPress and
Photoshop, also have large archives of tip and FAQ
files. But be patient the first time you go looking for
a FAQ. Often, several related FAQs will overlap on a
particular subject area, so you may have to check all
related FAQ files to find a specific answer.

If a Usenet newsgroup has a FAQ (most active
groups do), then you'll find it posted to the newsgroup at regular intervals — usually every few
weeks. While you could scan through the newsgroup for the file, an easier solution is to consult the
Usenet FAQ Archive, where every newsgroup FAQ is
archived and updated whenever it changes. Finding
other FAQs may take a little luck the first time, but
it's usually pretty easy. Try using Yahoo, Lycos, or
InfoSeek (see chapter 3) to search for "←the sub-
ject→ FAQ." If a FAQ exists, there's a good chance it
will be returned as one of the matching files. And,

Usenet FAQ Archive

ftp://rtfm.mit.edu/pub/usenet

If you don't know the name of the most appropriate newsgroup, you have to look around or
ask around. Don't be afraid to post questions
to what may be inappropriate newsgroups.

continued on next page

Current directory is /pub/usenet

Up to higher level directory

message	639 bytes	Mon Jul 17 16:47:00 1995	
alt./		Thu Jul 20 01:00:00 1995	Di
alt.2600/		Wed Jul 26 10:48:00 1995	Di
alt.abuse.offender...		Fri Jul 21 00:22:00 1995	Di
alt.abuse.recovery/		Fri Jul 21 00:22:00 1995	Di
alt.abuse.transcen...		Fri Jul 21 00:22:00 1995	Di
alt.activism/		Mon Jul 24 01:16:00 1995	Di
alt.adjective.noun...		Mon Jul 24 04:54:00 1995	Di
alt.adoption.agency/		Fri Jul 21 04:12:00 1995	Di
alt.adoption/		Fri Jul 21 04:11:00 1995	Di
alt.aldus.pagemaker/		Mon Jul 24 04:53:00 1995	Di
alt.aldus/		Mon Jul 24 04:53:00 1995	Di
alt.alien.visitors/		Tue Jul 18 00:59:00 1995	Di
alt.anarchism/		Wed Jul 12 00:22:00 1995	Di
alt.angst/		Wed Jul 5 01:05:00 1995	Di
alt.animation.spumco/		Thu Apr 27 18:58:00 1995	Di
alt.animation.warn.		Fri Jul 14 18:27:00 1995	Di

You have to build up a repertoire of good information sources for finding resources you don't know about. (I use Lycos, InfoSeek, newsgroups, and, when all else fails, dumb luck.) Unfortunately, there is no one index of all FAQs.

once you find a few useful Web pages, such as the Usenet FAQs Web page, finding new FAQs will get easier and easier, because they tend to link to each other. And hey, it's okay to ask in the most appropriate newsgroup or mailing list if and where a FAQ exists after you've made a few unsuccessful searches.

Usenet FAQs

http://www.cis.ohio-state.edu/hypertext/faq/usenet

USENET FAQs

This document contains a list of all USENET FAQs found in news.answers. The document is alphabetized by topic (more or less). Many of the FAQs in this list are presented in the same format as they appear in the newsgroup, while others have been further processed and split into additional documents. For more information on all aspects of this project, see the technical notes.

A few of the documents are provided in hypertext by the FAQ maintainers, rather than in converted plaintext. Those documents are shown with titles in italics.

This FAQ software was written by Thomas A. Fine.

Please send comments and complaints to webmaster@cis.ohio-state.edu.

New!

There is now a very limited search capability. This is not a full text search; only the newsgroup names, archive names, subjects, and keywords are searched. Click here to try it. (If your browser doesn't support forms, it might support index searches. Click here to try that method.)

New!

There is now a listing by newsgroup.

A, B, C, D, E, F, G, H, I, J, K, L, M, N, O, P, Q, R, S, T, U, V, W, X, Z

1

Be sure to check the Web sites of major software and hardware manufacturers, too, for advice. For example, the Tips & Techniques section on Adobe's

Adobe's home page

http://www.adobe.com

home page lists various tip sheets from Adobe's graphics gurus. They cover techniques for honing

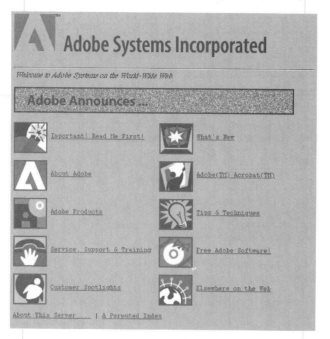

skills over specific subjects using various Adobe products. Wander over to the Photoshop page and you'll discover all kinds of information about Photoshop, including hardware requirements and even ordering info for training kits and books.

Photoshop page

http://www.adobe.com/Apps/Photoshop.html

Or hey, maybe you just need some objective feedback on a layout. Email a fellow designer in Tucson, or L.A., or Bangkok, for that matter, and attach your formatted document. Do you have a Macromedia Director question? Email that Director wizard you had lunch with last week. Ask her how she would handle the problem, and attach your preliminary Director shell. If she's as good as she said, your problem will be solved in minutes.

One thing about the Internet: It gives vent to a lot of people who are more than willing to give advice. Sometime when you've got a few extra minutes, join in a little Internet Relay Chat (see chapter 3 for details). Ask a question and you'll be amazed at all the advice you'll receive from total strangers. Of course, some may be better than others. And then there's Mr. Bad Advice. Got a problem? He promises he'll answer your question the worst he can and tell you exactly what you didn't need to know! Where would our poor world be today without the Internet?

Mr. Bad Advice

http://www.echonyc.com/~spingo/Mr.BA

Got a problem?
Ask Mr. Bad Advice!

That's right, kids!

Email your questions to Mr. Bad Advice and he'll answer them as worst he can!

You can always count on Mr. Bad Advice to tell you exactly what you didn't need to know.

Send your questions by email to the address below and your questions will appear here, answered, in hopefully a tolerable amount of time.

Mr. B's first piece of advice: **take your time!**

Thanks, and stop by soon.

Please send your problems to spingo@echonyc.com. **Make sure** to put

ATTN: MR. BAD ADVICE

in the subject of your email, lest it get, uh, misplaced, that's it, *misplaced* en route. Thanks!

PLEASE NOTE: Due to the bewilderingly voluminous amount of email received at BA HQ, Mr. B regrettably will *no longer* be able to answer each and every query received. He knows, that sucks. Sorry.

On To The Advice!

Be Part of a Design Community

One of the aspects of earlier ages that is so attractive is the "small town" sense of community that seemed to pervade people's lives. Life was apparently lived at a slower pace, one that allowed time to be an active part of the community. Today, while we live at a faster pace, we can use tools on the Internet to reconnect with peers, friends, and family, and redefine community for our time.

Keep Up with the Latest Trends

Keeping up is a very personal activity for most designers, and it takes various individual forms. Some designers spend a lot of time immersed in design journals and the latest annuals; others listen to music or garden. An article in an old issue of the Minnesota AIGA newsletter (not available online— not all the good stuff is on the Net!) called this latter option "Head Farming." Activities for keeping fresh with the latest in design can be very formal and structured, or very informal and intuitive. However the inspiration and information comes, getting it is essential in an idea business like graphic design.

The Internet offers a broad range of informative opportunities for designers, from organized to free-form. Newsgroups and mailing lists are semi-structured sources for ideas (see chapter 3 for more details on newsgroups and mailing lists). A good mailing list for Web designers is the Network Communication Design or NCD list in Japan. I joined and was recently involved in a discussion about GIF transparency problems—how different browsers react, where software can be found to help, what tricks and techniques help appearance, etc. The question came from Belgium, and the answers came from all over: Austria, Japan, Canada, the U.S.A. The dialogue was technical at times—"I use an 8-bit

Head Farming

"Thinking hard and the physical cramping, rapid breathing, and induced stress" of design are best dealt with by a random physical endeavor that compensates for the brain-intensive nature of design work. "Designers should use intuition...but intuition works only if your mind is well fed."

Karl Schweikart, "Head Farming," p. 2

NCD

http://ncdesign.kyushu-id.ac.jp

continued on next page

adaptive-diffusion palette...."—and more artistic at others—"if you pick colors that are nearly the same value...." The answers often include references to the latest software versions, as well as rumors about what's coming next. Wide-ranging and current, the voices and opinions of experts are constantly updated on the Internet.

Design chat is the most open and free-form opportunity to stay current. Chat is real time, so by definition you get the most current of current information available on the Net. designOnline has a design chat room called "dezine café," but not being very

designOnline

http://www.dol.com

chatty, I've never stayed there. It's a cafe where designers gather for everyday conversations on topics such as data dada, graphic guerrillas, and truth+ design. You'll have to try it yourself.

A much more organized source for design-related information is a book list or annotated bibliography, such as the one at the <u>University of Tampere in Finland</u>, or the excellent one about multimedia de-

University of Tampere in Finland

http://www.uta.fi/~samu/graphic_

design_books.html

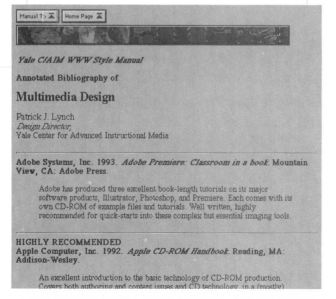

Graphic design books

Graphis Poster '94
Graphis, 1994
xxx p. : ill. (col.) ; hardback
The annual Graphis Poster book isn't quite as interesting as one might expect. The posters are from skilled hands undoubtedly, but true cutting edge and innovation is a bit lacking in my opinion. Good mainstream publication nevertheless.

Looking Closer: Critical Writings on Graphic Design
Allworth Press, 1994
xxx p. : ; paperback
Graphic design discussion, criticism and general writings from various magazines, such as Print, Emigre, Eye, Aiga Journal as well as some brand new ones. Issues range from modernism and deconstruction to typography, language and social agenda. Interesting stuff if you didn't catch this the first time around and definitely something that I'd like to see published more. On the other hand, the writings themselves are not all that excellent, some a bit light I might even say.

sign at the <u>Yale Center for Advanced Instructional Media</u>. The latter list includes links to some valuable Web documents. One of these—Visual design

Yale Center for Advanced Instructional Media

http://info.med.yale.edu/caim/Biblio_

Multi-media.HTML

Yale C/AIM WWW Style Manual

Annotated Bibliography of

Multimedia Design

Patrick J. Lynch
Design Director,
Yale Center for Advanced Instructional Media

Adobe Systems, Inc. 1993. *Adobe Premiere: Classroom in a book.* Mountain View, CA: Adobe Press.

Adobe has produced three excellent book-length tutorials on its major software products, Illustrator, Photoshop, and Premiere. Each comes with its own CD-ROM of example files and tutorials. Well written, highly recommended for quick-starts into these complex but essential imaging tools.

HIGHLY RECOMMENDED
Apple Computer, Inc. 1992. *Apple CD-ROM Handbook.* Reading, MA: Addison-Wesley.

An excellent introduction to the basic technology of CD-ROM production. Covers both authoring and content issues and CD technology in a (mostly) for the user interface, Part 1: Design fundamentals—is an electronic version of a recent scholarly summary of the issues of visual interface design. While bibliographic Internet resources are primarily lists of printed material, because they are on the Net they have the potential to be lists of the most recently published material, an important issue if you want to stay current.

Or maybe you'd like to take a little visit to Sweden. You could visit the <u>Graphic Arts Technology</u> at Royal Institute of Technology in Stockholm. Sounds like a great program, but they take only 16 students a year. Better check it out!

Graphic Arts Technology

http://www.gt.kth.se/info/GT.info.eng.html

Grafisk Teknik   Click <u>here</u> if you want to <u>go to home page</u>.

<u>This document as a Adobe Acrobat file in pdf-format</u>

Graphic Arts Technology at Royal institute of Technology, Stockholm, Sweden.

Table of Contents

- <u>What is Graphic Arts Technology?</u>
- <u>Education programme</u>
- <u>Courses</u>
- <u>Optional courses</u>
- <u>The Master Thesis</u>
- <u>Types of teaching</u>
- <u>Equipment</u>
- <u>Research</u>
- <u>Results from earlier research</u>
- <u>Industry collaboration</u>
- <u>Labour-market</u>
- <u>About the Division Graphic Arts Technology</u>

What is Graphic Arts Technology?

Find Conferences

Need to locate a conference? Once again the Internet, with its email, IRC channels, newsgroups, mailing lists, and Web sites, is a great place to look. Maybe you'd like some information on that upcoming AIGA event? Check out the Events link at <u>AIGAlink</u>. For local events, you can either telnet (see chapter 3 or, if you really want to get into it, Adam Engst's *Internet Starter Kit*) to your chapter's

AIGAlink

http://www.dol.com/AIGA

continued on next page

AIGA_link_ on designOnline™

a project of **AIGA**philadelphia

The purpose of the AIGA is to advance excellence
in graphic design as a discipline, profession, and cultural force.

The AIGA provides leadership in the exchange of ideas
and information, the encouragement of critical analysis and research,
and the advancement of education and ethical practice.

Welcome to AIGAlink

| **Home** | What is AIGAlink? | AIGA | Events | Gallery | Back to designOnline |

This page is maintained by the AIGAlink committee. It takes advantage of Netscape and HTML 3.0.
AIGAlink is a project of **AIGA** philadelphia the *first* AIGA chapter and the *first* AIGA chapter online. For more
information about **AIGAlink** or if you have any questions about this site please email SM Gassaway or the
AIGAlink web editor JosephJohn Clark.
9 February 1995 / **10 July 1995**.
1995 Copyright AIGA philadelphia

bulletin board or send off a quick email to the chapter's president.

Don't forget to check out relevant newsgroups for upcoming conferences, too. A quick check of the comp.graphics newsgroup found "Coming Soon! World Wide Web—Chicago," and the press release pointed to the DCI Events by Technology Web page listing all kinds of conferences.

DCI Events by Technology

http://www.DCIexpo.com

 DCI

Welcome to DCI

Events by Technology:

Internet & World Wide Web

Client / Server & Databases

Object Oriented Analysis and Design

Business Process and Enterprise

Management Conference

Recent articles and ideas from George Schussel .

The Catalog (All technologies), Executive Services , What's New

Exhibitor Opportunities

Another good place to look for conferences is in on-line magazines. Check magazines like California's Monthly for Electronic Design & Graphics or even

California's Monthly

http://www.cea.edu/online.design

Welcome to Online Design

When OnLine Design was first published back in May 1992 as Northern California's Monthly for Electronic Design and Graphics, we envisioned the magazine "as a meeting place for creative users throughout the region." Our vision expanded to include Southern

the ever-popular site at HotWired.

HotWired

http://www.hotwired.com

Network

Friends and personal relationships are what make the world go 'round, and that brings us to one of the best things you can do on the Internet. It makes sense that the network of networks would facilitate interpersonal networking. Email makes it easy to keep in touch with friends and design acquaintances all over the world. Need career advice, looking for a job, or just want to meet some other designers in your area (or elsewhere)? Contact a friend via email. The Internet makes it easy to stay in touch with anyone, anywhere, if he or she is online.

I recently met a wonderful young designer at an AIGA Chapter Retreat whose work I had seen and admired. We've extended our acquaintance on the Net and hope to help each other in areas of common interest. We've exchanged career advice, business information, client prospects—all online. We're far enough apart geographically that the normal competitive shadow doesn't cloud our sharing.

A few good Web sites to check out include design resumés at designOnline's site, The Graphix

design resumés

http://www.dol.com:8o/Root/people/

resumes/resumes.html

Exchange, or even the more general **Employment** section on Yahoo.

Graphix Exchange

http://www.rust.net/TGX_WWW_pgs/

TGX.html

Employment

http://www.yahoo.com/Business_and_

Economy/Employment

Another, more organized means of networking is to contact a site such as **Designlink**. There you'll find online portfolios, job and career information, a directory of designers complete with hotlinks to their email addresses, plus a list of professional organizations and vendor information. Many design firms

Designlink

http://www.designlink.com

continued on next page

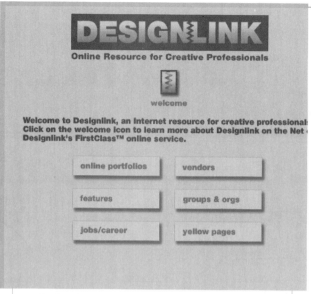

have individual home pages on the Net, so you can visit them directly and drop an email message, tell them what you like about their work, ask how they did a project, or ask who they know that does similar work. Some companies, such as vivid studios (http://www.vivid.com), even post positions available within the firm. However you hook up, get connected and network.

Get Inspiration

It happens to all of us. We hit a dry spell; we need some inspiration. It's tough being creative every minute every day. Maybe it's time to take a day or so off to unwind, or then again, maybe it's time to find some inspiration on the Internet. Step back and take a fresh look at the Internet as a vast repository of creative work. A couple of quick searches and you can wander at your leisure through the work of your peers. Want to take a stroll right now? Visit AIGAlink (mentioned previously), or Clement Mok designs, or designOnline, or The World Wide Web Virtual Library on Design, or even Zender + Associates, our home page. You're sure to get inspired.

The World Wide Web Virtual Library on Design

http://www.dh.umu.se/vlib.html

Clement Mok designs

http://www.cmdesigns.com

Zender + Associates

http://www.zender.com

continued on next page

continued on next page

Welcome to the Clement Mok designs WWW Site!

Design

This list is divided in various sub-topics. It's my goal that each topic will contain any relevant information, academic and commercial sites aswell as mailing lists, news groups and different supporting subjects.
Please mail webmaster@designum.umu.se with additional sites, suggestions of alteration or anything else that the list might gain from.

Items starting with ! are newly added to the list. Last update **95 07 03**

Related Topics of the Virtual Library

Architecture
Art
Computer Graphics & Visualization
Furniture & Interior Design
Human Computer Interaction

Fashion Design

Academic sites

The Syracuse University has a Fashion Design department online.

And why not visit a few of the many online galleries or virtual museums? Fortunately, bandwidth is not an issue when visiting online museums and galleries via the Internet. Since their images are for viewing only, low-res 72 dpi images suffice. When was the last time you visited the Louvre? Need a break? Check out the WebLouvre. You won't be alone. More than a million people visited it last year.

WebLouvre

http://mistral.enst.fr/louvre

WebMuseum, Paris

The WebMuseum network

Please take a couple of seconds to switch to the closest site in the ever-expanding WebMuseum network; this should dramatically improve the speed of data access.

- NORTH AMERICA:
  - **USA – Florida**: OIR, University of Central Florida
  - **USA – North Carolina**: SunSITE University of North Carolina
  - **USA – California**: emf/het, Berkeley
  - **Canada – Ontario**: Atkinson College, York University
- SOUTH AMERICA:
  - **Chile**: SunSITE University of Chile
  - **Brazil**: PUC – Rio Datacentro (Rio de Janeiro)
  - **Brazil**: Edugraf
- OCEANIA:
  - **Australia**: University of South Australia
- ASIA:
  - **Japan**: SunSITE Science University of Tokyo
  - **Singapore**: SunSITE National University of Singapore
  - **Korea**: CAIR, Korea Advanced Institute of Science and Technology (Daejon)
- EUROPE:
  - **England**: SunSITE Imperial College (London)
  - **England** *only* Southern Records (London)
  - **Germany**: Fritz-Haber-Institut der Max-Planck-Gesellschaft (Berlin)
  - **France**: Conservatoire National des Arts et Métiers (Paris)
  - **Italy**: CINECA-Interuniversity Computing Center
  - **Ireland** *only* University of Limerick
  - **Poland**: SunSITE ICM, Warsaw University

You may want to begin your visit with a welcome from the museum's curator. Then visit some galleries. Most have instructional text providing historical backgrounds to their works. Or, maybe you'd like to spend some time with cave paintings from the Paleolithic era. Whatever. Enjoy!

Nothing to do tonight? How about visiting a few galleries—online galleries. You may even want to contribute a few works of your own! No problem. Just send your work over the Net to freeSpace or another of the online galleries that give you a chance to exhibit your work for that 15 minutes of fame Andy Warhol promised.

freeSpace

http://www.rca.ac.uk/freespace

continued on next page

free Space

Thank you to everyone who sent work to **freeSpace**. The show finished on the 18th June. Here is some information about the project which I thought you might find interesting.

14,000 people visited the gallery in London.
141,307 people visited the web site, most while the show was live!!

The youngest participant **Sebastian Fleet** was **4 years old**, here is his Zebra picture. Work ranged from photographs of sculptures and oil paintings to computer generated imagery.

Entries came from the following countries: **Singapore, Japan, Estonia, Chile, Canada, America, Britain, Australia, Czech Republic and Sweden.**

I have now graduated and can be contacted from the 15th August at:
Philips Corporate Design, Building SX, P.O.Box 218, 5600 MD Eindhoven, The Netherlands.

Thankyou to everyone for participating!! Helen Charman

free Space   **Electronic arts event**

Other cool sites include the AIGAlink virtual gallery,

AIGAlink

An exhibition of graphic design excellence
in the Philadelphia region,
sponsored by AIGA/Philadelphia.

Four nationally recognized figures
in design were invited to judge
over 350 entries, representing the
diverse design community
in the region.

To avoid the false sense of consensus

AIGAlink virtual gallery
http://www.dol.com/AIGA/door.html

Grafica Obscura, the place, and A Global Canvas: The Museum Book of Digital Fine Art.

Grafica Obscura
http://www.sgi.com/grafica

The Museum Book of Digital Fine Art
http://www.mcp.com/hayden/museum-book

the place
http://gertrude.art.uiuc.edu/ludgate/the/
place/place2.html

continued on next page   *continued on next page*

GRAFICA*Obscur*

Collected Computer Graphics Hacks

Curated by [Paul Haeberli]

▼▼

Welcome to Grafica Obscura, my computer graphics notebook. This is a compilation of technical notes, pictures, essays and complete junk that I've accumulated over the years. For maximum enjoyment, check the [viewing notes] provided.

Contents

[A Paper Folding Project]
    Here are step by step instructions on how to make a folded paper sculpture.

[Japanese English Advertising Slogans]
    Beautiful and poetic word combinations from Japan.

[A Gallery of Pictures]
    A collection of digital pictures. This includes photographic and synthetic images.

[Synthetic Lighting for Photography]
    Modifying photographic lighting as a post process.

Collaborate within Your Firm

Technically speaking, the Internet really doesn't offer many ways with which you can collaborate with others within your office. Yes, you can use various Internet services such as email or an internal Web server for in-house electronic publishing. In fact, internal servers provide not only group access to the Internet but a host of other benefits as well, from sharing resources and software utilities to office-wide address, phone listing, and schedule information. But even these may require TCP/IP for a trip across the office, even though those cute little electrons really never leave your building or its local area network.

Then again, using the Internet to conduct research could be construed as collaborating within the office. A senior designer might ask an assistant to research a topic over the Internet. Maybe you need a picture of Groucho Marx. I just overheard one of our designers say he couldn't find one. Somebody else took a look on the Net and a few minutes later Groucho's big-as-life smooz was on his screen. He saves the file, writes a brief email message to his soon-to-be-pleasantly-surprised colleague, and attaches the Groucho image.

The Internet does, however, offer real benefits when you want to collaborate with fellow designers located in another office, say a satellite office in Denver, or better yet, maybe a little beach front in Nassau. Internet email alone can be of tremendous help, keeping designers up-to-date with timely communications. I've been amazed in writing this book at how useful email has been, particularly in reducing the time it takes to get feedback from our development editor located in another city. Okay, he's not on the beach in Nassau, he's in Indianapolis. But hey, you wouldn't trade, would you, Steve? On a more serious note, Steve has just reminded me that you could also pass files back and forth via an FTP site. Instead of emailing a file, you could simply upload it to an FTP site where it would become available to anyone wishing to download it. Not too much privacy, but hey, it works!

Draft a note, attach a file or two, and email it. It couldn't be easier, and I don't know how it could be any faster. But there are some occasions when written matter alone just doesn't cut it. No problem. How about an Internet telephone call? Excuse me, Ma Bell, and you Baby Bells, too, but you can call for free, anytime, anywhere in the world. Now that's collaborating! Chances are you have an A/V Mac in-house. If not, just add some inexpensive speakers and a microphone to your system. Then all you need is the software that enables you to place calls over the Internet, and you're ready to reach out and touch someone. Products such as Electric Magic's NetPhone (Mac-only for now) even enable you to initiate and control Internet calls through the Web.

Electric Magic

http://www.emagic.com

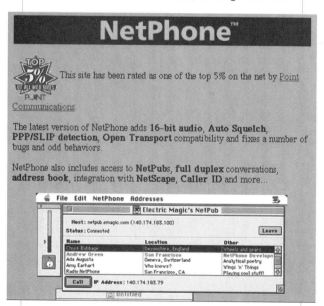

Better yet, reach out and see someone. Conduct an Internet videoconference—collaboration with sight and sound. Sound neat? Consider how your firm could use Internet videoconferencing for collaboration among designers located in different offices — talking, sharing documents and files, and making revisions. Or if you don't want to see or be seen, you could use IRC for a text-only conference, or set up a virtual office space by creating your own MUD. You sure could save a lot in FedEx charges and travel back and forth. Consider it today; you may find yourself using it tomorrow. (See chapter 5 for a more thorough discussion of this exciting technology, as applied to collaboration with your clients.)

As we've seen, the Internet has much to offer to us designers in connecting to our peers. In the next chapter, we'll explore its use in connecting to our clients. Remember them? Our bottom line? Oh, yeah!

Chapter 5

Connecting to Clients

This chapter hits the bottom line—our clients,

and how to connect to them and work with

them using the Net.

Act II

Scene 3

Casey and Steven preparing to conduct a videoconference over the Internet with Sharon, their most important client.

Steven: "Okay, Casey, ready for our Internet videoconference with Sharon? Here she comes. Hey, Sharon. Glad we could meet up this way. What's the weather like out there today?"

Sharon: "Here, I'll point the video camera on my monitor out the window."

Casey: "Hi Sharon. Looks like another beautiful day in sunny southern California. Sure beats our snow!"

Steven: "Sharon, you're really going to like what we've got to show you today. Why don't you open up your chalkboard window so you can see the PageMaker file for the annual's cover."

Sharon: "Wow! That really does look great, guys. Just a quick comment, though. Could you move the subtitle up and over to the left just a bit? Here, I'll show you."

Steven: "Oh, I see. You'd like to align the subtitle with the graphic element just above it. That's a good idea."

Casey: "Yeah, here, let me change the file in my computer so you can see how it really looks on yours."

A few brief minutes later, cover art was approved

and the client proceeded to mark up suggested changes throughout the entire report, which Casey and Steven were then able to make on the spot. The result? Approval for all finished art changes throughout the annual—far more efficient than if they had met in person without the ability to make changes on the fly. No need to spend several hundred dollars for travel. Absolutely no wasted time. A happy client, well-satisfied with her selection of these two talented, effective, and efficient designers who have mastered the use of the Internet in connecting to their client.

This scenario may be a bit futuristic, but just a bit! The technology needed for this kind of accomplishment is almost here. Really, the only thing limiting us is the issue of bandwidth, which should be improved in the not-too-distant future. Stop and think about it for a minute: You'll probably be doing this with your clients in the near future. You, too, will use the Internet to conduct a videoconference spanning thousands of miles and several time zones to "meet" with your most important client. In this chapter you'll discover all kinds of ways to use the Internet in your business—today—to connect with your clients. We'll look at ways in which you can find new clients, do research on and for clients, and even collaborate with them online.

Find New Clients

The Internet can play a significant role in helping you find new clients and promote the services of your firm. Although many Internet services can be of help in doing so (for example, you can email prospective clients, pointing them to a Web site containing your portfolio — or maybe even sending them your portfolio in Adobe PDF format), we'll take a look at what is arguably the most important arena for designers: the Web. Putting up your own Web page to advertise your services is easy and effective. In this section, I'll talk about what you should consider while creating your own Web site and promoting and publicizing it. Linking to and from other sites, lots of them, is really what this is all about, so other people (and companies) know where to find *you*.

Creating Your Web Page

One of the best ways to think about your own Web page is as an online capabilities brochure. This is your chance to show your stuff. Many clients will be requesting that you design their Web site, so make sure they know right off the bat that you've mastered the medium of the Web (see chapters 11 and 12 for specific design strategies).

That said, most of what you'd consider putting in your brochure applies to your Web page as well: a clear message, crafted presentation, and the obvious contact information. But on the Web, you can do even more because of its multimedia capabilities. Feel free to link audio files to your site, as appropriate, or put up animations you've worked on that potential clients can download and view. You can also bring an interactive dimension to your Web page, by including on your site a direct email connection to you, by providing some useful content that will impress visitors and bring them back (see chapter 8 for how your clients can do the same), and more. There are limitless possibilities, but the key is this: Design a site that fully expresses who you are and what you can do. "If you build it, they will come."

Probably the best way to get ideas for your own Web page is to explore what's already out there. You'll find a plethora of sites advertising the services of individuals and design firms. For example, designer Brad Johnson has set up a beautiful site for his firm; these Web pages feature his clients and projects,

Brad Johnson

http://www.dnai.com/~bradj

examples of his work, and a way to contact him via email and snail mail. Another example is the home page of Zender + Associates, which we set up to tell the world about us.

Zender + Associates

http://www.zender.com

A good place to begin your exploration is in the Graphic Design section of Yahoo, the popular Internet directory. Aim your Web browser at http://www.yahoo.com/Business_and_Economy/ Companies/Communications_and_Media_Services /Graphic_Design.

continued on next page

When you're ready to get going on your own Web site, the first thing you need is a place to put it. Web pages (which are HTML documents, if you remember from chapter 3) should be placed on the hard drive of a server that is constantly connected to the Internet. Chances are, your Internet access provider (see chapter 2) offers such a service, either for free or for a monthly storage fee. If not, there are plenty of other providers and companies who can help you out (you can find a list of them in Yahoo). And it doesn't really matter where your Web pages are stored geographically, since anyone can access them from anywhere. Talk with these providers about exactly how to set up your site, upload your HTML documents to their storage space, and so on.

As far as the actual creation of your Web pages with HTML, see chapters 11 and 12 for the software you'll need and some tips. This book isn't a step-by-step HTML tutorial (there are plenty of other online and offline resources that do that), but these chapters contain valuable information and suggestions to keep in mind.

Promoting Your Web Page

Okay, you're up on the Web. One of your techno-designers caught HTML fever and after soliciting everyone's input, he's constructed your home page. You've got some great links, and you can't wait for some clients to stop by for a visit. But how in the world do they find your page? You can:

1. Glue a phone to your secretary's head with an order to call each and every one of your clients to tell them your new URL—but they'll forget.

2. Advertise your URL—but you don't advertise.

3. Or maybe promote your home page by putting links to it in places your clients are likely to find. Yeah!

Registering with Search Engines

The first thing you want to do is register the URL for your home page with the most popular search engines. All WWW search engines, such as Lycos, attempt to catalog as many documents from the Web as possible. Search engines do this by loading and cataloging every document listed in a database of URLs. Every link on these documents is automatically explored by the search engine, and any new documents found are cataloged. This process continues over and over again as long as the search engine is able. Some search engines make it easy and let you add your own URL to its database of initial pages to search. This ensures that people will be able to find your page if they conduct a search using appropriate keywords.

Carnegie Mellon's Lycos search engine has a form that you can fill out to automatically add your page to those that will be cataloged. If at some point you wish to remove your URL from the catalog, you may do so by using a different form.

Lycos
http://lycos.cs.cmu.edu/lycos-register.html

continued on next page

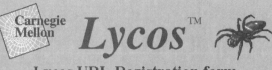

The WebCrawler search engine works in a similar fashion.

WebCrawler

http://webcrawler.com/WebCrawler/ SubmitURLS.html

InfoSeek, a commercial venture, is among the most popular search engines. However, it does not have a form you can use to register URLs. As long as you place your page in a few prominent locations—sites that are visited frequently—you should make it into this catalog.

InfoSeek

http://www.infoseek.com

continued on next page

"The best way to search on the Internet"

Free Net Search Service. The most popular way to search the Web with over 1 million queries answered daily.

- Search the Web for FREE!

InfoSeek Search. Our easy-to-use and very affordable service gives you quick access to Web pages, Usenet news, continuous newswires, and business, computer, health and entertainment publications.

Members Only
- Search
- Information about your account
- Free trial over? Sign up as a paying member

For our Guests
- How to get your free trial
- Free demo and basic information

What's **new and cool** at InfoSeek
What people are saying about InfoSeek
More information about InfoSeek

InfoSeek Corporation
2620 Augustine Drive, Suite 250
Santa Clara, CA 95054

And finally, there's Submit It! — "The fastest way to publicize your Web site." Now we're talking! What a great service! And it's free! A few more exclamation points, please!!

Submit It!

http://submit-it.permalink.com/submit-it

Submit It!

The fastest way to publicize your web site.

Sponsored by

Internet NOW! : An Advertising Cooperative.

Submit It! is a free service designed to make the process of submitting your URLs to a variety of WWW catalogs faster and easier.

Use the checkboxes below to select the web catalogs and robots that you wish to register your site with. Then fill out the form with information about your web site.

After you submit the completed form the cgi script will return a page with submission buttons for all the sites you selected. All of your information will be encoded in that page and no more typing will be necessary. Use that page to register your site with the catalogs.

Registering with Catalogs

Yahoo

http://www.yahoo.com

There is a form for submitting URLs for

consideration at http://www.yahoo.com/

bin/add.

Yahoo is probably the most popular subject-organized catalog (or directory) of the World Wide Web,

but there are also other useful directories, such as GNN's Whole Internet Catalog, The WWW Virtual

GNN's Whole Internet Catalog

http://www.gnn.com/gnn/wic

Send email to gnnews@ora.com to add

your URL.

Library, and EINet Galaxy. Each of these has a method for contributing new URLs. Unlike with the search engines, your URL will not be automatically added to these directories. Instead, your URL will be added only if the people behind the directory

The WWW Virtual Library

http://www.w3.org/hypertext/DataSources/

bySubject/ Overview.html

The Virtual Library is descended from the first

continued on next page

EINet Galaxy

http://www.einet.net

There is a form for submitting new URLs to

Galaxy at http://www.einet.net/cgi-bin/

continued on next page

attempts to catalog the Web. It is a collective effort, with each subject maintained by different individuals. The list of maintainers and their email addresses is at http://www.w3.org/hypertext/DataSources /bySubject/Maintainers.html, which is available via the Virtual Library home page.

The WWW Virtual Library

This is a distributed subject catalogue. See **Category Subtree**, **Library of Congress Classification** (Experimental), Top Ten most popular Fields (Experimental), Statistics (Experimental), and Index. See also arrangement by service type ., and other subject catalogues of network information .

Mail to maintainers of the specified subject or www-request@mail.w3.org to add pointers to this list, or if you would like to contribute to administration of a subject area.

See also how to put your data on the web. All items starting with ! are *NEW* (or newly maintained). New this month: Genetics Caenorhabditis elegans (nematode) Developmental Biology Drosophila (fruit fly) Epidemiology Journalism Mycology (Fungi) Pharmacy (Medicine) Physiology and Biophysics Roadkill Yeasts

Aboriginal Studies
        This document keeps track of leading information facilities in the field of Australian
        Aboriginal studies as well as the Indigenous Peoples studies.
Aeronautics and Aeronautical Engineering
African Studies
Agriculture
Animal health, wellbeing, and rights
Anthropology
Applied Linguistics
Archaeology
Architecture
Art
Asian Studies
Astronomy and Astrophysics
Autos
Aviation
Beer & Brewing
Bio Sciences
Biotechnology
        Pharmaceutical development, genetic engineering, medical device development, and related
        fields.
Chemistry

Galaxy | Add | Help | Search | What's New | About EINet

EINet Galaxy announces **Polaris**, an Internet advertising program.

EINet is changing and growing! Check out our job opportunities!

Galaxy is a guide to worldwide information and services and is provided as a public service by **EINet** and Galaxy guest editors. You can cruise the Galaxy with EINet's World Wide Web clients - **winWeb** for Windows and **MacWeb** for the Macintosh.

Topics

Arts and Humanities
        Architecture - Art History - Language and Literature - Museums
        - Performing Arts - Philosophy - Religion - Visual Arts

Business and Commerce
        Business Administration - Business General Resources - Consortia

explore it and feel it to be appropriate for their catalog. But don't worry—if in fact you started a significant new Web page, you are likely to be included in at least some of these catalogs.

Registering with What's New Lists

If you want your home page to receive a lot of exposure, you might also submit it to be potentially

annotate? Other. This link is listed on the Galaxy's home page.

included in the Netscape and NCSA "What's New" lists. These Web pages are regularly updated lists of new sites on the Web, read by thousands every

Netscape

http://home.netscape.com/escapes/
submit_new.html

NCSA

http://www.ncsa.uiuc.edu/SDG/Software/
Mosaic/Docs/Docs/whats-new-form.html

N EXPLORING THE NET

TELL US WHAT'S NEW

Do you have a new net site you'd like to add to our What's New pages? Fill out the enclosed form to submit your entry. Not all entries will be chosen. Void where prohibited by law.

What kind of site is it?

What does your content consist of? Is it a a personalized art exhibit? A stab at crass commercialism? Corporate PR and Information? Political Propagana? Something more intellectual than that?

Please Choose a content type ▼

Who are you?

Are you a commercial site? A corporation? Joe Public with something good to show? Pick your category:

Pick your site ▼

Resource Information

URL: The main link to your resource.

URL Title:

week. If your site is really interesting, it may also be included in a "What's Cool" list, such as Netscape's list, which is a sure way to gain quick exposure.

Submit an Entry to What's New

To submit an entry describing a new Internet service, fill out all the fields in the following form, then select the "Submit entry" option at the bottom. If your Web browser does not support forms, you may submit by email. If you have problems or questions about submitting, send a message to wn-comments@ncsa.com

The What's New Page does not currently accept submissions for personal home pages, material of an offensive nature, or adult entertainment listings. We also try to keep the What's New Page as a place for new Web "sites" (those with added-value information, hypertext, etc), not single text files, announcements, or product promotions.

The current turnaround time from submission to publication is 10-14 days.

Title:
The name of your resource.

Primary URL:
The main link (home page) to your resource.

Organization responsible for content:

Location of resource:
City

State/Province (two-letter code if in US):

Other Methods

As I mentioned early on in this section, linking is where it's at in using your home page to advertise your services. It's the ultimate form of networking. Make it your goal to get as many contacts as you make on the Net to link to your site. It won't be long before lots of folks will be lining up to take a peek at your great work. What, the design of your site isn't that great? Hey, that's why you bought this book in the first place, isn't it? Listen, we've worked hard to get you this far, and for one reason only—to get you to read the good stuff in the back of this book! That's right. Read on and your site will look great, too.

Back to the matter at hand: There are plenty of other methods you can pursue to promote your Web page. For instance, you could post a brief description and URL in appropriate Usenet newsgroups. Or, you could locate mailing lists covering topics related to your page and mail a description to them. Hey, and don't forget the mundane: Include your URL in your email signature, put it on your letterhead and business card—you could even print bumper stickers (who knows, it might start a fad!). But again, what's most important is to always ask the maintainers of other related pages to include a link to your page. If you do, though, don't forget to return the favor and include a link back to their page. Finally, be sure to include a link back to your page with every site you design for your clients. This is a great way for clients to sample your wares.

All in all, you'll be surprised at how quickly your page will be discovered once you get the word out in a few appropriate places.

Research Clients

Great! Your URL is linked here and there, you're registered with a few directories and lists, and you've found some new clients. Or, maybe more accurately, the new clients found you. That's even better. In fact, that's what promoting your services on the Internet is all about.

Now that you've got new clients, you can turn to the Internet once again to do a quick search and take a look at their Web pages. You'd be surprised what an analytical review of a Web site can reveal about a company and its culture. What, your new clients don't have Web sites? I bet they want one. Time to get to work! Chance are, though, that if they don't have a Web site, you're not going to find much other information about them on the Net.

But it can't hurt to try. First, search for information related to the company using Lycos, InfoSeek, or another search engine. You could try a WAIS search, but WAIS indexed information is largely limited to academic and research organizations. WAIS is a good idea for companies to organize and distribute information, but it takes a lot of work to set up and to index, and it's largely limited to static files. Most companies would rather just set up a Web server to distribute information about their companies.

Doing Market Research

Then again, perhaps the most productive research you can do on the Internet is not *on* your new clients but *for* them. As you can imagine by now, the Internet, with its megalibraries of information, is an ideal research assistant. It never ceases to amaze me how many clients come to our firm for excellent design executed in a beautiful manner, yet have so little idea of what they want to communicate. Suddenly, we take on a larger role, not only designing, but also analyzing and developing content, their content. And that content is often built upon research, rolling up our sleeves and learning all we can about a client, their market and industry, and their competition.

To learn more about a certain market or industry, there are a lot of places you could go. The most obvious is the Web, where more and more companies and information sources are going online every day. First, try the same catalogs and search engines we've been talking about all along (see chapter 3 for a more thorough list). You'll probably find all sorts of other companies immediately, and what better way to get familiar with a marketplace than to compare all the competitors?

There are also specific business directories on the Web, many devoted to particular industries (check out Yahoo's Business & Economy section). And no doubt, in your searches you'll come across other valuable Web, Gopher, and other sites that pertain to the specific market you're researching. The Net tends to reward this kind of research—the more you look, the more you find.

Keeping Up with Your Clients

Okay, now you've got those new clients, you've learned a lot about them and their industry, and you're doing some great work for them. Don't stop now—the Internet is a great source of timely news as well, helping you keep in touch with your clients and what's going on in their world.

As you can see by this example, "timely news" can help you stay on top of your clients' business. That means you know them better, and therefore can serve them better. When your client's position in its market is shaken, you can know early and react accordingly. And when you hear via the Net about your client's successes, you can quickly take credit! The

---

timely news

A few months ago, the president of one of our long-time clients suddenly resigned. This surprised us; we'd just met with him a few days earlier to review the company's plans for next year's annual report.

As is often the case, the company made sure to wait until late in the afternoon, after the stock market had closed, to announce the

continued on next page

vast amount of information available on the Internet is staggering, and can absolutely keep you on top of things.

Collaborate Online

Several technologies exist today that enable you to use the Internet to collaborate with your clients, whether they are in the building next door, across town, or halfway around the world. Some of these tools may be in their infancy, but your understanding of their capabilities and a little experimentation with them now will prepare you for the major changes they will no doubt bring to the way you work with clients—how you communicate, how they see your work, even how you submit invoices for your services.

Communicating

There are lots of ways you can communicate with clients via the Internet: anything from simple email messaging when face-to-face or even voice-to-voice communication is not called for, to fairly sophisticated videoconferencing. You can even use Internet Relay Chat or MUDs to create "virtual meeting spaces" online. Each of these services can prove useful in communicating with your clients on an ongoing basis. (For details on how to get started with these services, see chapter 3).

Let's take a brief look at Internet videoconferencing and NetPhone, services we see great potential for in our firm. What really makes desktop videoconferencing systems appealing is not so much that they enable users to view one another on their computers, but that they create a shared on-screen workspace in which two or more users, in distant locations, can simultaneously work on the same document vis-á-vis a "chalkboard." Although in the early stages of development, this feature, when

president's resignation. We may have been surprised, but the company's marketing director was shocked when we called first thing the next morning asking about the situation. "What!? How in the world did you guys hear about that?"

No problem! Thanks to an automatic Internet news searching application we use to keep tabs on our clients, news of the president's resignation was tucked away in each of our email baskets, patiently awaiting our arrival the next morning.

Once again, the Internet and its services brought us timely information with which to communicate on an important matter to an important client.

refined, will most likely become of paramount importance to designers.

It's this videoconferencing capability, enabling you to collaborate with a client, making notes and changes the other can see while cutting and pasting from other files, all in real time, that demonstrates this technology's real potential. Here's an idea: Set down this book for a few minutes and think about your firm. How will using videoconferencing over the Internet to collaborate with your clients impact your business? When you consider the time and money this could save you, suddenly it's not too hard to justify the cost of a couple of videoconferencing systems and that new ISDN line.

Of course, other technologies utilizing the Internet provide similar collaborative capabilities, albeit without the on-screen image of your client or yourself. Hey, if you're like me, that may be better anyway. "Could you just change the typeface? Move that headline a bit to the right. No, not that far, now down a little. That's right, but the blue is too green. I really don't like that photo. Well, maybe we better just change that typeface back again." Okay, what kind of faces are you making? Want your client to see them? You might be better off considering applications that enable you to share files with clients without the videophone window. Only one problem: Most of the software to accomplish this isn't much more than wispy vapor trails rising from the pages of computer magazines and manufacturer's press releases.

One promising new software application that *does* enable you to phone your clients anywhere in the world via the Internet is Electric Magic's NetPhone. And it doesn't cost you anything beyond the local call to your Internet access provider! All that's required are inexpensive speakers and microphones and the appropriate software on both ends of the

Electric Magic's NetPhone

http://www.emagic.com

continued on next page

NetPhone™

 This site has been rated as one of the top 5% on the net by Point Communications.

The latest version of NetPhone adds **16-bit audio, Auto Squelch, PPP/SLIP detection, Open Transport** compatibility and fixes a number of bugs and odd behaviors.

NetPhone also includes access to **NetPubs, full duplex** conversations, **address book,** integration with **NetScape, Caller** ID and more...

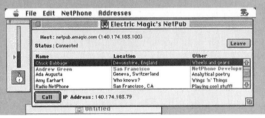

connection. After that, it's unlimited free calls on the Internet—although be forewarned that the transmission quality isn't all that great. Warning: Teenagers, after learning of the availability of this technology on the computers of their designer-type parents, have been known to commandeer said computers, erroneously thinking the computers have become their own. Imagine! (See chapter 4 for a more thorough discussion of using NetPhone.)

As I mentioned earlier, you can also use text-only Internet services for living communication, if that suits your purpose. Set up your own temporary IRC channel, schedule a time to meet, and you can have people from all over the world "meeting" at once. And if you email those Quark files to them beforehand, you can talk about what revisions should be made. You could also set up your own MUD, a "virtual office" that describes the surroundings, and allows you to do the same sorts of things. As the Internet continues to evolve, no doubt even more communication options will appear.

Exchanging Comps

I can see it now. You'll be sitting in your office in

Denver, alternating your glance out the window to the Rockies and back again to your computer, on which you're sharing a QuarkXPress layout with your client back in Boston. *"Oh, really? Not me!"* Yeah...you will! Not excited about this technology? Can't understand why you'd want to do this? You will. It'll be economics, pure and simple, and electronically connecting your office to your client's will forever change the way you do business. Remember, service is the name of the game. There are lots of great designers, but in the end it's service that often differentiates one from another.

It's really not that hard to exchange comps over the Internet. You could simply compress your Quark file and attach it to an email message and send it off. Or, if your client doesn't have Quark on his machine, just save your file as Adobe Acrobat PDF and upload it to your own or your client's FTP site. As soon as you do, your client can download it and take a look. Of course, everyone else who has permission to access that FTP site can see it too.

This is also a great way to distribute hypertext progress charts or low-circulation newsletters, saving paper and postage charges. Maybe you set up a Web page that requires a password to access. On that Web page, you and your client keep the ongoing progress charts of projects, and at any time either of you can update the charts right on the Web. It's always current and it's always available.

Pride and security aside, there are obviously limitations to so casually sharing files in this way with clients. Want them to mark up your files? Is it okay if they open them up and make changes? Hey, just who is the designer around there, anyway? You'll have to work out the issues, but the Internet holds forth great promise in sharing your work with clients. Relax, before long we'll all being doing it.

Billing

Hey, the technology is there; use it. Ask your firm's office manager to just complete an electronic invoice and email it to your client's payable department. They receive it, process it, and electronically deposit funds to your account. It's as simple as that: no more paper, no relying on good old Uncle Sam to lose the mail, no more waiting for "the check in the mail."

Of course, it may not be quite that simple yet, but I bet you it will be before too long. Might as well get started now. Go ahead and email that invoice. See what happens. Maybe you'd better make it a small one, though!

Collaborating via a BBS

Another way to facilitate collaboration with your clients, or better yet with a number of clients, is to establish a private BBS. This way you can collaborate with clients that aren't even connected to the Internet—and you can make sure that your information and files stay secure, something that you can't really guarantee on the anarchic Internet.

All your clients have to do is use a modem to connect to your BBS. You can use the BBS to distribute files and electronic mail between you and your clients in the same way you could using the Internet. One problem: Unless your clients are located locally, they will have to pay long-distance charges to reach your BBS. But the benefits might outweigh the costs.

Well, put this chapter into practice and you'll have one connected design firm. Seriously, with a little thought and effort, your use of the Internet to connect to your clients can bring very big dividends. In chapter 6 you'll learn just how productive using the Net can be when connecting to your suppliers and vendors.

Chapter 6

Connecting to Suppliers and Vendors

This chapter presents attractive opportunities

for improving our collaboration with our

suppliers and vendors.

Act II

Scene 4

Casey and Steven screaming through another productive day on the Net.

Casey: "Man! It's been a long day, but a productive one!"

Steven: "And we're not done yet. Hey, Casey, did you get a chance to look for that illustration we need for the annual?"

Casey: "Yeah, after lunch I visited a free Internet clip art site, did a quick keyword search, and found a couple of images that just may work. Another click of the mouse and they were emailed to me."

Steven: "Good. Let's choose one right now so we can manipulate it and place it in the layout. Before we leave, we can load all the files onto the server and set it to upload the annual to the digital press."

No big deal...just *major productivity*. In just a few short minutes, Casey and Steven searched through thousands of images to find just what they needed and downloaded it for their immediate, hassle-free use—and then actually sent their finished electronic art files over the Internet to an on-demand printer in a city thousands of miles away. The Internet, and their use of its efficiency, effectiveness, and timeliness, resulted in Casey and Steven compressing yet another set of what could have been very time-consuming tasks into but a few brief moments at the end of another productive day.

This scenario may not be common today, but before long it will be. We'll be using the Internet all the time to find stock photos and clip art, acquire fonts, download software, get tech support, send pre-press files electronically, and more.

Locate Stock Photos and Clip Art

You know how difficult it is to find just the right photo for a comp layout? The hassle of paging through book after book of stock photos (man, how can they afford to publish these books, anyway?). Well, now you can do it the easy way: by using the Internet to connect to the Web sites of any number of well-known stock houses, such as Black Star or Tony Stone Images (http://www.tonystone.com).

Black Star

http://www.blackstar.com

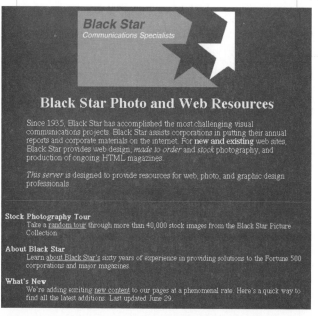

Try <u>Graphics on Call</u>, for instance. Just visit the site and type in a few keywords for the image you're

Graphics on Call

http://www.pacific-coast.com/GOCDemo.
html

Stock Graphics from <u>Pacific Coast Software</u>

Save money. Save time. It's like having your own personal assistant who can search through thousands of photos for you -- instantly! Use our incredible high-speed search software to find, preview, and purchase individual photographs from professional-quality stock photography CDs--over the internet! And even FEDEX can't beat our blazing delivery speed...because we deliver product at near-light-speed directly to your email inbox: **no charge, no tax, no hassle.**

Every image you see here is for sale, and you don't have to buy an entire CD to get it! Browse at your leisure **for free**, then buy as many photos as you want -- using a credit card or First Virtual. Remember, these are **exactly the same photos** you would get if you bought an entire CD, but at a fraction of the cost because you only buy the ones you need.

<u>Enter Graphics on Call</u>

Come back often; we'll be adding thousands of pictures every month!

[Back to Pacific Coast Software Home Page]
Copyright 1995 Pacific Coast Software

looking for, and sit back and relax for the couple of seconds it takes the computer to do its search. Don't like any of those images? "Waste" a few more seconds searching at another stock house Web site, say <u>The Stock Solution</u>. Once you've found just the right image, most stock houses on the Internet will email a low-res electronic version of the photo to

The Stock Solution

http://www.xmission.com/~tssphoto/
tssphoto.html

THE STOCK SOLUTION

A Stock Photo Agency

Images for Lease

The Stock Solution (TSS) is a stock photo agency, representing the images of about 100 photographers. Our library of 200,000 images is available for use by publishers and advertisers. Our <u>copyrighted images</u> can be leased for a variety of uses, i.e. brochures, newsletters, magazines, multi-media presentations, and even personal uses.

The TSS Online Image Library

The How and Why of Stock Photography

- <u>What is Stock Photography?</u>
- <u>Rent or Own? (Traditional Stock vs. Clip-art)</u>
- <u>Leasing Stock Images for Commercial or Publishing Use</u>
- <u>Leasing Stock Images for Personal or In-house Use</u>
- How to do a <u>custom photo search</u>
- <u>How We PRICE Our Stock Photos</u>
- <u>How to Order and Acquire Our Images</u>

you or enable you to download it via an FTP site to paste it into your layout. Once your client approves the photo, a quick call or an email to the stock house people and they'll express the original or a high-res electronic file to you. Sure beats those stock photo books, doesn't it?!

Companies such as PhotoDisc offer the hybrid option of stock photos on CD-ROMs, yet also making

PhotoDisc

http://www.photodisc.com

them accessible via the Internet. You can download free samples to use and browse through entire collections of photos before submitting your order online.

Sounds easy. It really is. But there is one problem still unsolved: bandwidth, or perhaps more accurately stated, the lack thereof. Once greater bandwidth becomes readily available, downloading high-res photos directly to our computers will make this process even more efficient. For the time being, however, downloading a 50 MB high-res 8¨ x 10¨ color photo requires a significant amount of time, about five hours using a fast 28.8 Kbs modem. Even over an ISDN line, it would still take something like two hours. If your design firm is anything like ours, that's a problem! (Unless, that is, you really need the photo and you don't mind letting your computer work at night while you sleep. Hey, that sounds pretty good. And after all, a couple hours of long-distance charges in the middle of the night may be cheaper than FedEx anyway! Order that photo. It'll be waiting for you in the morning.)

Paying for photos downloaded over the Internet is still a bit problematic, since it's not necessarily safe to send your VISA card number across the Internet. But things are changing daily. Netscape, for example, has server software that companies can use for making credit card transactions secure when you visit their Web site. Other companies are investing in "virtual banks" that enable you to buy things with electronic cash (which is, unfortunately, backed up with your *real* cash).

There's a lot of high-quality clip art on the Net, too. Clip art Web sites are great places to visit when searching for just the right image. For more clip art than you've ever dreamed of, check out Sandra's Clip Art Server. If you can't find what you're looking for there, you'd better reach behind your computer and pull that Internet connection!

Sandra's Clip Art Server

http://www.cs.yale.edu/homes/sjl/clipart.

html

Sandra's Clip Art Server

Local Clip Art Archive

These are copies of clip art collections from other archive sites that I've found while looking for artwork for decorating WWW pages. I have not attempted to edit the collections in any way (except to do format and filename conversions), so expect to find some duplicate images and some files with low-quality graphics.

If you want to use these images in your own WWW pages, I request that you not make direct links to individual image files. Please copy the files you want to your own server instead.

If you want to grab these files en masse, please download the corresponding tar file(s) instead of fetching every image file separately. Tar is the standard Unix archive format. There are also tar programs for the Macintosh and DOS, but **please** don't waste time sending me mail if you can't figure out how to unpack the tar files or how to display the images. I **cannot** help you with PC or Mac software questions, so **don't ask**.

Update: Because of server load problems, I am now providing only the tar files from this site. The individual image files are now being served at UIUC, courtesy of Peter Leppik (p-leppik@uiuc.edu). If you are interested in setting up additional mirror sites, please send me (loosemore-sandra@cs.yale.edu) mail.

- **Funet Collection**: this is a copy of the huge clip art collection on ftp.funet.fi. The pictures were collected from a variety of sources, including various public-domain Amiga, Atari, and Macintosh clip art collections. The collection was originally contributed by Gareth Blades (gareth@blades.wcp.co.uk).
  - Individual images

Acquire Fonts

Imagine it's 11:30 at night. Your eyes are burning from staring at that layout all day long. It's due at your client's office first thing in the morning, and suddenly you realize you need Garamond. But not just any old Garamond—you need that special Garamond with the Old Style Figures. Now what do you do? Simple. Just launch Netscape or your favorite Web browser, pull down your Bookmarks menu to the home page address of one of your favorite font houses, and load the font directory. Find the Garamond font you need and click to download it to your computer, along with the obligatory invoicing required.

Wait a minute! This really isn't quite possible today. Although they're working on it, the major font suppliers haven't yet been willing to open the vaults containing their valuable copyright-protected fonts to potential cyberspace thieves wandering the notoriously security-less Internet. This is not to say, however, that you cannot procure fonts over the Internet. There are, in fact, plenty of freeware fonts available, though they may or may not meet your professional standards. Want to take a look anyway? Check out the Internet Font Archive. From there you can link to any number of sites, including the mac.archive.umich.edu Font Archives, from which you can download any of more than 500 different fonts.

And then there are those innovative folks at designOnline with fontsOnline, Alphabets, Inc.'s unique font marketplace on the World Wide Web. The fontsOnline interface incorporates a patent-pending process that allows the user to examine the fonts on an interactive feedback page. Designers can choose to preview a font using any short phrase of their choosing, which will then be rendered by the

Internet Font Archive
http://jasper.ora.com/comp.fonts/Internet-Font-Archive

mac.archive.umich.edu
http://jasper.ora.com/comp.fonts/Internet-Font-Archive/mac.archive.umich.edu/index.html

fontsOnline
http://www.dol.com/fontsOnline

continued on next page   continued on next page

The Internet Font Archive

Table of Contents
Introduction
The Archives
Commercial Foundries
Type Libraries on CD

Query the Server

Introduction

The *Internet Font Archive* (IFA) grew out of my attempt to collect all of the fonts available on the Internet in a single place. Rather than trying to mirror the font archives on the Net, the IFA is a database of fonts utilizing the hypertext functionality of the WWW to point to the other archive sites. The database contains information about each font and a thumbnail sketch of a few characters.

In addition to fonts available on the Net, the IFA database now includes fonts from several commercial foundries and type CDs.

If you know of a free font that isn't in the IFA, or if you represent a commercial foundry and you'd like to have your fonts added to the IFA, please tell norm. Send comments and suggestions to Norman Walsh (norm@ora.com).

At present, the IFA contains only Adobe(R) Type 1 fonts. MetaFont (TeX) fonts and Type 3 fonts are likely to be added next. If anyone contributes a TrueType rasterizer, TrueType fonts will be added as well.

> **Disclaimer:** The fact that a font is available over the Net does not mean that it can legally be used in all applications. In fact, it's possible that it is being distributed illegally. For this reason, very few of the fonts in this archive are available from jasper.ora.com or any other ftp server at O'Reilly. Please don't ask me to make them available; get them from the server(s) that already provide them.

The Archives

The fonts are arranged alphabetically by server (but note that some fonts appear on more than one server). You can also query the server using regular expressions to locate a particular font or fonts

This file uses standard HTML 2.0 tags. If your browser understands tags from the HTML 3.0 draft specification, you may find this alternate presentation more appealing visually.

Font Archives at mac.archive.umich.edu

PostScript Type 1 Fonts

There are currently 509 fonts in this section of the Internet Font Archives.

Alphabetical Font List

A: 31 fonts: **Aarcover** to **Averoigne**
B: 31 fonts: **BODIDLYbold** to **ButnerBold**
C: 53 fonts: **CHANLPlain** to **CyrillicItalic**
D: 27 fonts: **DavysBigKeyCaps** to **Durendal**
E: 18 fonts: **EBrantScript** to **Eviscerate**
F: 18 fonts: **Faktos** to **Futhark-Gothic**
G: 26 fonts: **GREEKnor** to **GrungeUpdate**
H: 22 fonts: **Handwriting** to **HuntSpeedBall**
I: 11 fonts: **INDUSTRIAL-Regular** to **Ismini**
J: 9 fonts: **JMDWulfila-NormalItalic** to **Juliet**
K: 21 fonts: **KOI8-Terminal** to **KrtRussell**
L: 24 fonts: **LampoonBrush2** to **LynzFont**
M: 35 fonts: **MacKeyCaps** to **Muriel**
N: 11 fonts: **Nauert** to **Nviray**
O: 9 fonts: **OSWALDblack** to **OxNard**
P: 24 fonts: **PalPhon** to **Publius**
Q: 1 font: **Quadrata** to **Quadrata**
R: 22 fonts: **RRHeralds** to **Ruffian**

fontsOnline server and returned to the Web client as a downloadable graphic. If desired, the font can be ordered directly through the system, and will be available for FTP downloading once the credit card or other payment information has been authorized. The entire Alphabets, Inc. library is also shown in an exclusive Adobe Acrobat PDF format catalog, designed to be viewed directly online with the soon-to-be-released Acrobat Reader features in Netscape. In addition, these PDF catalog pages can be downloaded and printed locally at high resolution

continued on next page

to show the detail and characteristics of the fonts. Hey, why not give it a try. And for the more adventurous, you can also acquire A*I font animations by bYte a tree productions and other creative types.

In addition, there are any number of other font-related services available via the Internet that are also quite worthwhile. One such site is Graphion's Online Type Museum, where you will find information

Graphion's Online Type Museum

http://www.slip.net/~graphion/
museum.html

about the history and practice of typesetting. Or you might want to visit the Internet Font Browser to search through hundreds of type faces, or the Will-Harris House to view the *Typofile* Magazine that claims it "blows the lid off the type scene! Cross

Will-Harris House

http://www.will-harris.com

Internet Font Browser

http://cuiwww.unige.ch/InternetFontBrowser.html

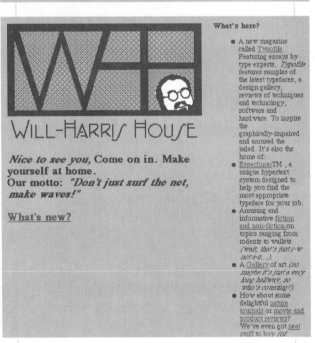

Bars! Counters! Bowls! Sans Serifs!" By the way, while you're at the Will-Harris site, be sure to try out the Esperfonto hypertext system to help you find the most appropriate type face for your next job.

Other sites you might check out include Letraset's home page and TypeLab, a kind of interactive conference on type.

TypeLab

http://www.dol.com/TypeLab

Letraset

http://www.letraset.com/letraset

TypeLab Barcelona 1995

- 21 September to 25 September 1995
- When & Where
- Temporary Program
- TypeLab Space
- How to participate in TypeLab
- Give a lecture! Write an article!
- Contacts for Registration

TypeLab itself

- What is TypeLab?
- TypeLab Content

There's no question that as the Internet becomes more secure, we will look to it as a major medium through which to purchase the fonts we need. Begin now to use it as a research tool to locate the fonts. Before long you'll be taking delivery of those fonts directly to your computer over the Internet.

Download Software

One of the really great advantages to connecting electronically via the Internet to suppliers is the ability to download software. Need that new upgrade? What about those software fixes you read about but never quite knew how to find? And then there are the hundreds and hundreds of great freeware programs, and still hundreds of other inexpensive, and often even better, shareware programs. You can download them all whenever you need them.

Commercial Software

Although there's a vast library of software available over the Internet, very little of it is conventional commercial software, such as Photoshop or QuarkXPress—although electronic distribution of commercial software is likely to start sooner or later. You will, however, find a certain degree of free software from commercial developers, mostly things like viewers for files generated by Adobe Acrobat and Virtus VR. Software like this will usually be found on the commercial developer's home page. For example, you can download Adobe's Acrobat viewer from http://www.adobe.com.

In addition, the Internet is a great place to find upgrades, patches, and fixes for your commercial software, too. How many times have you suddenly encountered a bug in your software? Now what do you do? You're working on a rush project, and of course it's the middle of the night, when there is no way you can reach the manufacturer. I've been there! No problem: Just connect to the Internet and visit the manufacturer's Web site. Locate the patch or the fix you need and download it. Might as well download the free upgrade while you're at it. Give it a try. Mac users can visit the Apple Support and Info

Web site to download all kinds of upgrades and patches. Windows users can do the same at Microsoft's site. Actually, the same holds true for most major manufacturers.

Apple Support and Info Web
http://www.info.apple.com

Microsoft
http://www.microsoft.com/Products

major manufacturers

Adobe: http://www.adobe.com

Canon: http://www.canon.com

Corel Corporation: http://www.corel.ca

Hewlett Packard: http://www.hp.com

HSC Software: http://the-tech.mit.edu
/KPT/contact.html

IBM: http://www.ibm.com

Macromedia: http://www.macromedia
.com

NEC: http://www.nec.com

WordPerfect: http://www.wordperfect
.com

Virtus: http://www.virtus.com

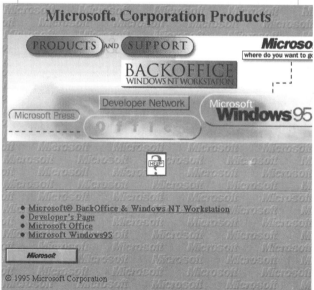

Shareware and Freeware

Elevate shareware to a new level, thanks to the Internet. Shareware is software distributed for free, giving you a chance to try it out. If you like it and want to keep it, all you have to do is send in a required payment, usually very reasonable, to the software's creator. Prior to the recent onslaught of Internet users, getting shareware was cumbersome at best. But now, all you have to do is conduct a few searches to find what you're looking for and download whatever you need. Just don't forget to be a good Internet citizen. Send in the required payment for whatever you want to keep and use.

You'll find piles and piles of extremely useful shareware and freeware software on the Internet, utilities that will do everything from change the background colors on your screen to convert Microsoft Word files into HTML. As you probably have gathered, browsers for the Web are usually free. Most other useful Internet utilities, such as FTP, Telnet, and Gopher clients, are also free. And then there are really great apps such as StuffIt Lite (ftp://ftp.utexas.edu/pub/mac/compression), a file compression program really helpful when sending files back and forth over the Internet.

By the way, if you're interested in the history behind the shareware concept, visit Jim Knopf's site, where you'll see he is the self-declared Father of Shareware. For a visit to a totally new kind of share-

Father of Shareware

http://www.halcyon.com/knopf/jim

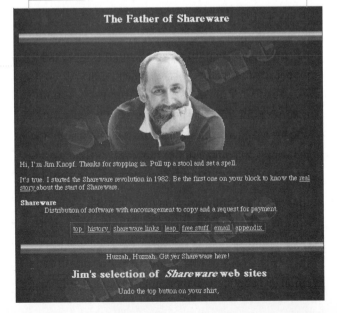

ware site, check out Shareware Central's interactive shareware page.

Shareware Central

http://www.intac.com/~dversch/swc.html

Welcome to Shareware Central!

This page was last updated on 7/11/95.

Welcome to *Shareware Central* sponsored by Q*D Software Development. *Shareware Central* is not just another shareware site. In fact it's a totally new concept. *Shareware Central* is an interactive shareware catalog. At *Shareware Central* users get to read program descriptions written by the authors themselves, download the program(s) of their choice, and can also contact the authors directly via hypertext links to the authors' e-mail addresses. In certain case users can actually experience an interactive demo of a particular program.

Like the World Wide Web, *Shareware Central* is an ever-changing phenomenon. We are open to all suggestions and comments. Within the weeks and months ahead, as more shareware authors become aware of our service, we plan on considerable expansion.

For more information on the *Shareware Central Interactive Catalog* and to visit the catalog, you may choose from the menu of hypertext links below.

- Note to all visitors
- Submissions to the Catalog
- Visit the interactive *Shareware Central* catalog
- Make comments or suggestions
- Visit Q*D Software Development's home page.
- Credits

And then there is freeware—software for free, available for downloading over the Internet. The whole freeware thing is almost too good to believe. And some of this freeware you can find is great. Getting it is as easy as visiting a few archive sites on the Web. Want to download a great email application? Here's how great life on the Net can be: Just visit Qualcomm's home page. Click for information on Eudora Light. Click again to download the application to your computer. Install it and then send your first email back to Qualcomm thanking them for

Qualcomm's home page

http://www.qualcomm.com

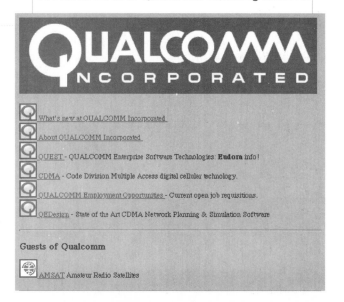

Guests of Qualcomm

what is undoubtedly one of the best bargains on the Net!

Where do you find shareware? Well, mainly in software archives. The biggest, oldest, and most useful archives are maintained by universities. Macintosh sources include the vast Info-Mac archives at Stanford University (ftp://sumex-aim.stanford.edu/info-mac) and the University of Michigan Mac Archive (ftp://mac.archive.umich.edu).

Because these sites are so busy, they are difficult to connect to. Many mirrors—sites containing copies of the entire archive—have been set up to lessen the load on the main archives. If you are denied access to an archive, you will usually be notified of available mirror sites you can try. The most useful mirror I know of is maintained by America Online at ftp://mirrors.aol.com. For Windows software, check out the California State University at San Marcos Windows Shareware Archive (http://coyote .csusm .edu/cwis/winworld/winworld.html) and The Center for Innovative Computer Applications at Indiana University: PC/Windows FTP Archive (http://www.cica.indiana.edu/cgi-bin/checkftp). Yahoo's shareware listings (http://www.yahoo.com /Computers/Software/Shareware) can also be helpful. (See chapter 3 for more information on finding software).

Get Technical Support

Remember the last time you had a computer-related problem? You called the manufacturer's toll-free (hopefully!) customer service line. You were put on hold long enough to have probably rebuilt the darn thing, and then suddenly the tech comes on the line, gives you a few nanoseconds to describe your ailment, and finally searches his well-formed cerebrum for a totally unique phrase that is sure to help. Something like, "Gee, that's the first time I ever heard that one."

Ever been there? Bet you have. You can say good-bye to all of that if you're comfortable with the Internet, by taking advantage of other avenues of support such as mailing lists, Usenet newsgroups, and a vast assortment of resources on the Web. It helps if you know a few <u>tips</u> along the way.

Mailing Lists and Usenet Newsgroups

The easiest way to get answers to your problems probably isn't a call to a manufacturer's technical support line. Instead, try subscribing to any one of the thousands of different mailing lists and Usenet newsgroups, perhaps a few related to desktop publishing and graphic design. There are lists for PageMaker, QuarkXPress, Photoshop, Illustrator, Director, and more (see chapter 3).

You'll be in good company. All kinds of people sub-scribe—some are experts, some are novices. A question posted to one of them is likely to be an-swered pretty quickly by one of the experts. And, since other people can read your question and the ensuing responses, your query is likely to help other people with similar problems. It may take longer to receive a response than a call to the manufacturer, but it will be a lot less stressful, and you can get back to work on other projects in the meantime. And, in an age when many manufacturers charge for technical support, mailing lists and newsgroups are free.

If you take this route, be sure to follow the threads of conversation and try to answer some of the questions posted there. These discussion groups de-pend on give and take between all their subscribers. Just by scanning the subjects of the messages in a list, you may be able to get a fix for a program or find out about a bug before you ever run into the prob-lem. It's good preventive medicine.

tips

Fast technical support to the rescue. Just do it once—call the company's technical support line, be patient and hold on long enough to get past those sexy voice mail voices and finally reach a real, live technical support human being. Here's the secret: Get his or her name and *email address*, and let the tech know you can communicate over the Internet in the fu-ture. You'll never again have to hold and hold and hold and.... Next time you need some help just zip off a quick email.

Home-Grown Web Pages and FTP Sites

Like other subject areas, it can take quite a while to find a really useful Web page, but once you do, it will likely lead to other useful sources of information. As an example, a good place to start for information related to desktop publishing is the DTP Internet Jumplist. The page contains an extensive

DTP Internet Jumplist

http://www.cs.purdue.edu/homes/gwp/dtp/dtp.html

list of design-related information. Another example is the FTP archive for the Photoshop mailing list. This archive contains software updates, many FAQ

Photoshop mailing list

ftp://export.acs.cmu.edu/pub/PSarch

and tip sheets written by other users covering all aspects of Photoshop, shareware and freeware filters and plug-ins, and more. Another useful site is the

University of New Brunswick <u>Graphic Services page</u>.

Graphic Services page

http://degaulle.hil.unb.ca/UNB_G_

Services/GSHomePage.html

Also be sure to check a search engine such as InfoSeek or Lycos for new information that is constantly generated. It doesn't take long, and the journey toward a needed piece of information usually leads to enough useful info on related topics to make the extra time spent worthwhile.

Manufacturer's Web Pages

Often the best place to find technical support is at the product manufacturer's Web page. The first place to check for a manufacturer's page is the manual included with your hardware or software. With the growth of the Internet, it is becoming increasingly common to provide official corrections to the documentation and software patches online.

If all else fails, just try plausible addresses, such as http://www.adobe.com for Adobe (Adobe has a great <u>Service, Support, and Training</u> page), or do a few searches on one of the various search engines. (See the list of some manufacturer's Web pages earlier in this chapter.)

Service, Support, and Training

http://www.adobe.com/Support/Service

.html

continued on next page

Adobe Service, Support, and Training

Information for Users & Developers, Application Notes, Technical Notes, Developer and SDK information, Training, and User Group information.

Support and Sales Phone numbers

FaxYI: Application Notes

Notes on specific Adobe application products, organized by platform and application. Indexes include:

     Macintosh / Power Macintosh - Technical information
     Windows / DOS / OS/2 - Technical information
     UNIX and NeXT - Technical information
     Adobe Consumer Products Index - Technical / Sales

Technical Notes for Developers

Notes on Adobe technology, file formats and interface specifications like TIFF, OPI, PPD, and AFM, communications protocols, the PostScript language, and the Display PostScript System.

Adobe Developers Association

Membership information, Software Development Kits (**SDK**'s), Developer Resources,

Send Prepress Files

A general lack of bandwidth (surprise, surprise!) is currently the main problem we face in sending prepress files over the Internet. Although this holds forth great promise for connecting designers to a variety of suppliers and vendors, doing so makes more sense with some, given this constraint, than with others. If and when the bandwidth issue is solved, we will routinely exchange finished art files with prepress suppliers over the Internet.

Actually, this can be done today, yet almost no designers and very few prepress suppliers have the fast T1 lines in place that are mandatory to do so. Having said this, however, one of our suppliers, a high-quality color separator, routinely receives and sends prepress files back and forth between Cincinnati and New York via the Internet. Just the fact that the Internet is being used to do this today points to the probability that many design firms may do so in the not-so-distant future. For the time being, though, don't lose the phone number for your local courier service. If you're interested, keep your eye on prepress Web sites such as these:

• Online Prepress Service

Online Prepress Service

http://www.wco.com/~billn

• PrePRESS Main Street (http://www2.prepress.pps.com)

• Global Prepress Center

Global Prepress Center

http://www.ledet.com/prepress

This jump list is designed to hold links to businesses, information, and resources for those involved in professional desktop publishing, graphic arts, prepress, and printing. The Global Prepress Center has been sponsored by PrimeSource Corporation. Please make sure to visit them (and register there!) before you go.

The Global Prepress Center is maintained as a service of Prepress Online. Prepress Online offers WWW development and network support services for the graphic arts industry.

Please sign our visitor's log before you go. If you have a graphic arts related WWW site and would like to have it added to the Global Prepress Center, please leave a comment with your registration. If you already have a site, listings are free. If you would like Prepress Online to program a site for you, prices start at $125 per year.

• PrePress Online (http://www.mindspring.com/~sledet/po)

● <u>The Bureau</u>

The Bureau

http://bureau.com

Connect to On-Demand Printers

The world of graphic arts is indeed changing. Without the Internet and its direct connections between clients and printers, we would have never seen the recent advent of electronic digital printing presses known for their on-demand printing. Although hampered by a lack of bandwidth, on-demand printers are cropping up everywhere.

Just install a T1 line between you and the printer and then it's as simple as choosing a printer over your network. Just drag and drop that Quark file on the direct digital printer icon, and off your file goes, not to your laser printer or the Tektronix in the room next door, but to the digital press down the street or across the sea.

Independent design firms may not be employing this technology just yet, but those of you working as in-house designers for large corporations know all about this high-speed, high-quality printing from your desktop to the digital press anywhere in the world. Once again, this is an incredible display of technology, thanks in great measure to the Internet. Try it out. Call a local on-demand printer or, for that matter, check out DocuNet Digital Document Services, or BusinessGraphics on the Web.

BusinessGraphics

http://www.busgrfx.com/busgrfx/bushome.html

DocuNet Digital Document Services

http://www.netudoc.com

So, in this part of the book, you've learned how to get the most from the Net, and in the process you've connected to your peers, to your clients, and to your suppliers and vendors. In part III you'll be using your newfound expertise to help your clients use the Net, sharing, telling, and selling online.

PART III

HELPING CLIENTS USE THE NET

Part III

PART III SUGGESTS WAYS WE DESIGNERS CAN
IMPACT OUR CLIENTS' BUSINESS THROUGH CRE-
ATIVE USE OF THIS NEW MEDIUM.

Chapter 7

CHAPTER 7 BEGINS THE DISCUSSION WITH HOW
WE CAN HELP OUR CLIENTS USE THE INTERNET
BY INTRODUCING MODELS FOR IMPROVING IN-
TERCOMPANY COMMUNICATION AND COLLABO-
RATION.

Chapter 8

CHAPTER 8 EXPLORES MODELS FOR HELPING
CLIENTS INFORM THE WORLD ABOUT THEM-
SELVES, THEIR PRODUCTS, AND THEIR SERVICES
VIA THE INTERNET.

Chapter 9

CHAPTER 9 TAKES THE GLOVES OFF AND ILLUS-
TRATES SOME BARE-KNUCKLED MODELS FOR
ONLINE COMMERCE.

Act III

Scene 1

A 15th floor meeting room in the offices of BigCorp. A Communication Team Meeting is in progress with Carol from Corporate Communications, Bradley from Customer Support, Duane from Information Systems, Nick from Marketing, and Gloria from Public Relations all in attendance, team leader, Abig Shot presiding. The atmosphere is charged with hope and stress.

Team Leader, Abig: "Okay, let's get back on task, there's another meeting scheduled in here in ten minutes. Let's go around the table and summarize your findings. Gloria, what are the top priorities for Public Relations?"

GLORIA: "WE THINK NEW PRODUCT ANNOUNCE-MENTS ARE A NATURAL FOR THE INTERNET. WE THINK THERE'S EVEN POTENTIAL TO SMOOTH THE PROCESS OF HOS-TILE TAKEOVERS, BUT WE NEED INFORMED HELP. ALL WE HAVE ARE IDEAS."

Abig: "Nick, what about Marketing?"

Nick: "Marketing likes the idea of cutting our print catalog run. We'd save a lot just in paper, and we could keep an electronic catalog updated a lot cheaper than reprinting—at least that's the projection—and the newsletter makes a lot more sense on-line. We project the total savings could let us double our media budget for the first quarter. We could sure use it."

Abig: "Sounds great, Nick. Bradley?"

Bradley: "Like I said, umm, if we made a list of our most common customer requests, uh, you know, complaints and such, if we put those all in one place where customers could find them, I think they call it a Frequently Asked Questions file or something. FAQ is it, well, we think we could trim our customer support phone service and redirect some of that energy to our on-site support team. I mean, we'd really like to do that, because, as you know, last year, we ahhh..."

Abig: "Thanks, Brad. Carol?"

Carol: "We can put the annual report online tomorrow, no problem. But I believe we need some input in the Corporate Communications area. We're not certain what all's appropriate on the Internet. Should we limit ourselves to free advice or hard sell ourselves, or some combination.... We aren't sure. We want more input."

Abig: "We'll come back to that in a second. Duane, what about Information Systems, can you..."

Duane: "I'm not worried about the connection. That part's virtually done. We're online now. Where we need help is from Carol. And probably somebody from Gloria's area. It's not our job to figure out how to promote the use of electronic forms and email. These services are no good if we can't get people to give up their paper. We'll waste our time. And we'll need support from product development people.... Just a second...."

Duane reaches to his pocket protector for his calculator/digital personal assistant.

Duane: "Yes, Ron is the guy's name. Ron Teckwiz will have to tell us exactly which technical information he wants us to put up on the server. We can't decide for him."

Abig: "Is that it? Nick, get hold of Bill at SOS Design and get them to help us develop a

strategy and get it implemented. Carol, you manage this team and make sure you fill SOS in on this meeting. I want **design expertise** on this from the start. We don't want this to erode our identity or conflict with our marketing. Anything else? Let's do it, people."

There is a lot that can be done on the Internet and designers need to know about it. This sprawling network is developing so quickly and so dynamically that businesses are discovering that building a solid strategy to fully employ the commercial opportunities on the Internet is an extremely challenging feat. Your clients can expand markets, update publications, reduce paper consumption, microtarget customers, connect to vendors worldwide — quickly, easily, and inexpensively 24 hours a day on the Internet.

In part II, "Getting the Most from the Net," we covered a variety of topics about how designers can use the Internet for connecting to peers, clients, and suppliers. Well, all these opportunities are available to your clients as well and they need your help to sort out which ones are most effective and how to implement them. As a graphic designer, an expert in information strategy and design, you hold the keys.

Chapter 7

Sharing Online:
Collaboration

This chapter begins the discussion with how we can

help our clients use the Internet by introducing

models for improving intercompany

communication and collaboration.

Act III

Scene 2

Three days later a subteam meets in the basement in the Information Services area, just outside the mainframe computer system.

Carol: "Here are some options for introducing email and electronic forms. As you can see, there are distinctly different strategies for internal customers and field salespeople. Our experience shows that the field people will be a lot more resistant to change than headquarters staff."

Duane: "Who's going to pay for these materials?"

GLORIA: "IF WE SUCCEED IN CONVERTING HALF THE PEOPLE, THEY WILL PAY FOR THEMSELVES."

There are two classic ways to improve an organization's bottom line: reduce expenses or increase income. Doing both at the same time is great, but doing just one will help. The easiest way to help our clients make money on the Internet might not involve bringing in any income at all. Reducing expenses is a no-brainer on the Internet.

Yet, graphic designers aren't accountants. We're in the communication services business: We identify, conceive, and develop things that help our clients communicate more effectively. Designers add value to information. If data were a rocket, graphic designers add boosters. We help our clients communicate with themselves, their clients, stakeholders, communities, and peers. Those we serve count on our expertise to advise them on all aspects of communication practice, including explosive new media such as the Internet.

While the Internet is a powerful vehicle for improving communication on every level, intercompany communications, the grease that smoothes and improves organizational operation, can be greatly enhanced by wise use of the Net. Because the Internet is such a powerful and cost-effective vehicle for speeding and enhancing communication, it can save our clients significant money. While improving intercompany communication is not a big revenue item for most graphic design consultancies, smart designers inside and outside the organizations we serve should be prepared to advise them in its use.

Low-Cost Communications

Companies do not need to "make money" on the Internet in order to justify an Internet investment. The Net is a high-quality, low-cost communication vehicle that can save an organization hundreds of times the cost of installing a connection by cutting down the need for faxes, overnight deliveries, and long-distance calls.

The resulting communication process enhancements can improve the effectiveness of how individuals, departments, and companies perform, help them automate their business processes, and even transform the nature of their work/service/product.

Internal and External Email

Expediting internal communication through the use of interoffice mail has many obvious advantages. It reduces "telephone tag" while enabling both (or more) parties to communicate when most convenient for each. Email is less intrusive than the phone; it enables instant messaging, but without the tension of a live phone call. Email enables time shifting, so you can send and respond when it's convenient for you. Email will also automatically produce an electronic record of the communication, so you can track when you talked with whom and what was discussed.

With email, forwarding information from other sources is almost effortless. You can send graphics information or enclose files or programs with the click of a mouse (see chapter 3). Email encourages not only low-cost, instant communication, but also collaboration as employees exchange files (see the section coming up).

Speed

For an example of how one could cut cost while improving communication, consider the sales process of a company that depends on applications to qualify a new prospect for a sale, such as an insurance company. It is the prospect's first exposure to the company and how responsive it will be to him. He is at a very "closable" state in that he is filling out forms trying to qualify to buy the product. Once the application is written out, it is taken by the agent to her office and then sent to the home office the next day, arriving days after that. It is then routed from the mailroom to the appropriate department, where the information is then keyed into a database and medical background is followed up on, etc. This will take at least another week. If any information were not included satisfactorily, the process must start over. Once it's approved, the agent will be notified by fax or mail and she will contact the new customer. Total time will be at least three weeks.

What if the form were electronic, part of the company's Web site? It would have been instantly in the home office database. If not completed correctly, the form would be rejected upon sending and the prospect would have the chance to correct it on the spot. No information would need to be rekeyed into the computer at the office—just do the medical background follow-up and email the results. Total time? Perhaps three days, maybe a few more. In the meantime, the prospect could get all the information he wants about the company, its products, the industry, and strategies by exploring the Web site of the company.

Interoffice Collaboration

As new paradigms for transacting business emerge, new opportunities for designers are available in assisting clients with internal and external communications, moving toward a paperless office, telecommuting, and using groupware to collaborate.

Moving Toward a Paperless Office

Until the advent of the Internet, the paperless office, long promised by the use of the computer, had not materialized. No matter how forward-thinking you were, there was simply no easy way to transfer files long-distance without resorting to hard paper or hard U.S. mail.

Today, simply viewing Web sites does eliminate much of the need for paper; however, hard copy is still often desired. Likewise, email requires no paper until the occasional hard copy is needed. Forms can be telecommunicated. In the case of a client who requires forms be manually completed on paper, the company's complete range of forms can be provided to local offices on CD-ROM, eliminating the need to print, ship, and store paper. A form would be printed out locally only as needed, with no inventory and no waste.

Forms

For designers, a profitable (albeit mundane) source of income can be in designing electronic forms for entities such as insurance companies, financial and medical institutions, and so on.

---

paperless office

A friend of ours was approached by one of her clients (a pharmaceutical company in the U.S.) about a new kind of incentive program. The company wanted to save money and contact its sales force in a more innovative way. Shipping manufactured goods from the U.S. to Europe is very expensive, especially with tight deadlines. She proposed using a highly interactive internal Web site in which parts of the site were updated every day, and others on a weekly basis. Whether the proposal was ever accepted or not, this solution was a way to have an almost paperless promotion. Forms, updates of sales numbers, video, music, and

continued on next page

The paperless office isn't here yet, but for the first time, Internet tools such as email, FTP, and the Web are making such an office truly possible. More and more, intercompany memos are being sent via email, not via hard copy. Regular schedules are posted on publicly available networks, not on the cork bulletin board. Files are being sent electronically, not via someone walking five flights up to hand a disk to the production department. New opportunities are finally opening up, resulting in less paper and more productive work.

Extending One's Reach Through Telecommuting

Telecommuting enables users to widen their geographic scope and increase their reach to an ever-expanding and dispersed circle of coworkers. Yes, the world is definitely getting smaller.

There are many examples and applications for telecommuting, including traveling salesmen staying in touch with their office and customers, regional and branch offices communicating with each other and headquarters, employees checking into the office while at home or on a business trip—or checking in when on vacation. And this doesn't just include email. Users can set up live meetings over the Internet using IRC or MUDs; they can "call" each other using NetPhone; they can even videoconference with CU-SeeMe (see chapter 3).

But the first example of telecommuting that comes to my mind is when in 1993 our midwest design firm worked on an annual report for our client in Montana, using a copywriter who lived in Idaho. After an initial meeting in which we all met face to face (this could just as easily have been a videoconference), we all returned to our own corners of the world and began to produce. Although many phone calls were still utilized, all copy files were exchanged electronically via CompuServe, without

other incentive items would have been available online.

telecommuting

Telecommute America (http://www.att.com/ Telecommute_America), a joint effort of government agencies, nonprofit organizations, and corporations that include the EPA, the Association for Commuter Transportation, and AT&T, promotes this new paradigm of work. For additional information, a discussion group, free how-to brochures, and related links, check out AT&T's Web site (http://www.att.com).

travel, expense, rekeying, or waiting for express mail (the copywriter's remote location wasn't even covered by most express mail companies' next morning guarantees). Email file transfer through CompuServe was extremely efficient; no copy needed to be rekeyed, and most importantly it enabled a creative person to live in the remote location of her choice without sacrificing business. The ease and logic of this setup boggled my mind and challenged my views on where I choose to live and why.

Although our design firm still has our CompuServe account, our Internet server now gets the lion's share of our traffic, as it hosts our mail server and Web site. We transfer files through FTP and as attached documents to email files internally and externally. Even as we produce this book, telecommuting with our out-of-town publisher literally on a daily basis over the Internet is a tremendous time- and cost-saver.

Using Groupware

Integrating an organization's Web site with its business processes and management systems is facilitated by the use of groupware. When Web sites can link, relate, and therefore utilize applications such as customer tracking systems, collections and management, loan processing, tech support, and so on, the productivity and efficiency normally gained in the main offices can be expanded to satellite offices or to the field. I am not suggesting that designers need to become expert at these systems or applications—only that you should be aware of them and understand that the need for integrating them into many of your clients' Internet solutions may be demanded in the future. These can add a lot of substance to a site.

Groupware is an entirely new class of software and was developed to enable teams of people to

Groupware

Groupware providers include the following:
continued on next page

integrate their knowledge, work processes, and applications to improve business processes. Groupware is unlike operational systems, such as databases and spreadsheet programs that capture and track data (for order entry and inventory management, for example). Groupware accesses an organization's data warehouse and enables it to be shared with users internally and externally. For example, a manufacturer can provide descriptive product and inventory data to its marketing and salespeople, as well as to customers.

Oracle (http://www.oracle.com)

Red Brick Systems (http://www.redbrick.com)

Sybase (http://www.sybase.com)

A sophisticated system in the groupware arena is Lotus Notes. Notes is software that not only improves the effectiveness of how an individual or workgroup performs a job, but in many cases transforms the nature of that work and the relationships among customers, vendors, and business partners. Lotus refers to this class of applications as strategic systems.

Lotus Notes

(http://www.lotus.com)

Notes enables an enterprise to create a "corporate memory" of its experience, expertise, and unique business knowledge. The software is document-based, composed of reports, faxes, letters, scanned images, and even video and sound. It can be utilized to improve customer service, sales management, product development, communications... virtually any aspect of organizational activity. Notes can link users in a single location, nationally, and even worldwide. Related products and techniques also allow integration of relational databases so information can be shared with all members of a workgroup, regardless of time, and synchronized across geographically dispersed sites.

Lotus has numerous case histories that illustrate how Notes applications have improved productivity. One study found an average return on investment with Lotus Notes to be 179 percent, with a 2.4-year payback.

Integrating systems such as this into Web sites can deliver a lot of benefits and should be considered when developing Internet strategies for your clients.

Designing and implementing groupware solutions for clients require a depth of technical capability that most design firms can't offer. Unless unusually strong in programming and networking, design firms should utilize outside help in providing these services. A strategic alliance with a firm that specializes in networking and programming services can be a mutually beneficial relationship. They have a built-in customer base in which they could get additional fees for getting online (and even an ongoing revenue stream), yet lack the design skills to effectively develop a site. Conversely, as a design firm, you always find it a challenge to prove technical expertise for larger-scale projects, especially when dealing with technical types within a prospect's organization. Look for mergers and virtual corporations to form, linking designers and DTP professionals with networking and programming companies. Prepress houses, as they protect their market share in publishing, also will expand into Net-related services.

Research Online

The Internet, from its inception, has been an extremely useful research tool. As a designer, you can help your client take advantage of this immense pool of information. Businesses can use the Net to learn more about their industry and marketplace, their customers, their competition, legal and ethical issues, and more—basically the same kinds of things you as a designer can use the Internet for. Because so much of this topic is covered in chapters 3 and 5, I won't go into too much detail here.

To demonstrate the ease of doing research on the Internet, all you have to do is click on the Net Search button in Netscape. Type any subject of interest into the keyword form, and seconds later hyperlinked text from the InfoSeek search engine scrolls down your screen with brief introductions of the search results. Doing this is extremely helpful for demonstrating to clients and others who are skeptical about the Internet: "Why would I want to be on the Internet?" Just ask them, "What are you interested in?" and type it in. Most people immediately see the Net's value in a very personal way.

If you're researching something about the Internet itself, from culture to protocols, the definitive sources can be found online. However, in subject areas other than internetworking, even areas of computer science, an old-fashioned trip to the library is tough to beat. The Internet is unparalleled in terms of how quick and how easy you can find resources. Try to use it for its strengths instead of as a cure-all elixir. For example, online card catalogs can make the act of research quicker and more convenient. To save time, try to find the books or articles you are looking for by using your computer, before going to the library.

Internet Search Tools

For a list of various search engines, check out W3 Search Engines, a Web page that organizes engines by the subject matter in which they specialize: information services, software, people, publications, news/FAQs, documentation, and a category for other interesting things (jargon, acronyms, etc.). I'll review some of the Internet research tools below, but for a more complete list, also check out chapter 3.

W3 Search Engines
http://cuiwww.unige.ch/meta-index.html

A very good explanation of these and other Internet tools is the EARN Guide to Network Resource Tools at http://www.earn.net/gnrt.

continued on next page

W3 Search Engines

This documents collects some of the most useful search engines available on the WWW. Omissions are the fault of the maintainer. Suggestions for additions are welcome! **Submit** buttons have now been added to accommodate non-Mosaic browsers.

NB: If you find this page especially useful, why not install a local copy on your machine? It will work from anywhere. *[The original source of this page is at CUI]* You may also be interested in trying out Martijn Koster's CUSI (Configurable Unified Search Interface), and the External Info page at Twente University.

Looking for:

- Information servers
- Software
- People
- Publications
- News/FAQs
- Documentation
- Other Interesting Things (Jargon, Acronyms, WIRED ...)

Last update of original source on November 25, 1994.

Last update of this copy on January 12, 1995, by trs and completed with free database search engine on January 17, 1995, by Karl guggis@iam.unibe.ch

Information Servers

List-based WWW Catalogs

[submit] [   ] CUI World Wide Web Catalog

Web Search Engines

InfoSeek (http://www.infoseek.com) is one of the best Internet search engines, containing a very good index of webspace, as well as indexes of newsgroups, various wire services, computer periodicals, and more. Not surprisingly, InfoSeek is a commercial venture, and access to its full power costs money. A very good, useful demonstration search is available for free.

Lycos (http://lycos.cs.cmu.edu) is probably the largest, busiest WWW search engine. It has a flexible, form-based interface, and searches an index containing keywords from over 700,000 documents.

WebCrawler (http://webcrawler.com) is not as large or as flexible as InfoSeek or Lycos, but is not nearly as busy as these, and is often more than adequate. WebCrawler is operated free of charge by America Online.

Web Directories

Yahoo (http://www.yahoo.com) was started by two

Ph.D. students as their own hotlist of sites. It is now probably the best subject-oriented directory of the World Wide Web, and is turning into a commercial venture.

The WWW Virtual Library (http://www.w3.org/hypertext/DataSources/bySubject) is one of the earliest attempts to catalog the World Wide Web and is still growing rapidly. Each subject area is maintained by a volunteer.

Maintained by O'Reily and Associates, the publishers of the paper *Whole Internet Catalog and Users Guide*, GNN's Whole Internet Catalog (http://gnn.com/gnn/wic) is a well-organized, easy-to-use directory. As a bonus, each link has a short abstract describing it.

Another directory, EINet Galaxy (http://www.einet.net) is similar to Yahoo, but not quite as large.

Other Net Search Engines

As chapter 3 explains, your clients can also search valuable non-Web services on the Internet, such as Gopher, FTP, and WAIS. Each has its own specific tools for effective searching.

If you wish to search just Gopherspace, use Veronica. There is a directory of all Veronica servers listed at gopher://gopher.scs.unr.edu:70/11/veronica.

If you wish to search for files located on public FTP servers, use Archie. Archie servers contain an index of documents on virtually every anonymous FTP archive on the Internet. A form-based Archie client, which may be used with any form-aware Web browser, is located at http://www-ns.rutgers.edu/htbin/archie.

WAIS stands for Wide Area Information Servers. Instead of simple keyword searches, WAIS makes subject-oriented searches possible. The number of

WAIS servers is much smaller than other types of information servers, but the information on them is easier to find. Most WAIS servers are academic in nature. To use WAIS, see chapter 3. To learn more about WAIS, check out http://www.earn.net/gnrt/wais.html.

Internet News

Scan news sources for information about customers, competitors, and product or industry news. The Internet is a tremendous tool for following news of all sorts, from personalized insights via a newsgroup to official daily reports from news services.

As discussed in part II, participation in newsgroups and mailing lists will produce timely answers and opinions from the most qualified experts in the world in almost any area of interest imaginable. To search through a list of Usenet newsgroups and LISTSERV mailing lists by keyword, check out http://www.nova.edu/Inter-Links/cgi-bin/news-lists.pl. Again, check out chapter 3 for more details.

For a comprehensive list of other news sources on the World Wide Web, investigate Yahoo's news list at http://www.yahoo.com/News. There is more than enough to satisfy even the most addicted news junkies. Also, check out News Link, which claims to

News Link

http://www.newslink.org

Main menu | Newspapers | Broadcasting | Magazines | Special links

About NewsLink | Register | Send for file | Take survey | Update list

Please sign our guest register and jump to our 1,715 free links, updated daily:

Your name:

Organization:

E-mail address: *(form requires valid address)*

⚪ New user .. ⚪ Previously registered guest
⚪ Journalist .. ⚪ Reader .. ⚪ Student/educator

[Register and continue]

be the Web's most complete news resource, featuring 323 newspaper, 273 broadcast, 268 magazine, and 335 special links, plus up-to-date surveys and consulting information.

For news reports customized by topics of interest, NewsPage offers a subscription service that filters over 15,000 stories from over 500 news sources and

NewsPage

http://www.newspage.com

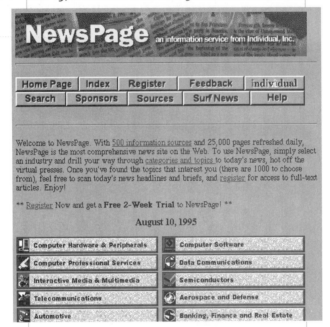

categorizes them by topic. Users can bookmark topics of interest, and every day by 8:00 a.m. receive news on only those topics selected. They can then scan concise briefs of articles, and select which ones to read for the complete story.

Even though commercial online services such as AOL, Prodigy, and CompuServe are not technically part of the Internet, they do offer some valuable news services that are worth mentioning. While almost all commercial services effectively access the news through various publications and news wires, many of these also have the ability to filter the news by topics of interest, adding value to news access.

CompuServe's Executive News Service enables users to create custom folders that they can program by keyword to scan numerous newspapers, wires, and periodicals worldwide for up-to-the-minute information relating to the criteria that they dictate, folder by folder. Users can create folders using search criteria such as a competitor's name, or follow a current issue by combining keywords (such as copyright+Internet), stock ticker symbols, or other subjects the user desires. For instance, users can keep one folder for competitor's news releases, one for supplier's news, one for news on the stocks they hold, one for industry news, and even one for Chicago Cubs news! The Executive News Service is considered an *extended feature* by CompuServe, which means in addition to the monthly fees for basic services, there is an additional $2.40 per hour charge (recently dropped from $4.80) while accessing this feature. When users enter the Executive News Service, the new files are already enclosed—there is no need to wait for searching, because the stories are automatically spooled into each folder as they are published. Users mark their stories for retrieval without taking the time to read them while in extended services (minimizing access charges). They can then take the time to read the stories, print, delete, or forward them, and all this can take place while only spending a few minutes of metered time.

Software Updates

Finally, your clients can also instantly access software bug fixes via the Net—just like we talked about in chapter 6. As companies are more and more reliant on computers and software, it is now critical—not just a convenience—to be notified of bug fixes and upgrades to the tools they depend on every day.

Every major hardware and software company from Microsoft (http://www.microsoft.com) and IBM

(http://www.ibm.com) to Adobe (http://www.
adobe.com) and Apple (http://www.apple.com)
have Internet support sites (Web, FTP, etc.) to provide users with announcements, advice, and answers, as well as fixes and patches. The Apple
Computer home page offers an information and
product support menu that includes hardware, software, and customer support, as well as a list of service providers. The Products & Support area
features hyperlinks to information on various software products and includes an FTP link to free software, patches, support, and bug fixes.

While the Internet offers so many new and exciting
promotional opportunities for your clients, companies need to understand its potential for enhancing
communications, operational systems, and collaboration as well. We wanted to introduce that point in
this chapter, stress that designers need to be aware
of these benefits, and suggest that your clients will
value the guidance you provide for them in these
areas as much as the visual and marketing-oriented
work you traditionally provide...maybe even more!

Chapter 8

Telling Online: Public Relations

This chapter explores models for helping clients

inform the world about themselves, their products,

and their services via the Internet.

Act III

Scene 3

The Public Relations meeting area outside Gloria's office.

GLORIA: "LET'S SUMMARIZE THE STRATEGIES FOR TELLING PEOPLE THE LATEST AND GREATEST WE HAVE TO OFFER. ROBERT IS IN CHARGE OF FINDING APPROPRIATE NEWS-GROUPS AND FORUMS. SANDRA WILL DEVELOP CONTENT FOR THE 'SALT LICK.' I'LL TALK WITH BILL AT SOS DESIGN ABOUT IDEAS FOR COUPONING, CONTESTS, PROMOTIONS, AND HOW TO TIE ALL THIS TOGETHER. AND BRADLEY... BRAD, WHAT IS IT YOU WANTED HELP WITH?"

Bradley: "Yeah... everybody in customer service is talk-ing about how we can automate, you know, sort of gather the most common questions all in one place, and maybe get legal to help write answers to some of those.... You know, if we give bad answers, the company..."

GLORIA: "I THINK I UNDERSTAND. HOW DOES THIS SOUND: I'LL..."

In addition to streamlining your clients' internal communication and collaboration, you can also help your clients take advantage of the Internet's tremendous opportunities for promotion and "soft sales." While the existing models highlighted in this book are businesses' first attempts at adapting what they already know into a new Web world, and while these adaptations already show great potential for us all, they will pale in comparison to the innovations that have yet to be conceptualized, the new extensions that this media will generate as it unfolds. New software applications, compression schemes, hardware, and bandwidth will open up possibilities that are difficult to envision. And instead of shoehorning existing business models into an infant medium, whole new approaches to this uncharted way of communicating will evolve, or more likely, explode.

In this chapter we explore how organizations are currently using the Internet to improve customer service, sell softly, and augment traditional public relations efforts. These models will serve as the foundation for the innovative models of the future.

Improve Customer Service

What can the Internet do for customer service? A lot. The Net can drastically increase the responsiveness to customers and vendors alike at a fraction of the cost. Customer service systems on the Web can be designed to alert a service representative upon a customer login; they can automatically check the customer record, link to a database and assist with problem-solving, process a sale and/or service call, respond to the customer, and create management reports. Moving these tasks from the traditional operational systems increases the quality of the data, shortens the time needed to perform the tasks, adds additional benefits and features to the system such as tracking and monitoring, and gives all appropriate parties the ability to share the information in real time (see the section on groupware in chapter 7 for more information).

The posting of FAQs (Frequently Asked Questions) to a client's Web site can eliminate the need for a high percentage of service, consumer, or engineering questions, reducing the number of 800 toll-free calls as well as the labor costs associated with fielding these repetitive <u>requests</u>. In sensitive situations, a consistent and well-scripted response written by the legal or public relations department

requests

Sun Microsystems (http://www.sun.com) launched an online email program designed to answer customers' technical questions and to distribute software fixes and updates. In the first year of its use, this program reportedly reduced the use of the toll-free telephone support line by over 90 percent, and cut support costs by over $1,000,000 annually. Sun did this while increasing the amount of information, reducing the response time of customers receiving fixes and updates, and most importantly, increasing customer satisfaction ratings. In short, for less money, with fewer people, in less time, Sun provided a higher level of support by utilizing the Internet for customer service.

can skillfully disarm the potential harm to corporate image or even financial liability that could be associated with an inappropriate response an operator might give in a high-pressure or tedious situation.

Both <u>UPS</u> and <u>Federal Express</u> have launched

United Parcel Service

http://www.ups.com

Federal Express

http://www.fedex.com

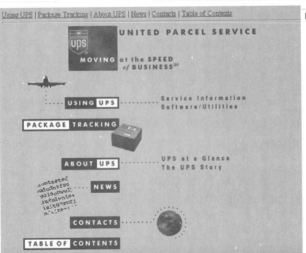

continued on next page

Web sites that not only offer information about the corporation and its services, but include features that enable users to easily track the progress of their packages by entering the shipping number of the package in question.

As designers we need to be aware that these options are out there, so we can best service our clients as they explore how to best use the Internet. When and if the technical aspects of setting this up ourselves becomes too great for us to handle in-house, we can serve as liaisons between our client and the programmers and providers required to accomplish these results.

Soft Sell

By using the Internet to sell softly, a company creates a positive public image and positions itself as a leader in a specific field or appeals to a niche marketing area. There are a number of ways to accomplish these goals, including participating in newsgroups and other Internet services, giving away free samples, and using the "Salt Lick" strategy.

Participate in Internet Services

Participating in a newsgroup or mailing list on the Internet (or a forum on CompuServe or AOL) within areas of interest to a market not only creates a valuable source of information for companies, but can be a very effective public relations tool. A strong presence in the right group(s) can powerfully and efficiently cultivate a corporate image of experience, expertise, and even caring to an ideal demographic mix. Subscribers to many of these groups number in the tens of thousands, all indicating a specific area of strong interest. These groups create extraordinary value for your clients with needs to penetrate market niches that are difficult and inefficient for traditional media to reach.

For instance, a company that specializes in the duplication and packaging of software and CD-ROMs has potential sales that may come from less familiar territory than the usual software developers. Business could possibly come from desktop publishing professionals, designers, advertising agencies, and even corporate communications or training departments in medium- or large-sized companies. The relatively few and dispersed people that are timely prospects are hidden in these diverse markets.

An effective and low-cost way to reach them would be to aggressively monitor all multimedia newsgroups and forums and contribute whenever there is a discussion or question regarding unit pricing, distributing, preparing, or defragmenting a hard drive before cutting a master CD-ROM, and so on. In each communication, the participant can leave her email address (jsmith@duplipak.com) or link to a full Web site (http://www.duplipak.com) for more information. This method properly promotes her expertise within good Netiquette because, first of all, she is providing value to the group, and second, they have asked for it to be provided in a posted question.

However, this does open the door for those with less integrity to work with a cohort to set up the "sales message." Someone can post a prestrategized question designed to maximize the opportunity to allow the "seller" to advertise his expertise through the scripted response.

So what is appropriate? While there is very little black-and-white on the Internet, there are some guidelines:

- Bulk, unsolicited advertising is poor Netiquette and just plain lazy. Like any other selling, if you have a sincere desire to serve an industry or market instead of exploit it, you will be much more successful.

- Take the time to <u>lurk</u> in a group—make sure it is an appropriate forum for you and/or your client. Do not risk alienating the members by posting a press release or any other solicitation, no matter how softly stated, before understanding how the group responds to similar material.

- Make sure to read the FAQ files regarding preferred and acceptable use policies. In short, *do your homework*.

- Post only to appropriate groups—i.e., if your client has software that runs only on a Macintosh, don't post to all computer groups.

- Write carefully and objectively; don't sensationalize. It is helpful if you disclaim any attempt to promote, as in: "I am not trying to sell any product here, only to answer the question the best way I know. I offer this for educational purposes. My employer happens to be one of the best...and is an expert in.... Our experience tells us... If I can be of any additional help, feel free to contact me at..."

lurk

Lurking means taking the time to observe in a newsgroup or mailing list without participating. A user "lurks" until understanding the tone, personalities, culture, and nature of the group.

- KISS: Keep It Short, Stupid. Members of news-groups often flame verbose writers for burning up the bandwidth with needless rambling, especially whining. Keep the <u>signal-to-noise ratio</u> down. Keep to the point. Try to not exceed two screen lengths.

- Remember the culture of the Internet: communal, interactive (not one-directional speeches), altruistic, collaborative, and content-oriented.

Of course, these guidelines can be applied to any Internet service your client participates in. As the Web evolves, for example, there will be increased opportunity to "participate" on a Web site, making that yet another medium in which businesses can make their presence known.

Give Away Free Samples

Free samples are perhaps the most common form of "selling" on the Internet. From the beginning, the communal culture of the Web was peer-to-peer collaboration, people helping people. Abundant and useful freeware has always been there for anyone with a modem and a computer. A short jump from freeware is shareware, programs that are free to anyone who wants to try the software—in hopes that the user will like the product and do the right thing by sending in the usually very reasonable charge to get documentation and notification of bug fixes and updated versions, and to support ongoing enhancement efforts.

There are many examples of freeware, shareware, and marketware distribution methods that create tremendous marketing opportunities. Check out how these applications are distributed: Adobe Acrobat Reader (http://www.adobe.com/Software. html), Eudora (http://www.qualcomm.com/quest/ QuestMain.html), <u>Netscape</u>, RealAudio Player

signal-to-noise ratio

This is a Net term for how much of the discussion is solid content (signal) and how much is unnecessary, longwinded babbling (noise).

Netscape

continued on next page

(http://www.realaudio.com/products/player.html),
and StuffIt Lite (http://www.aladdinsys.com).

Netscape's distribution model for its Internet browser is called marketware. It is free for education, nonprofit, and evaluation use. All others are expected to pay for using the software. Using this strategy, Netscape was able to capture approximately 75 percent of the market.

http://home.netscape.com

Distributing the products <u>for free</u> helps the credibility of the developer, eliminates customer resistance to trying the product, and builds as well as defends an immediate market for cross-selling. The success of this model stems from how it capitalizes on the

for free

id Software showed Net-savvy, foresight, and astute marketing flair by using the Internet to freely distribute the first episode of DOOM, its best-selling computer game. The results were historic. DOOM burst across the Internet, triggering enthusiasm for the product and creating an international user base as it became absorbed onto the hard drives of the world. It didn't take long for id to make a fortune selling commercial versions and sequels to its passionate ranks.

http://doomgate.cs.buffalo.edu

What's New

Quake screen shots

culture of the Internet to build relationships within this new market.

This method of selling (or is it giving?) also has numerous variations. A product can be free for a specified amount of time, free for number of searches, free for access to article briefs then charge for full stories, free via a coupon for a sample of merchandise, free to individuals (so as to create a market that businesses then cannot ignore), free for a limited version of full commercial software (such as Eudora), free for a free chapter or issue to encourage a subscription or book sale, and so on. The possibilities are endless.

Designers can use their creative and marketing savvy to conceive innovative ways to use the free sample strategy to build market share and customer/prospect involvement for their clients. Concepts can include such ideas as contests, quizzes, puzzles, gimmicks, and much more. Expect to see more of these traditional promotional activities on the Net...and expect to see new, innovative strategies as well.

The "Salt Lick"

The objective of the "salt lick" strategy is to continually draw people to a site by publishing information services, directories, announcements, hotlists, databases, coupons, trade or industry news, sports scores, incentives, or any other content of interest and value. These can be targeted to the Internet community at large or to a niche market within it. Once the traffic arrives at the site, the goal is to pull users through the hyperlinks to the more overtly commercial site underwriting this "public service."

Again, there are numerous variations to this approach. Two common examples are the Library model and the Sponsorship model. Both seek to position the company as a good corporate citizen by

---

industry news

Security APL, a portfolio accounting and performance measurement firm, set up the Security APL Quote Server, which gives stock quotes with a 15-minute delay (according to SEC rules). This method brings people back to the site many times a day. Their target market, investors, are the only surfers drawn to the site because of the nature of the information they are providing. Once people are there, the

continued on next page

---

content of interest

Mountain Travel * Sobek, an adventure company, has a beautifully designed site that has formation about the company, news from field, a form for requesting its Trekking catalog, and a great "salt lick" concept: a way personalize any of over 200 wonderfully p tographic postcards, which I assume w taken on the expeditions, and send them

continued on next page

unsolicited sales message waits behind a clickable logo of Security APL, ready to pounce on casual clickers.

http://www.secapl.com/cgi-bin/qs

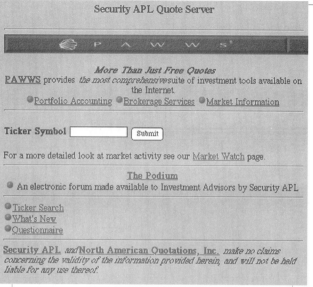

anyone on the Web. The recipient is notified via email and sent to the Mountain Travel * Sobek Web site with a password to retrieve his private postcard. This not only pulls the sender to the site to send cards, but guarantees the recipient will visit the site as well.

http://mtsobek.com/mts

providing valuable content to a specific market, in a medium whose culture resents commercial enterprise.

Library Model

The Library model entails creating or assembling the content, building the site, as well as doing ongoing maintenance and administration. If done properly, the value of the content will create a magnet for the targeted demographic group, bringing people in large numbers. It will also generate the originator's desired positioning and image, that of a generous benefactor graciously providing a free public service. And of course, as always on the Internet, it is considered appropriate to quietly provide a hyperlink to the company's Web site, where the awaiting commercial messages are more acceptable.

Examples of this model include Netscape's site, which provides many links and valuable information. Another would be AT&T's Toll-Free 800 Directory, which provides an excellent service online while not letting you forget the company behind it.

Toll-Free 800 Directory

http://www.tollfree.att.net/dir800

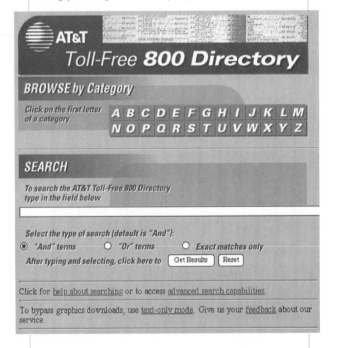

One of the negative aspects of this approach is that while there is inherent pressure to publish your clients' most valuable ideas and information in order to dramatize the value of their contribution, protection of that intellectual property is difficult and faces serious exposure to plagiarism as well as exploitation by the competition.

Sponsorship Model

Sponsorship is very similar to the Library method, with the exception that the sponsoring party does not conceptualize, own, build, or maintain the service, much less generate the information. In this case, the company studies the demographic mix and size, as well as the perceptions (image projection) of existing sites, selects an optimal site, and negotiates a fee for having a presence there, thus supporting the altruistic efforts of the service and generating goodwill. This is similar to an oil company sponsoring a winning Indy car.

Examples of this model include companies that advertise on Netscape's Internet Search page, as well as the numerous sponsors of Guide to the 1996 Olympic Games.

Netscape's Internet Search

Numerous advertisers sponsor Netscape's site. See the bottom of this Web page for the Sponsor Index.

http://home.netscape. com/ escapes/ internet_search.html

Guide to the 1996 Olympic Games

http://www.atlanta.olympic.org

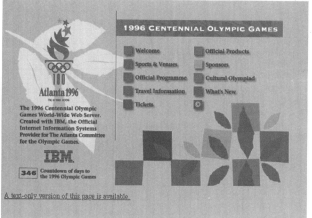

The Sponsorship model should be viewed from two different commercial perspectives. The first, as stated above, is when a commercial enterprise finds an appropriate "fit" with a noncommercial site and pays for a presence there. In the second perspective, a typically noncommercial content provider builds a site that offers a free service to the Internet community and then aggressively seeks sponsorship, thus creating a commercial and often quite profitable business.

free service

Yahoo (http://www.yahoo.com), an Internet index site started in 1994 by two electrical

continued on next page

Usage Tracking

While it is easy to see that quality content will need to be financially supported in order to be maintained, one factor complicating sponsorship has been a lack of credible and neutral tracking information—i.e., a Nielson of the Net.

In the past, freeware Unix programs have been the only way in which electronic publishers have been able to get tracking information in the form of basic analysis of log files. Sophisticated software packages are now available, such as the suite of products from Open Market (http://www.openmarket.com). They do give valuable information about usage, yet lack the impartiality desired by advertisers. Also, there is the fact that many "hits" could come from the same surfer on the same night, so tracking hits is often unreliable. Software packages attempting to address the inaccuracy of the hit method by trying to distinguish unique machines via their IP addresses are an improvement, yet flawed in other ways.

But promising new commercial tracking services have appeared and offer validation of site usage for a monthly fee. One example is Digital Planet's NetCount. Starting at $300 per month, NetCount reports the number of hits and sessions, analyzes

engineering Ph.D. candidates, Jerry Yang, 26, and David Filo, 28, began as a personal hotlist of Web links. They named it Yahoo, which stands for "Yet Another Hierarchical Officious Oracle," and decided to make it available on the Web. They allowed users to add their own resources to the database. As it grew, they added sections such as "What's New," "What's Cool," and "What's Popular," and they were among the most visited areas on the Internet. The site drew more than 200,000 visitors a day and the founders were overwhelmed by the visibility it was getting.

Staunch ideas about advertising on the Internet led them to develop a business model in which they obtain sponsorships, licensing, and even limited advertising. They believe that while the Internet should be free, some commerce is needed to support it, and the choice is whether to make people or advertisers pay for it.

---

hits

A "hit" is one request for a file located at a specific URL on a server. By compiling statistics out of the request log from your WWW server, you can determine how many times a specific file was requested. Since the IP address where the request originated from is also recorded, you can make exact statements about the number of computers your page has been viewed on. By making adjustments for multiple people using the same computer, you can begin to estimate the number of people that have viewed your page.

Digital Planet's NetCount

http://www.digiplanet.com/DP1/netcount.html

We are now accepting beta testers for NetCount 1.0b.

This is your opportunity to test drive our webtracking system for FREE!

About NetCount

NetCount in the News

Fact Sheet

More information about NetCount

Apply for Beta-Test

other usage patterns, and tracks hits from one site to another so the effectiveness of online ads can be judged. In the latter case, NetCount's recording software runs on both the advertiser's server and the one at the ad placement site. The log files are then compared at NetCount's computers.

Other new commercial tracking services include I/PRO (http://www.ipro.com), WebTrack (http://www.webtrack.com), and iAudit (http://www.iaudit.com).

These tracking services are important to us as designers because they allow a pragmatic measure of how successful our work on the Internet is. And remember, this is different from print in that you can continue to use this information to enhance and improve the site (your work) long after it is implemented. But even before reaching the point of judging the effectiveness of your work, you will need to justify to your clients the costs of creating a presence on these sites, and until they can understand the true demographics, they will be reluctant to sponsor or advertise there.

Augment Traditional Public Relations

You can also use the Internet to communicate your clients' public relations messages to their markets. You can post news and press releases about new products, contracts for new business, awards, promotions, and so on, to Web pages, newsgroups, or even email.

You can design and locate company newsletters on your clients' Web sites or email them to a mailing list that has been built up over time, but I would caution you to be careful not to fall into the category of unsolicited direct mail. These lists should be comprised of prospects and customers that have asked for the information, or all the goodwill you are trying to generate can come crumbling down in an avalanche of <u>flame</u> mail.

A good analogy here is that you can put out as nice of a welcome mat to your own home as you want, but never burst into another person's home without an engraved invitation. Don't even knock on their door. Once you're invited, however, continued mailings, press releases, and even electronic company brochures and catalogs can be emailed to eager recipients.

A soft-selling corporate ad on the Web, with the equivalent of a complete capabilities brochure or catalog for harder selling, laying one mouse click behind it, can be very effective. These ads can help a company provide more information, garner greater participation from the viewer, and offer timeliness to the content.

Utilizing a full corporate Web site will enable your clients to expand their market or develop new markets that would be difficult to reach efficiently with traditional media.

Consider <u>Sony</u>. Its major market niche is young adults, who are very difficult to reach through the

flame

The act of flaming is when people who don't agree with what you have done or said let you know in the form of angry email. These messages are often belligerent and question your judgment, sanity, lineage, etc. Flame mail can come in the hundreds (even thousands) and bring your mail service to a screeching halt. If you plan on being outspoken on the Web, wear asbestos!

Sony

http://www.sony.com

print medium. They are transient, moving from apartment to apartment, to their parents' home and out again, and from town to town as their careers stabilize. They have changing patterns of media preferences, and are often students who switch dorms and take summers off to return home or to travel. But as a generation that embraces technology, they remain a strong component of the Internet's demographics. Also, of course, many universities, colleges, and even high schools provide their faculty and students with free access to the Internet (and high-speed access at that). The nature of the Internet environment differs from traditional passive media and makes it ideal to reach this market, or more to the point, for this market to reach Sony. Sony created its Web site to appeal to this niche, with bold graphics and content about consumer electronics, movies, music, and electronic publishing. This is exceptionally good PR for Sony because it is able to connect with this elusive group in an environment the young adults are comfortable in, providing content of interest to them, promoting Sony and its products, as well as managing to make a corporate statement that Sony is "hip" in doing so.

Finally, Web sites can also expand existing goodwill an organization enjoys in traditional markets to this new environment.

Announcing Fantasy Football '95 | Mickey Mantle remembered

A SERVICE OF STARWAVE AND ESPN

| SELECT SPORT | ZONED OUT! | SPORTSTALK | ESPN STUDIOS |

The top stories as of August 15, 1995, 10:54am ET

Overflow crowd likely for Mantle's funeral

Redskins snare top pick Westbrook with $18 million

Red Sox steamroller flattens Yankees' AL East hopes

Just what the doctor ordered: Griffey OK to play

Couples, Strange add experience to Ryder Cup team

Winnipeg's spirit fails; Jets in holding pattern

- The Wire

Scoreboards

existing goodwill

ESPNET SportsZone is a good example of a successful cable station (ESPN) complementing its sports news service and generating good PR in the process. SportsZone is loaded with features and interviews, plus late-breaking stories and scores. This is a good example of how companies can leverage their existing business to capitalize on a new market.

http://espnet.sportszone.com

This section introduced the power of the Internet for meeting your clients' Public Relations goals, from generating a positive image and building goodwill to softly selling. Using the Web for this kind of promotion is an excellent strategy because it takes advantage of the ability to communicate worldwide at very low cost, and providing information and services for free matches the original culture of the Internet.

Chapter 9

Selling Online: Electronic Commerce

This chapter takes the gloves off and illustrates

some bare-knuckled models for online commerce.

Act III

Scene 4

A phone conversation in the BigCorp Marketing Department.

Nick: "Hi Bill, Nick at BigCorp.... Good, how've you been?... Great. I just got out of a meeting with our Communications Team and we need your help.... No, no, not that. We may *never* get *that* off hold; in fact, it's not even a print project, it's about the Internet. Last time Kit from your office was over here we kicked around a lot of ideas for ways to save money and do a better job.... Yeah, Kit is great, and that got us thinking. We've run some numbers and think we could really cut our catalog print run down, maybe even in half.... That's right.... No, we're not pulling back, not at all. You know what's happened to paper cost.... Right, eight increases this year. I know, it's awful. Well, we need to control that cost and the best way is to reduce the amount of paper we buy.... I know. I know what you mean. We can set up a site that is secure enough to place the order interactively right there online.... No, I haven't checked, but both Netscape and Open Market have products that claim to be transaction-secure.... Right. Credit cards, and probably options for skeptics, fax form, and the like. We think it's something that we need to investigate. I need you to give me an idea of what it would cost to get us set up on an Internet site…. I understand. That sounds all right. When can you come over so we can get this thing moving?"

Ever been in a gold rush? Everyone with the same good idea at the same time? That's a good analogy for marketing on the Internet. How often does the chance come along to improve quality *and* really reduce cost? That's the promise that is luring companies onto the Internet to sell their products and services. The Web's combination of global coverage, information depth, dynamic flexibility, and personalized consumer contact make it a marketing medium of unprecedented potential.

The Internet is not a mass market like network television, where advertising is targeted to an audience of millions. It is a collection of ever-increasing and evolving individual communities. I remember the first time I got online with Mosaic and experienced the Web. I thought, "What a wonderful metaphor—Mosaic. So descriptive of what I'm seeing. The Internet, composed of what seems like millions of individual pieces/sites. Each jewel unique and wonderful in itself, yet together they weave the texture of a composite image so rich and full."

All these micromarkets have their own culture, rules, and customs. What kind of advertising and sales are appropriate on the Net? The answers are as varied as the number of communities you are trying to reach for your clients. This is the opportunity for designers, for if generic, broadbrush, mass-market advertising is all that is needed, designers would have a hard time differentiating themselves from DTP professionals and technical types. On the Internet, knowing how to read a market and communicate your clients' messages in an effective, memorable, and unique way is and will always be paramount.

Standards, Practices, and Security

There has never been a more promising and exciting medium for global sales and marketing than the Internet, yet the lack of standards and practices for online commerce have been a hindrance to wide acceptance. We can best explore this through an example. CommerceNet was formed to facilitate the use of an Internet-based infrastructure for electronic commerce; to enable efficient interactions among

customers, suppliers, and development partners; and to speed time to market and reduce the costs of doing business.

The following info comes from the CommerceNet Web site.

CommerceNet is a nonprofit consortium of companies and organizations whose goal is to create an electronic marketplace where companies transact business spontaneously over the Internet. CommerceNet will stimulate the growth of a communications infrastructure that will be easy to use, oriented for commercial use, and ready to expand rapidly. The net results for businesses will be lower operating costs and a faster dissemination of technological advancements and their practical applications.

---

promising and exciting medium

The Web enables businesses to sell directly to customers, with no middleman, no expensive information channels, and no delays. It reduces distribution expenses to the cost of a delivery, provides uniform access to consumers anywhere in the world, and widens your clients' markets.

CommerceNet

http://www.commerce.net

The charter of CommerceNet includes:

- Operating an Internet-based World Wide Web server with directories and information that facilitates an open electronic marketplace for business-to-business transactions

- Accelerating the mainstream application of electronic commerce on the Internet through fielding pilot programs. Pilots include transaction security, payment services, electronic catalogs, Internet EDI, engineering data transfer, and design-to-manufacturing integration

- Enhancing existing Internet services and applications and stimulating the development of new services

- Encouraging broad participation from small, medium, and large companies and offering outreach programs to educate organizations about the resources and benefits available with CommerceNet

- Serving as a common information infrastructure for Northern California and coordinating with national and international infrastructure projects

From this example alone, one can see the great potential for online commerce. CommerceNet provides a forum for industry leaders to discuss issues, deploy pilot applications, and from these efforts it will help this emerging industry evolve to common standards and practices so that users will see a seamless web of resources, and online commerce blossom.

In addition to standards and practices, another big challenge to direct selling on the Internet has been a lack of security. People are uncomfortable with sending confidential messages or credit cards over what is generally agreed on as an unsecured environment. Two companies have taken a lead in changing that and creating innovative secure software solutions for the Web: Netscape and Open Market.

Netscape

"Netscape Internet Applications, a new family of turnkey software applications that enables companies to conduct full-scale electronic commerce on the Internet, are the first applications to integrate high-volume transaction processing, real-time data management, easy-to-use interfaces, and secure communications for creating sophisticated online services and large-scale businesses on the Net. All of the applications feature a tightly integrated relational database-management system and are based on industry-standard protocols and interfaces." Examples of companies using Netscape software servers can be found through its Web site in the Galleria section.

http://www.netscape.com/comprod/ netscape_products.html

COMPANY & PRODUCTS

KILLER APPS

Netscape Communications offers a full line of open software to enable electronic commerce and secure information exchange on the Internet and private TCP/IP-based networks. All Netscape products are fully compatible with other HTTP-based clients and servers and are designed to deliver secure communications, advanced performance, and point-and-click simplicity to companies and individuals who want to create or access information services on global networks.

If you are interested in purchasing any Netscape software product, please head over to the Netscape Store and fill out our handy online form or call 415/528-2555.

MONEY & INVESTING — UPDATE — from THE WALL STREET JOURNAL.

NETSCAPE BROWSER PRODUCTS

NETSCAPE NAVIGATOR
Netscape Navigator is a powerful commercial point-and-click network navigator optimized to offer performance up to ten times that of other browsers. It provides a common feature set and graphical user interface across computers running the Microsoft Windows, Macintosh, or X Window operating environments and offers security features such as encryption, authentication, and data integrity, enabling customers to take advantage of the full range of commercial on-line offerings.

NETSCAPE NAVIGATOR PERSONAL EDITION
Netscape Navigator Personal Edition offers a dial-up Internet connection combined with automatic account creation and configuration for a range of leading service providers.

Open Market WebServer

Available NOW!

Order today using our online form!

Test it today, for FREE!

The Open Market WebServer is the first product in a line of advanced software that forms the foundation for electronic business solutions. It meets the business challenges of companies demanding World-Wide Web servers capable of hundreds of simultaneous connections. The Open Market WebServer sets the standards for functionality, performance, and unrivaled interoperability with the net's most popular browsers.

The Open Market WebServers offer the following features:

- High performance
- Standards
- Flexible access control
- Enhanced logging features
- Easy installation

High Performance: The Open Market WebServer has been designed from the ground up to offer the highest levels of performance. The WebServer's multi-threaded architecture runs benchmark tests 5X faster than other freely available Web servers, and supports over 1,000 concurrent client connections, several times the capacity of any other existing server.

Standards: All Open Market WebServer products are based on Web standards:

- Common Gateway Interface (CGI/1.1), the standard interface for server scripts
- HyperText Transport Protocol (HTTP/1.0), for interoperability with all existing Web clients

Open Market

Open Market's server software provi for high quantities of simultaneous c nections, transaction-level security, bil services, payment processing, cont management tools, advertising syste and customer profile reporting. O Market has created a complete, end end solution to electronic comme putting together all of the pieces ne sary for merchants and buyers to carry secure business transactions in an e tronic medium.

http://www.openmarket.com/omi/ products/secureweb.html

When you're helping to design and implement secure sites—ones as technologically sophisticated as the examples in this section—expert knowledge of hardware, software, servers, LANs, WANs, firewalls, and so on is mandatory. This will demand that unless you are unusually strong in these areas, you will need a technology partner (see also the discussion of strategic alliances in chapter 7). Select this resource early and make sure their expertise is integrated in your design and development process from the very beginning.

Selling Information

The information selling model is similar to the Library model discussed in chapter 8, because in both models the site developer creates or assembles the content and builds as well as maintains the site. Both use the "salt lick" strategy. However, the objective isn't the same as the Library model's: to continually lure users into a content area, hoping they will seek information about the gracious benefactor who supplied this wonderful public service. Instead, this site's objective is to provide content that is so timely and/or valuable that users will *pay* for access to it. This typically occurs through subscription-based fees or database retrievals on a per-search basis.

Quote.Com is an example of a subscription service that provides financial market data to the Internet

Quote.Com

http://www.quote.com

Quote.Com

First in Financial Information

OVERVIEW
Quote.Com is a service dedicated to providing **quality financial market data** to the Internet community. This includes current quotes on stocks, commodity futures, mutual funds, and bonds. It also includes business news, market analysis and commentary, fundamental (balance sheet) data, and company profiles.

New users should look at the overview of our services. Subscribers may retrieve current quotes on your portfolio.

We believe that you will find quite a lot to interest you, so we suggest that you put *http://www.quote.com/* in your Bookmarks or Hotlist right now!

HOW TO REGISTER
Quote.Com is free for limited use, but you must register in order to use it. Subscriptions (unlike samples or free trials) provide access to some of the best, most timely investment information available anywhere. We have gained commendations for our unique

community. This includes current quotes on stocks, commodity futures, mutual funds, and bonds. It also includes business news, market analysis and commentary, fundamental (balance sheet) data, company profiles, and much more. It has some public service free services such as stock quotes (off-peak hours), and a basic service tier for $9.95 per month for 11 additional subscription services. Site licenses are also available. An interesting note: To be a member, you must supply a valid email address and every week or two they will send you "informative" messages, they claim "This is our way of verifying that you are a current user." These messages may also contain advertising of products and services relating to financial investing. If a subscriber does not want these messages, he or she may *not* continue to subscribe to Quote.Com. It is clear that this selling model depends on advertising income to complement subscription income.

For an example of a per-search payment setup, check out UnCover. It is an online table of contents, index, and article delivery service for approximately 17,000 magazines and journals. Around six million

UnCover
http://www.carl.org/uncover/unchome.html

UnCover is an online article delivery service, a table of contents database, and a keyword index to nearly 17,000 periodicals.

Click here to access the UnCover database.

For more information about UnCover, select one of the following:

UnCover information

Instructions for using UnCover

The latest UnCover Update newsletter

An archive of UnCover Update newsletters

A glossary of UnCover terms

articles are available through a simple online order system, and 5,000 citations are added daily. Table of contents information is entered into the database as the journals are received from the publishers, so issues are indexed online at about the same time that they arrive in libraries or on the newsstand. Searching the UnCover database is free; users then pay only for the articles they order. Articles cost $8.50 U.S., plus a copyright royalty fee. You can pur-chase an UnCover access password for $900 U.S. per year and receive a $2.00 discount on every arti-cle you order. Payment methods include credit cards, deposit accounts, or a monthly invoice for a billing account.

Newspapers have always been a prototypical model of timely and valuable content providers in the print world. Now, as they begin to see future advertising dollars slipping away and finding their way to the Internet, it is not surprising to see them finding their way to the Net as well. Perhaps the most ambitious of the newspapers has been _USA Today_. When this organization decided to publish a paper that was

USA Today

http://www.usatoday.com

not provincial and would be delivered daily nation-wide, the biggest challenges it faced were coordi-nating several regional presses, absorbing the costs of higher-quality paper and color printing, and of course distributing its product. Incredibly, not one of these challenges exist when publishing on the Internet. *USA Today*'s original vision of a national daily newspaper also coincides with the strengths of the Internet, in that a disperse geographic market is not a problem on the Net. New visions may include opportunities for personalizing papers and adding user-defined and -oriented content, such as local interest stories to capitalize on small local markets as well as the dynamics of the Internet itself.

To demonstrate how much *USA Today* is embracing the Web, it is also offering Internet access as part of its services. *The Arizona Daily Star* (http://azstarnet.com) is also selling Internet access.

Several publishers, such as The Tribune Company, Advance Publications, and Time Warner have committed to using Open Market as the primary back-end manager for their sites, employing transaction-level

Time Warner

Time Warner is reported to have 100 journalists working on content development, as well as a commitment to Open Market of more than $1 million to build and manage the commercial portion of its Pathfinder site, an electronic publication with content organized by Today's Headlines, News, Money & Business, The Learning Center, Kidstuff, Sports, Home & Hobbies, and so on. Needless to say, content providers predict that the Internet will supply a strong source of paying consumers for their products and have begun jockeying for position.

http://www.pathfinder.com

security, billing services, payment processing, content management tools, customer profile reporting, and more in preparation for selling information.

There are already many examples of newspapers online and in business.

The *San Jose Mercury News* is online as the Mercury Center Web. Some of the information here is currently brought to the Internet community at no charge through the sponsorship of advertisers. Advertisements appear at the bottom of many

pages and are linked to more detailed information. Other information is available on a subscription basis, which began April 17, 1995. That includes the full text of Breaking News, Today's Newspaper, Comics, and the Dave Barry page. News summaries, special collections, and classified ads are available at no charge.

The Wall Street Journal's current electronic venture on the World Wide Web is its Money & Investing Update (http://update.wsj.com), a continuously updated electronic publication containing business and market news. This is a good example of testing the Web waters, adding infrastructure and getting all the kinks out before launching a subscription site. By early 1996, the entire paper, including Personal Technology and all of its other extensive technology coverage, will be on the Web in a full-blown Wall Street Journal Interactive Edition, which will also be updated around the clock. While the

Update will be free on the Web for a while, ultimately both of the new online Journals will be available to paid subscribers only.

Newspapers aren't the only information sellers out there on the Web. Another example of capitalizing on this new medium of distribution is *The Florida Law Weekly*. It publishes and sells subscriptions for its weekly law reports online at a steep discount from its printed reports version, and additional discounts to those subscribers who already receive the

printed version and wish to sign up for online reports as well. *FLW* reports the full text of the opinions of the Supreme Court of Florida and Florida's five district courts of appeal within days of filing, months ahead of the official reporter's advance sheet.

Supplements, disk-based books, CD-ROMs, and bound volumes are also available, demonstrating an excellent strategy for experimenting with digital publishing and offering a lot of alternative methods of distribution.

The biomedical field is continuously inundated with new information—more that 20,000 relevant journals and 17,000 new books are published annually. Current awareness of the newly published information is of vital importance to clinical decision-making, biomedical research, and the quality of patient care. Clearly, there is a need for accessing current and comprehensive biomedical information. In the 1960s, the National Library of Medicine (NLM) addressed this need with the creation of a computerized version of *Index Medicus*. In 1971, this online bibliographic database became known as MEDLINE. Today, MEDLINE is one of the most widely used databases in the world.

There are a number of ways to access MEDLINE. Through software interfaces to the NLM, or connec-

MEDLINE

http://www.sils.umich.edu/~nscherer/
Medline/MedlineGuide.html

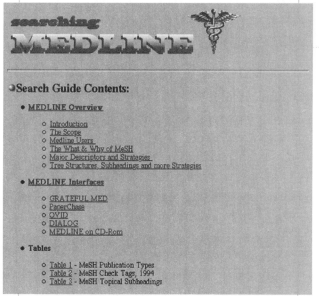

tions to services which have access to the index citation references of the NLM, one can remotely access MEDLINE without leaving the home or office. Each of the interfaces have unique features and pricing that distinguish them from each other, as well as their CD-ROM counterparts. See their Web site for more information on these options.

As you can see, selling information is still in its infancy on the Internet. But rest assured that this new information business is growing up fast. As designers, we'll be leading the way to making it happen, and can significantly guide our clients as they explore this new way of selling.

Selling Products

Businesses that utilize electronic or online storefronts seek to use the Internet as a medium in which to accomplish the same goals they have in the physical world. They want people to order goods and services in a rewarding and pleasing environment.

This method of selling has a variety of advantages:

1. Although it is online, this model otherwise fits a format with which businesses and customers are familiar and comfortable.

2. It is extremely more efficient than the physical model because virtual real estate sells for far less than physical real estate, there is no interior design or fixtures needed, and often companies hold no inventory by directly shipping from manufacturers or setting up "just-in-time" delivery arrangements. Electronic storefronts enable businesses to go directly to customers, without middlemen or sales commissions, quickly and efficiently, all with minimal employee overhead. These savings are even more exaggerated after the initial design and production of the site is complete, and although the start-up costs of an ambitious online storefront can sometimes rival its traditional counterpart, the marginal costs of maintenance are but a fraction of what they would be otherwise.

3. There is no limit to the number of products carried or how much and how often the product lines are revised. Electronic stores reduce distribution costs of those products and expands business boundaries. Additionally, the depth of information that can be provided about each item and its

applications, manufacturer, and options is, for practical purposes, without limits.

Purchases can be handled in a number of ways: on-line forms, fax forms, printing and then mailing forms, toll-free 800 numbers, or a combination of these. In fact, direct clothing merchant Lands' End uses all four ways!

Example Electronic Storefronts

Lands' End offers a complete electronic version of its catalog, saving on the cost of paper, printing, and distribution. This allows the company to reach new

Lands' End
http://www.landsend.com

International Direct Merchants of quality men's, women's, and children's clothing; domestics and soft luggage.

Continue ...

markets, enhance its marketing database to use in future electronic promotions at extremely low cost, keep information/inventory timely, and most importantly, formulate an Internet strategy. The Internet represents the single biggest fundamental change in the catalog industry's history. It cannot be overstated how important it is for companies such as Lands' End to understand and develop expertise in the newest and most efficient channel of direct distribution ever. Help your clients score early and score often!

Lands' End understands the importance of satisfying customer needs and wants. It also understands this medium is so new that in addition to the company not knowing what this market's preferences are, the consumers themselves don't have a clear idea. Because the methods that users prefer for making purchases on the Net are not clearly known or understood, Lands' End currently offers <u>four different ways</u> to purchase its products, which is sort of a real-world focus group solution.

Launching an online storefront with a secure software server aids in ordering products online via credit card, but it is not necessarily a mandatory feature for successful electronic commerce. For example, the Macmillan Information SuperLibrary Bookstore (http://www.mcp.com/cgi-bin/do-bookstore.cgi), which contains more than 1,100 computer-related books, is not a completely secure site. It doesn't recommend ordering with credit cards, but accepts them from shoppers who don't mind assuming the risk. Macmillan suggests setting up an account with the company through its fax form or toll-free number, and then ordering online sans credit card info as a safer option.

The realities of commerce on the Web today are that the majority of most buyers are not on the market yet. The average person on the Net today is male, college educated, employed, an early technology adapter, etc. If this profile does not fit your client's market, selling on the Internet may be premature. However, the <u>demographics</u> are changing quickly, and it is good strategy to get experience for when the medium blossoms. Lands' End's market is not there yet, but the company is learning valuable (yet remarkably inexpensive) lessons as it builds its infrastructure and expertise while the market matures.

If your client wants immediate sales, the offerings and the current demographics must be matched. Internet Shopping Network's (http://www.internet.net) offerings match the current demographics well. It positions itself as a computer superstore, but also offers shoppers Gourmet Foods and Wines, Gifts & Flowers, Electronics, a lifestyle category called

---

four different ways

"We offer four convenient ways for you to order: online, using our Electronic Order Blank; or by fax, phone or mail. For all orders, please include a daytime and evening phone number, email address or fax number where you can be reached—and let us know your preferred method of contacting you."

http://www.landsend.com/spawn.cgi?OTHE-ORDR0795?GRAPHIC?NODEPROD0795?gT325 z76xiDd8dxcJDIF

Now there's a memorable URL! :-(

---

demographics

For more in-depth demographic info, check http://www.cc.gatech.edu/gvu/user_surv and http://www.netsurf.com/surveys.htm

Living, and Office Goods. The Network sells hardware and boasts 20,000 software titles in stock. It also provides reviews from various computer magazines.

Internet Shopping Network reportedly operates with only a handful of employees, carries no inventory, and costs less than $1 per transaction (compared to about $5 per transaction for telephone operators). The company is moving toward actual software distribution via the Internet as well. It's not too difficult to look at this example and imagine some of your clients and/or prospects benefiting from this kind of practicality.

Another similar example is software.net (http://www.software.net), which offers close to 8,000 software packages for PCs, Macs, and different flavors of Unix. Cross-indexing aids in searching for products. Considerately, its site links to an extensive product review library. Demo programs and sometimes the entire product can be downloaded and installed with a few keystrokes or mouse clicks. Online transactions are fully encrypted and secure for shoppers using Netscape as their browser; toll-free telephone orders are accepted as well.

Exploiting the fact that electronic storefronts don't suffer from the same capacity problems that physical stores do and can offer an almost unlimited amount of product with an almost unlimited amount of information at a marginal cost, CDnow has an online music store that has almost every album made in the U.S., so when you find your favorite artist, you can discover everything he or she ever did (everything that still exists, anyway). CDnow is divided into two stores, Rock-Pop-Jazz-Misc and Classical. The stores are a little different, because with Classical music, it can be difficult to find what you want. You may specify several features of the album or performance you are looking for. You can specify the Composer, the Title of the album or composi-

CDnow
http://www.cdnow.com

continued on next page

LARGEST SELECTION IN THE WORLD
GREAT PRICES & LOWEST SHIPPING ON THE NET

OR, TRY THE SUPER-FAST TEXT ONLY STORE

| 2-6 DAY DELIVERY | NETSCAPE SECURE | WHAT'S NEW AT CDNOW | ALL-MUSIC GUIDE | MAGAZINE WAREHOUSE | GIVE US FEEDBACK |

CDNOW · THAT'S WHAT YOU CALL SERVICE

No other music store offers its customers as much as CDnow does. That's because at CDnow we know that being the best means more than just having a selection larger than anyone else... on or off the net. It means getting the music you order to you quickly and inexpensively. It means giving you information such as biographies, album reviews and track listings on the artists and albums you buy. Here are just a few additional points we think are important in serving you.

● 2 to 6 business day delivery for most titles

tion, the Performer, the Conductor, the Record Label, the Primary Instrument, the Genre, or any or all of the above. The site has reviews of the albums and biographies of the artists, along with "Links" that show relations among artists. CDnow also carries a catalog of over 6,000 imports, as well as VHS videos.

videos

Speaking of videos, Walt Disney's Buena Vista Pictures (http://www.disney.com) has a virtual cinema on the Internet. You can't buy anything there yet, but information, pictures, and short QuickTime video loops promoting the latest movie releases are available for downloading. You don't have need to be a fortune teller to see that distributing video across the Internet is on the horizon.

CDnow has low prices because of the savings it enjoys in reduced employee and floor space costs. The maximum total shipping and handling for any U.S. order is $4.94, no matter how many items from your shopping list are in your order. When you have found an album you want, you may put it in your shopping cart. If you decide to buy the album, stop by the Cash Register and make your purchase. CDnow can accept payments by Visa, MasterCard, and American Express, and checks as well as money orders. Credit card information is taken via phone, fax, or over the Net. CDnow assures users that it protects credit card information and does not release any card information to outside organizations.

211   D _ G _ I .

Illustrating the relatively low barriers to entry, Internet Underground Music Archive (http://www.iuma.com) was started by three University of California Santa Cruz students as a free service to provide online exposure for unsigned, independent bands and musicians. It now earns fees for showcasing each of between 500 and 600 artists with information, pictures, downloadable music samples, and discography, as well as profits from selling the artist's music on traditional media.

SandCastle Magic's Web site very effectively enables visitors to learn about its "alternative to the garbage kids watch on TV today." It sells children's educational video products and is expanding its

SandCastle Magic

http://www.sandcastlemagic.com

Welcome to SandCastle Magic!

"Children's programming on commercial broadcast television remains the video equivalent of a Twinkie -- kids enjoy it despite the absolute absence of any nutritional content."

— Rep. Edward Markey of Massachusetts, Chairman US House of Representatives Telecommunications Subcommittee and Cosponsor of the Children's Television Act of 1990

We at SandCastle Magic want to give you an alternative to the garbage kids watch on TV today.

market online. The site has branches with information on SandCastle's mission, ways to become a distributor of its products, scenes from the latest video, testimonials, educational materials and a teacher's guide that accompany the videos for parents, and an email link to SandCastle and toll-free product ordering with an Internet discount (as in "Just tell 'em you saw it on the Web").

As an example of on-the-job learning, Pizza Hut (http://www.pizzahut.com) established its storefront on the Internet early in 1994 and generated an incredible amount of publicity that would have cost hundreds of times more if done conventionally. Although pizza deliveries were available only in Santa Cruz, California, the entire Internet community was aware of it, and Pizza Hut showed the world it was on the cutting edge. When people are discussing business on the Web, it is a common occurrence to hear "even Pizza Hut is on it." The positive image-building and positioning payoffs were staggering. Today, the actual ordering of pizza is a minor benefit to the justification of this virtual storefront, but it is easy to foresee a time when local stores will be coordinated and online (with one central URL advertised nationally). You will enter your address, make your selection (from the menu or a list of preferences from your past orders), print your coupon, and wait for the doorbell. Oh yes, and don't forget to hold the anchovies!

Virtual Malls

Virtual mall sites are Internet versions of the physical malls we're quite familiar with—a group of stores or, to continue the metaphor, a group of electronic storefronts. These have merit because malls will generally organize electronic storefronts into categories of products, enabling quick navigation for users who do not necessarily want to browse, or a organizational aid for those who do want to browse or "shop."

A stand-alone store has a more difficult marketing job to gain traffic. Shoppers must make a specific and intentional trip to that one store. Online storefronts have to answer the question of how shoppers will know their URL; to look it up or search the Net, the shopper must have a predetermined goal of finding that store or product instead of benefiting from built-in traffic and even impulse purchases.

marketplaceMCI

http://www.internetmci.com

In marketplaceMCI, a good example of a virtual mall, you can enter an assortment of storefronts to view products; retrieve product, service, and pricing

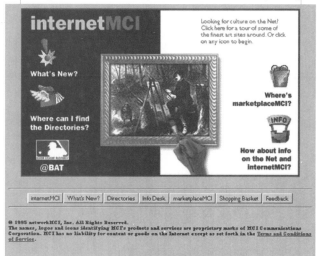

information; and order products and services. Upon entry into marketplaceMCI, encryption is initiated, keeping your entire session in confidence. This feature protects any transferred information, including credit card numbers, from third-party observation and abuse. Authentication techniques are also used to prevent an unauthorized third party from masquerading as a legitimate principal in a transaction.

As you browse through marketplaceMCI, you can select items from the various stores you enter to be placed in your shopping basket. At any time during the shopping process, you can either check out or modify or remove items in the shopping basket. Your shopping basket can be used to hold items from multiple stores, so you can continue shopping from store to store until you are ready to check out, at which point you can make all of your purchases at once. If not purchased within 12 hours after they are selected, items are automatically deleted from your shopping basket.

Once you have completed all of your shopping and your shopping basket contains the items you wish to buy, you then select the check out option to place

Authentication techniques

The technology is called public key cryptography, which differs from traditional methods by being asymmetric. This means that one can use a special pair of numbers called keys to encode and decode messages. One number is made publicly available; the second number is held privately. With the public key, anyone can encrypt a message that only the private key can decode. Similarly, the process works in reverse to authenticate messages. A message sent with the private key can be decoded with the public key and is thus proven to have come from the holder of the private key. For more information on public key cryptography, check out: http://home.netscape.com/newsref/ref/rsa.html.

your order(s). Check out is performed on a per-merchant basis, and you are prompted for your billing and shipping information for each merchant separately.

If you were to put your clients' site in this mall, they could expect page access reports, product sales reports, and storefront sales reports summarizing the total amount of purchases made in the store.

An example on a much smaller scale is First Virtual's InfoHaus (http://www.infohaus.com), one of Internet's first digital content marketplaces. It is a public access mall where anyone can open a shop and stock it with information products for sale. For a small fee, anyone can place text, image, sound, video, and even software online for purchase via downloading. Although the current 70-plus "merchants" offer mostly text-based materials, images and sound clips are also available for a few dollars. This site demonstrates that commerce can be done on the Internet at *extremely* low cost. It virtually promotes the ability to sell low-cost items, from a $2.29 cold remedy to a $3.79 How To Buy A Computer text file, all online.

A creative example of using a physical world metaphor for a mall, the Supernet's BarclaySquare uses a 3-D floor plan of a mall complete with shoppers walking on the stores' hot spots (which are

clickable imagemaps); the site even has a lift for changing levels in the mall.

In the 3-D world, multiple stores of a common theme seem to pull shoppers in larger numbers—

---

small fee

Account setup is $10 U.S. for sellers, $2 for buyers. Credit card information is transmitted over toll-free telephone lines, and orders are then done online and billed to the card. Sellers are surcharged monthly at 2 percent of sales, plus $0.29, times the number of transactions, plus $1.00.

Supernet's BarclaySquare

http://www.itl.net/barclaysquare

not unlike outlet malls do. As crazy as it sounds, you may want to consider linking your clients to their competitors, and by combining forces increase the impact and draw. For example, have you ever noticed how several antique stores seem to group together and all benefit from the increased traffic? Antiques World (http://www.webcom.com/~antiques) demonstrates this strategy in the electronic arena. Marian Dieter and Steven Sagri, a husband and wife team, are the entrepreneurs behind Antiques World. Marian has been a computer systems designer and consultant for 20 years, developing systems for Fortune 500 companies and other clients. Steve and Marian started a part-time antiques business 15 years ago, and Steve has been a full-time antiques dealer for six years. Together they have done shows, sold via mail order, run an antiques mall, and held auctions, and now they have their own antiques shop in Shaker Hts., Ohio. This unique combination of computer systems experience and wide exposure in the antiques field made them ideal developers for a project like Antiques World.

Here are some other virtual malls you might check out:

• Access Market Square: http://www.icw.com/ams.html

• Branch Mall: http://branch.com

• eMall: http://eMall.Com/Home.html

• The Internet Mall: http://www.mecklerweb.com/imall

• MarketNet: http://mkn.co.uk

• The Super Mall: http://supermall.com

• Downtown Anywhere: http://awa.com

• Electronic Auction: http://www.primenet.com/~auction

Combination Models

Throughout this part of the book, I've tried to high-light various models businesses are using for their Web sites. I've used these examples because they fit each model so well. But I don't want to convey that when designing an Internet solution for your client or yourself, you need to pick the singular model that best suits your goals and then design a site specifically like that. Real life is not that black-and-white. As you know, there is much more gray area. Successful sites often use a combination of any number of these models to offer interactivity, communication, free samples, quality content, sponsors, and advertisers, as well as the overt offer-ings of goods and services.

One of the best examples of combining these strate-gies is HotWired. This site has wonderful design, graphics, and content (see chapter 14 for an in-depth critique of the HotWired site), and mixes pieces of

HotWired ....

http://www.hotwired.com

most of the Internet business models featured in chapter 8 of this book.

• HotWired uses elements of the "salt lick" by offer-ing new and exciting content to keep users coming back.

- It uses the Library model by archiving old issues of *Wired* magazine, links, and product reviews.

- It uses the Sponsorship model by enabling SGI, Internet Shopping Network, and others to have a presence and hotlink on its site.

- It uses the traditional PR model, generating tremendous visibility by putting up one of the Internet's hottest sites.

- It utilizes online promotion of print product to increase demand online for print subscriptions.

- It uses the free sample model by letting users have access to the same content as its printed publication, although that content is delayed so as to not decrease the value of print subscriptions.

If we were to stretch a little more here, I think we could even come up with a few more, but I think the point has been made. To skillfully blend more than one strategy strengthens a site and helps to ensure its success in the same manner that diversifying a product line increases the sales, durability and flexibility of a traditional business.

If we wish to continue to serve our existing and prospective clients in their efforts to sell goods and services, we need to add Internet marketing to our arsenal. Just as with other media, when commercial interests begin to compete for the same audience, Net publishers will be challenged to attract them and to keep them, which is good for the medium and good for designers. To win market share, sites must have quality content, quality aesthetics, logical and clear navigation, as well as a solid conceptual foundation (see part IV). This bodes well for those skilled in designing and packaging information. Add strong technical capabilities and expertise in interactivity and interface design, and a bright future awaits you.

PART IV

DESIGNING FOR THE NET

Part IV

PART IV EXPLORES THE ISSUES, TOOLS, AND TECHNIQUES FOR DESIGNING INTERNET DOCUMENTS.

Chapter 10

CHAPTER 10 EXAMINES THE IMPLICATIONS OF DESIGNING FOR THE INTERNET AND SUGGESTS ESSENTIAL CHANGES IN THINKING DESIGNERS NEED TO MAKE IN ORDER TO USE THE NET EFFECTIVELY.

Chapter 11

CHAPTER 11 INTRODUCES THE SOFTWARE TOOLS NECESSARY TO CONSTRUCT EFFECTIVE WEB PAGES FOR THE INTERNET.

Chapter 12

CHAPTER 12 SUGGESTS SOME SKILLS THAT NEED TO BE DEVELOPED, AS WELL AS SOME TIPS AND TRICKS TO USE THOSE NEW TOOLS WELL.

Chapter 13

CHAPTER 13 TAKES A LOOK AT THE NATURE OF THE NEW MEDIUM OF THE INTERNET AND SUGGESTS CHANGES IN THE DESIGN PROCESSES THAT SHOULD ENABLE THOSE WITH GOOD SKILLS TO PRODUCE EXCELLENT RESULTS.

Chapter 14

CHAPTER 14 SHOWS SOME ACTUAL SAMPLES OF WORK DONE ON THE INTERNET. IT EXAMINES SEVERAL CURRENT WEB SITES AND OFFERS AN INSTRUCTIVE CRITIQUE.

Act IV

Scene 1

Kit, junior designer at a large downtown design consultancy, SOS Design, has just been called to the
boss' (Bill's) office to discuss a request from SOS's
biggest client.

Bill, 40-something design director: "Why would
BigCorp want to do away with paper? It's
beautiful, it's durable, it's been around for
thousands of years."

Kit, 20-something junior designer: "You don't understand—
electronic publishing is m o r e than that.
It's like Gutenberg. It's a publishing revolution.
There is no gatekeeper at some publisher determining what we can know or how
much we have to pay to know it. The Internet is there.
It's changing e v e r y t h i n g ."

Bill: "Isn't it just like a different format,
an electronic magazine…"

Kit: "It's n o t like that."

Bill: "What do you mean? People write things
and make them available from their computers."

Kit: "There are n o m o r e authors.
Users are the a u t h o r s .
C u l t u r e is the a u t h o r ."

Bill: "No authors?
Somebody has to write this stuff!"

Kit: "Everybody does. N o b o d y does."

Bill: "Look, we've been making electronic docu-

No authors

"We can easily imagine a culture where discourse would circulate without any need for an
author. Discourses, whatever their status,

continued on next page

ments and printing them for years."

Kit: "It's not like that. Documents can call other documents; they can change daily, hourly—the document isn't a fixed thing. It evolves. It c h a n g e s. Everything's different."

Narrator: This conversation had happened before. The ending had been predictable until today. Earlier in the day, Bill received a call from their biggest client, BigCorp, asking them to develop an interactive information service for marketing its products on the Internet rather than printing them in several catalogs. Bill had thrown a six-figure price out, half-hoping it would discourage the idea, but the client didn't blink. Bill still wasn't quite used to being responsible for setting his own type—and now this! A whole new medium to learn. And his client was demanding it.

Bill: "Kit, I guess I'll have to sit down with you and learn how to surf the Net. Good grief, I'm starting to sound like a computer geek."

form, or value, and regardless of our manner of handling them, would unfold in a pervasive anonymity. No longer the tiresome repetitions:

'Who is the real author?'

'Have we proof of his authenticity and originality?'

'What has he revealed of his most profound self in his language?'

New questions will be heard:

'What are the modes of existence of this discourse?'

'Where does it come from; how is it circulated; who controls it?'

'What placements are determined for possible subjects?'

'Who can fulfill these diverse functions of the subject?'

Behind all these questions we would hear little more than the murmur of indifference:

'What matter who's speaking?'"

Michel Foucault. "What Is an Author?" *Bulletin de la Societe française de Philosophie*

Act IV

Chapter 10

Shifting Paradigms for a New Medium

This chapter examines the implications of

designing for the Internet and suggests essential

changes in thinking designers need to make in

order to use the Net effectively.

Act IV

Scene 2

Still in Bill's office.

Narrator: The truth was, the computer had changed the face of SOS Design years before. The drawing boards were all but gone, replaced by computer workstations. The whole typesetting industry had disappeared practically overnight. Most projects now go directly from computer to final film with no mechanicals, no tissue overlays, no color breaks. Communication between designers and suppliers is confused. Neither is exactly sure what he or she needs to tell the other to do, because not only have their means of communication changed, but their roles as well. Designers, or rather their computers, are doing some of the work formerly entrusted to camera operators and strippers. And their prepress suppliers aren't exactly sure what to expect from SOS designers either. Files come in from different designers that are constructed so differently that they require vastly different amounts of effort, expertise, and money to plot successfully. No two designers seem to construct art the same way anymore.

Bill: "Kit, a little stability sure looks good some days. In spite of all the changes, at least we're still producing print projects. You know, ink on paper."

Kit: "Sorry Bill, can't help ya there."

Bill grumbles at the inevitable conclusion: He and the entire staff at SOS are being drawn into the emerging world of hypertext electronic publishing.

Bill: "No more ink on paper. Great, more changes."

Electronic publishing is more than just a change in material from ink and paper to phosphor and glass. It is a change in what information is. This change is so profound that we need a new way of thinking about how we communicate. While the definition of graphic design—the interaction of content and form to communicate—has not changed, the means of communication certainly have. Designers need to make a series of paradigm shifts to assimilate new ways of thinking about reading and learning.

We designers will not be able to appropriately use this new medium until the paradigm shift has been internalized. To internalize the changes, we need to experience firsthand the new medium of the Internet. In order to explore it fully, we must grasp its technical and philosophical issues. This means learning new software and network processes that form the backbone of the Internet. For some, particularly those practicing design the longest, this will mean more stress and reeducation. For most others, getting involved with the new medium will be exhilarating, even entertaining. But it is necessary. It can be enjoyable. And it is rewarding.

paradigm

The dictionary meaning is "an outstandingly clear or typical example or archetype." *Paradigm* is from the Greek compound word *paradeigma*, with *para* meaning alongside and *deiknunai* meaning to see or to show. A paradigm is a concept, often assumed or subconscious, that enables one to see and understand. It is not the thoughts we have, but the framework around which our thoughts are formed. In this sense, our paradigms are the mental tools or mindsets that we use to understand a situation.

Merriam-Webster's Collegiate Dictionary, Tenth Edition

Paradigm Shift: Text to Hypertext

TEXT	HYPERTEXT
linear	three-dimensional
sequential	random
author control	reader control
defined progression	open progression
limited context	broad context
limited association of ideas	free association
reading skills	research skills
attitude: granting expertise	attitude: confidence in own expertise
learn truth	make truth for self
info time = long	info time = brief

The most basic paradigm shift is from traditional text to hypertext. Hypertext is an extension of the idea of the cross-reference. A text is embedded with hot text links that connect immediately to additional texts, which contain additional links leading to more texts. It is a game of information hopscotch—users hop from document to document and concept to concept following an information thread.

Hypertext is a deceptively simple concept that requires a dramatic conceptual shift. In the past, an author developed a linear flow of thought for readers. Writing courses and English teachers have taught us to establish a thesis, support it with arguments, and finish with a summation, making a logical and linear flow of thought. In a hypertext document, individual readers select and develop their own line of thought through personal exploration of a variety of texts. At its best, hypertext encourages readers to select what is most relevant to

Hypertext

"A literature student, for example, reading a 'hyperbiography' of Edgar Allen Poe, might come across a reference to a poem. 'Clicking' on the title of the poem calls up a window with the complete poem in it. Reading the poem, the student finds an unfamiliar word, clicks on it, and the relevant dictionary definition pops up on the screen. Similarly, critical essays on the poem can be called up, or a digital copy of the original manuscript can be viewed, all without moving from one workstation."

Bob Cotton & Richard Olive, *Understanding Hypermedia*, p. 52

hypertext encourages readers

"Neilson points out that the value of hypertext

continued on next page

is that (compared with normal 'sequential' reading) it more closely models the way we think, allowing us to explore a subject area from many different perspectives until we find an approach that is useful for us. Using hypertext, authors would no longer have to write for a specific 'average' reader. They could include any level of detail, and allow the reader to decide how deep into the subject matter they wanted to go."

Bob Cotton & Richard Olive, *Understanding Hypermedia*, p. 24

their needs from a supplied palette of available information. Going through the process of reviewing, analyzing, assembling and drawing conclusions from data leads to more advanced understanding than merely observing bits of data individually.

In this way, the Internet adds value to data. It encourages understanding. The result of this process is that all readers become their own author/editor. A hypertext work is not a traditional book, but a selected body of information arranged in a logically addressed pattern that encourages exploration. The hypertext designer yields significant content control to the reader. (See chapter 13 for revised design methods to address this issue and chapter 14 for critiques of examples of how this has been accomplished.)

With greater control comes increased responsibility. Hypertext incorporates broad information palettes to grant greater freedom to readers, along with greater responsibility to understand, navigate, and associate appropriately. Some hypertext documents, such as early HyperCard stacks, are clearly limited, focused, and easy to navigate. Other hypertexts are significantly more complex and correspondingly more difficult for the reader to use. Interactive programs created with sophisticated authoring software such as Macromedia Director and Authorware are capable of creating more complex hypertext experiences. Interactive CD-ROMs allow great complexity because they provide an impressive quantity of information to navigate. As the volume of information increases and the tools to form links necessarily grow in complexity, navigation difficulties multiply for a reader—and for the designer creating a document easy for a reader to use. It is easy for users, who only view one page at a time, to get lost in a web of connections that clouds the perception of valuable information and blocks understanding.

view one page

"Unfortunately, only one piece of your Web site is visible at a time (the current page), so

continued on next page

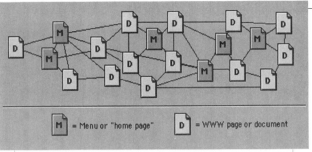

M = Menu or "home page"   D = WWW page or document

users instinctively begin to build a mental model that they use to predict the scope and structure of your Web. Although your Web pages may be extensively interconnected, you don't want the user's mental model of your Web site to look like this [see illustration at right]."

Patrick J. Lynch, Yale C/AIM WWW Style Manual, http://info.med.yale.edu/caim/ M_I_3.HTML

Challenges for Designers

As the richness and complexity of a hypertext document increases, obstacles to learning are created that need to be addressed by designers. In this regard, the Internet is not just a complex hypertext document, but a vast hypertext environment. The available texts are limited only by the quantity of information available on the millions of computers connected to the Internet. Because the scope and depth of information available on the Internet is vast, the means and capacity to assess it are correspondingly challenging. The price of admission to the Net's huge information storehouse is confusion of access. Designers need to understand the difficulty in order to design appropriate solutions.

For designers struggling to make this paradigm shift, the difference between text and hypertext is analogous to the difference between two-dimensional and three-dimensional space. In a humorous tale called *Flatland*, by Edwin A. Abbott, creatures living in a two-dimensional world are asked by revolutionaries to conceive of three-dimensional space. In a two-dimensional world, all things are linear and sequential. The two-dimensionalists end up imprisoning the three-dimensional heretics because the 2-D people are simply unable to think nonlinearly.

Designers need to think of communication in a different dimension. We are designing nonlinear, nonsequential documents for people who have lived their lives in Flatland. To help them navigate, we need to grasp both the communication potential and the obstacles presented by hypertext documents. This will enable both designers and users to take full advantage of the new medium of the Internet.

Expanded Context

The shift from text to hypertext thinking raises many important issues that designers are not equipped to answer, such as the impact the Net will have on our social fabric, or the ways it will change the way people think, or the way organizations are structured. Although it's not the designer's role to answer these questions, we should at least be aware and keep in touch with observations by experts such as researchers and social scientists.

One of the issues more closely related to the design task is context and how it is transformed by the Internet's hypertext environment. Context is necessary for understanding information. Lack of context is one of the surest routes to misinformation. The Net is an environment in which the user is immersed in the capacity for context. Additional information on any topic is a mouse click away. The very purpose of the Net is to make information on everything widely available. By way of contrast, television is a medium that limits context. A TV vegetable is a person who's a passive recipient of a preprogrammed information stream. It is futile to expect even the best evening news program to address the questions you may have. The medium precludes it. The Internet is context-rich beyond anything previously experienced.

context

According to Neil Postman, if information is without sufficient context, "if the event is entirely self-contained, devoid of any relationship to your past knowledge or future plans…you will in fact have learned nothing…. At best you are left with an amusing bit of trivia, good for trading in cocktail party chatter or solving a crossword puzzle, but nothing more."

Neil Postman, *Amusing Ourselves to Death*, p. 75

The issue of context exposes the need for the members of an information society to have adequate research and critical thinking skills. Are people prepared to use the Internet? Are our research skills adequate, or will poor research skills lead people to form wrong conclusions? Or do we even agree that it matters? Do we agree that there is any truth to discover, or is truth completely relative? What does it matter if a randomly patched-together collection of data leads someone to conclude that John Kennedy was never killed, or that Elvis was an alien, or that bombing Federal buildings is a wholesome idea?

Designers are in the business of piecing together information for clients and their audiences. We often add value to information by adding contextual clues. The clues may be as simple as a certain color (red to the word "apple") or as complex as layers and layers of related image content—but we designers add context. The Web gives us a whole new contextual field to glean, and to give to our clients and our readers.

We designers can respond to the Net's expanded context by shifting our paradigm. In particular, we can expand our own information research and analysis skills and, through our design, help users successfully find the context to answer their questions (see chapter 12 for specific skills we designers should learn). The responsibility for equipping our society with the skills to research appropriately and think critically lies with educators, parents, and ultimately with each individual.

Paradigm Shift: Media to Multimedia

MEDIA	MULTIMEDIA
single medium	multiple media
content constrained by medium	content dictates medium
static form	dynamic form
rigid	movement
focused experience	diverse experience
encourages single learning style	supports multiple learning styles

Another paradigm shift is from "mono" media to interactive multimedia thinking. Multimedia is the simultaneous expression of text, image, animation, video, and sound. It is made possible by digitization. Scanners convert drawings and photographs into numbers, video cameras convert moving images into numbers, audio recorders convert sounds into numbers, and word processors translate words into numbers. This common numeric existence makes it possible for previously incompatible media to coexist and interact freely in a computer. The result is a new medium with dramatic expressive power and unheard-of content richness.

A viewer of an interactive multimedia program is free to make hypertext-type links not just between texts but between documents of various media types. Text can link to image. Image can link to sound. Sound can link to video or animation and back to text again. Information can be presented in the form most appropriate to it. A bird song can be heard rather than described in words. The flight of a goose can be observed rather than defined.

Viewers exploring an interactive multimedia document are free to construct their own unique experience through interaction. The viewers control how

---

interactive multimedia

The Cyberspace Lexicon defines interactive multimedia as "programs and applications that include a variety of media (such as text, images, video, audio and animation), the presentation of which is controlled interactively by the user." It's also referred to simply as multimedia. The authors of the *Lexicon* draw a distinction between multimedia and hypermedia by defining hypermedia as "a communications medium created by the convergence of computer and video technologies," and requiring hypermedia documents to have no beginning, middle, or end.

In this sense, the Internet would correctly be called a hypermedia environment, while a given Web document could be hypertext, if it contained only words, or multimedia if it included words, pictures, and other media forms (sound, motion, etc.).

Bob Cotton & Richard Oliver, p. 112

they sequence the experiences, how long each event lasts, and which media to experience and which to ignore. The experience is dynamic, changing from user to user, rather than static and fixed as in a video. Someone using a multimedia program is more like a video producer than a video viewer, because the structure and sequence are under the direct control of the user.

Challenges for Designers

This democratic approach is very different from film, television, or video. Producers and designers are going to have to come to grips with the loss of control and emotional power that comes when the viewer is in control of sequence and duration. We are going to have to shift our paradigm away from one of strict control to guided exploration. It's not just designers who need to make this shift; government and business leaders are going to have to grapple with the incredibly flattened hierarchy that the Internet creates in their organizations and in society.

And we graphic designers are going to have to come to appreciate the expressive power of time-based media. The dimension of time and the illusion of motion add an incredible expressive dimension to design tools like typography. Bouncing type can convey happiness, sagging type sorrow. Adding interactivity gives the viewer a participative role unheard of until now. Designers must let the concept of user control and the powerful tools of time and motion sink deeply into their thinking about communication in order to design effectively for the Internet. (See chapter 13 for an expanded discussion on how to revise design methodology to accomplish this.)

The Hypertextual, Multimedia Internet

With hypertext everyone is his or her own author. With multimedia everyone is his or her own producer. On the Internet, everyone is both and more. The Internet is an interactive multimedia communication and information collection system of global proportion. It requires the paradigm shifts to hypertext thinking and to multimedia thinking, and then some. The Internet's World Wide Web supports interactive multimedia documents whose hot buttons can hop to millions of text, audio, or video documents all over the world.

From Monologue to Dialogue

The Internet requires a paradigm shift from one-way communication flow to two-way communication interaction because the Internet is a <u>two-way communication</u> medium. It not only offers information but collects it as well. We need to shift from the communication model of the monologue to that of the dialogue. We can develop a brochure that enables each recipient to return it with his or her own changes and additions. Authors from all over the world can add to documents on the Internet. All sorts of questions can be posed to a global audience and answers can be gathered and published. Internet documents can be dynamic forms of communication that encourage readers to participate.

These paradigm shifts will lead to a change in methods of designing to include more feedback and audience participation in the process (see chapter 13). Not only will design processes change, but designers will need to change as well. Ivory-tower individualism and professional egoism are going to have to fall in favor of a more inclusive, humble approach.

Part of the Internet's magic is its incorporation of most previous forms of interpersonal communica-

two-way communication

Sites such as Project 2000 (http://www 2000.ogsm.vanderbilt.edu) not only enable direct user feedback via typing written responses, but also provide statistics on the use of the site.

tion: People talk to each other over the Internet, people send and receive mail, people see each other on the Internet. Anyone on the Internet can create documents, express ideas, and gather responses. The information designed for the Internet can be dynamic or static, but the Internet as a medium is dynamic. It changes moment by moment.

talk to each other

Internet Relay Chat, IRC, enables people to type written messages in real-time, carrying on a written conversation though they may be continents apart. "IRC does not assume physical contact between users—either prior to or after communication via computer. Users of the system will, as the medium is international, know in person at most only a few fellow users. IRC allows—encourages—recreational communication between people who have never been, most likely will never be, in a situation to base their knowledge of each other and their methods of communication on physical cues."

Elizabeth M. Reid, *Electropolis: Communication and Community on Internet Relay Chat*, Honours thesis, University of Melbourne, Australia

From Limitations to Opportunities

Because its structure is global, the Internet shrinks space to irrelevancy. Location doesn't matter. This makes the Internet a powerful information distribution system. Personal publishing is nothing new. Anyone with access to a copier can produce multiple copies of his or her own work. But the Internet makes it possible to distribute copies of one's work instantly to a global audience.

Because distribution is electronic, there is virtually no cost. And because it is electronic, there is virtually no cost to revise, edit, update, and republish the information. We designers must make a paradigm shift away from the limitations on communication imposed by print technology. Previously accepted parameters such as the expense of full color, minimum quantity breaks of 2,500, and paper weight and mailing costs are all irrelevant. We need to change our thinking about the cost of information distribution, revision, and access.

This means that entire categories of information previously difficult or expensive to publish effectively are easily publishable electronically over the Internet. Any time-sensitive information that is updated regularly, such as a membership directory, is a natural match in this paradigm. Information needed by a small but widely dispersed audience, such as a change in training regimens for Olympic decathlon athletes, is another match. Any situations in which low-quantity print runs were previously an

expense of full color

"Why does color have to cost anything? In printing, color costs because of the machinery and technology involved. Printing presses transfer thin films of ink onto paper by means of metal plates and rollers. On press, each color requires a separate roller and plate set to form a unit.

Offset presses are large complex machines; the larger and more complex they are, the greater the number of color units they contain, the more they cost to build, maintain and use."

Mike Zender, *Getting Unlimited Impact with Limited Color*, p. 1

obstacle are perfect for on-demand Internet publishing.

The ability to gather information and the minimal cost involved in revising and distributing information make micromarketing possible (see part III, "Helping Clients Use the Net"). An audience of one can be reached with a personalized communication, advertisement, or offer. An auto maker could gather information about preferences from a group of interested buyers, make a special run of cars that fit their wishes, and send a personalized invitation to each prospect offering a special deal on his or her custom car. The combination of mass media distribution and individual product design and marketing is unique. The Internet is both global and individual. It is an ideal research and communication medium.

In one sense, the Internet has no real impact on design. The need for creative thinking and problem-solving is as great as ever. Ideas and concepts are still essential for communication. Internet design is still what design has always been—the relationship between form and content. Established designers, take heart! The Internet is simply a new medium for designers to do what they have always done.

In another sense, the Internet has a dramatic impact on design. The process of communicating on the Internet is different from any previous medium. Accessing, reading, and viewing information on the Internet use complex tools; there is a vast quantity of content available; messages are read in a more "skim and summary" fashion; and more advanced research skills are required by Net surfers. It's a new medium and it is creating a new class of learners, a new audience. In addition to requiring significant paradigm shifts, designing for the Internet requires new tools, new production skills, new communication skills, and modifications in the design process—all of which we'll explore in the coming chapters.

Chapter 11

Learning New Tools

This chapter introduces the software tools

necessary to design and construct effective

Web documents for the Internet.

Act IV

Scene 3

SOS Design, three weeks after the momentous call from BigCorp.

Bill: "Kit, have you seen that new site that offers stock photo research? It's quick and they only charge $4.95 an image."

Kit: "Haven't seen it. What's the U R L ?"

Bill: "I'll give you my bookmark. I'm enjoying laying out ads for the Net, but I'm still a little confused about how to get links to work on our home page."

Kit: "H e y, I just got a hot u p g r a d e to our HTML converter; let me s h o w you...."

Although it is hard to ignore the Internet or the hype about the changes it brings, it is possible to design very traditional-looking projects on the Internet. Ads on the Internet look remarkably similar to their print cousins. Internet books look remarkably bookish, and email looks a lot like snail mail.

In the early days of a new medium, it is common, perhaps necessary, for initial efforts to mimic work in the previous medium. Those creating documents in a new medium and those using the new documents are comfortable with the old form. As

Gutenberg developed moveable metal type, he created many ligatures and alternate characters, at least in part to give his printed Bibles the appearance of the hand-copied ones that were all that existed at that time. While this is understandable, it squanders the power and potential of the new medium. Making a successful paradigm shift is the first step in breaking free from the preconceptions formed by long experience in an old medium (see chapter 10). After we designers redirect our thinking, we need to learn new tools, acquire new skills (see chapter 12), and revise our design process (see chapter 13).

Why Specific Internet Design Tools?

The Internet is a computer medium. You can't do it with a pencil. It won't work without electricity. It depends totally on strings of 1s and 0s—the bits, bytes, and megabytes that roam in computers and ride wires, fibers, and microwaves throughout the world. And the Internet is driven entirely by software. The design tools for the Internet, therefore, are software tools for a computer medium. Current computer-based design tools are primarily print-oriented. They are designed to output files to various printers using a special page description language called PostScript. PostScript was not designed for the Internet, making software tools based on it unable to address the computer transmission and viewing requirements of the Internet.

Software tools for the Internet are in their infancy. Like early print design software, the software used to design for the Web is developing rapidly, with minimal direction by a specific guiding body, and without much input from the designers who need to use it. The more designers get involved with software developers, the more likely the Internet tools that developers produce will be the tools that designers want. Hopefully, like print design tools, Internet design tools will experience an initial period of rapid and unfocused growth followed by the development of mature standards and stable evolution. Translation: Internet design tools are crude now, but getting better quickly.

A brief visit on the Net illustrates one problem with current tools. The landscape is littered by a visually unsophisticated similarity. This is because, compared to our control over print, graphic designers do not have a lot of creative control on the Net. Internet standards provide very limited control over the visual form of Web documents. The reason that visual control has been so limited has to do with the nature of the Internet, a network of computer networks. To meet the challenge of distributing documents, developers have given the Internet a set of basic protocols (TCP/IP) to facilitate data transmission. These protocols solve information transmission problems very well. Once TCP/IP has delivered the data correctly, it is available for viewing—but how?

Each computer platform requires specific software to create and display each document. A document created on a PC may not be compatible with any software application available on a Macintosh, making it unviewable to Mac users. Yet for documents to be viewable on the Internet, they must be viewable not just on a Mac or a PC, but on PCs, Macs, Unix stations, and many other platforms as well, using different software on networks distributed all over the world. As you can imagine, encoding a document's visual form for viewing on an unlimited number of hardware/software computer platforms presents serious challenges.

An example of just one of these problems is type font availability. There is no way to ensure that every possible recipient of a given document will have the type font

"If you have ever received an electronic document from someone and you didn't have the font, then you know your computer will automatically revert all text information to the default font. The look, feel, line breaks, italics, boldface, and hyphenation of the file you received will be completely askew. The document, in almost all cases, is unreadable and unmanageable."

Patrick Ames, *Beyond Paper*, p. 88

type font that the document creator used in the original. First of all, fonts would be needed that would work on all computer systems. Second, if such fonts were used, it would be too cumbersome to attach font files, typically 40K, to each document, when often the documents themselves are only 10K. Using three fonts in a document would increase the size of a 10K file to 130K. The information overhead is just too great. Documents distributed internationally via the Internet must be viewable on any platform regardless of details involving font, software, and so on. So, how do we gain control? ASCII to the rescue.

The Text-Only Internet

The simplest viewable document form is plain or ASCII text. ASCII text documents can be converted for viewing or printing by nearly any computer system. Because the ASCII code simply defines keystroke characters, it is font-independent, or rather, the font is determined by what's available on the recipient's computer. Text-only documents are simple, which is an advantage. They are easily translated and small in size. They are flexible, but they have few formatting options. A large percentage of the documents on the Internet are text-only, in part because text-only documents work well with early Internet transfer protocols such as FTP (File Transfer Protocol), email, and Gopher.

ASCII

Short for American Standard Code for Information Interchange, *The Cyberspace Lexicon* defines ASCII (pronounced "ask-ee") as "A standard scheme for encoding alphanumeric characters so that they can be stored in the computer. Each character input from the keyboard is represented by 7 bits."

Bob Cotton and Richard Oliver, p. 20

Creating a text-only document is very similar to typing with a manual typewriter. Text-only documents have minimal text formatting options, and by definition have no hypertext capacity, no support for color images or other media types, and often uniform letterspacing. This makes text-only formats unprofitable for designers, because they offer minimal control over document structure and few options to improve appearance, enhance communication, and provide services for which clients will pay. As designers we may want to include access to this simple document type in a project, but we must accept severe limitations on the effectiveness of the document's form.

In part to overcome these limitations, a whole fascinating world of text-based communication icons, symbols, and mnemonics has evolved on the Internet to expand the expressive power of text-only communication. The smile :-) and the wink ;-) are two of the simplest. <u>Text-only illustrations</u> are more complex. e.e. cummings and many other

Text-only illustrations

One example of text-only "design" is an illustrated signature on an email document.

```
                          \\\///
                         / _ _ \
                        (| (.)(.) |)
     +-----------------------oOOo- () -oOOo-----------------------------------+
     |                              ........ Markus Q.   "Hawkeye" ........|
     |[][][][][] []  []   [] [[[][][][][] California State University San Marcos|
     |[]   []  [] []  []   []        [] ......................................|
     |  . [] .     [][] .... []  []        Homepage Address ....................|
     |.... [] ..... [][]  ... [][][] <www.csusm.edu/public/markusq/smiley.html>|
     |.... []  ..... [] [] . []  []    ......................................|
     |... []  ... []  []  . []      [] ..Tau Kappa Epsilon .... Scroll# 38 ...|
     |... [[]] ... [][] . [] [[[][][][][] .......Strong Bonds In Family .........|
     |......................oooO.........................And Brotherhood...|
     ^~~~~~~~~~~~~~~~~~~~~~~~(T  )~~~Oooo.~~~~~~~~~~~~~~~~~~~~~~~~~~~~~~~~~~~~~^
                            \K(     (  )
                            \E)     )#/
                              (1/
```

creative artists have demonstrated the wealth of graphic and linguistic expression possible with typewriter-like text, but the tool itself is severely limited, so much so that it tends to limit the quality of communication rather than enhance it.

The World Wide Web

While designers have little value to add to text-only documents, the World Wide Web offers designers a format with much richer potential. The World Wide Web (also known as WWW, W3, or simply the Web) is a hypermedia Internet architecture that works with plain text, but goes much beyond that to provide for formatted text with proportional spacing, hypertext links, color pictures, video, animation, sound, and virtual 3-D environments. The ability to integrate all these communication forms interactively, with significant formatting control across networks and computer systems, is what makes the Web particularly interesting to designers.

A word of caution, though: The Web is still developing. Not all Web users can take advantage of all these features. In some cases, instead of an image, the user's computer simply displays a small icon indicating the place where an image was supposed to appear. *Potential* is the operative word for multimedia design on the Net.

FTP is an adequate protocol for exchanging ASCII files, but the more robust, multimedia files of the Web demand a more dynamic format, such as HTTP (HyperText Transfer Protocol). HTTP goes a step beyond transferring files to establish a dynamic working partnership between the document sender (the server) and the document recipient (the client). The Web's real strength, via HTTP, is its combination of a dynamic viewing mechanism and a dynamic file transfer and retrieval mechanism. This means the Web has good answers not only to the problem of Internet information transfer, but the problem of viewing as well.

There are two essential processes that make Web documents viewable. One is the markup language that governs the document structure; the other is the software browser that interprets the markup language and enables the receiver to view the document.

The current standard markup language for the Web is HTML, HyperText Markup Language. HTML uses descriptors called tags to supply formatting instructions for documents. These tags are used to create and govern the visual form of Web documents. HTML instructions include control over relative or precise placement of objects and format control over text. The growing body of recognized HTML commands also provides more sophisticated

markup language

"Historically, the word *markup* has been used to describe annotation or other marks within a text intended to instruct a compositor or typist how a particular passage should be printed or laid out....

Generalizing from that sense, we define markup, or (synonymously) encoding, as any means of making explicit an interpretation of a text....

By markup language we mean a set of markup conventions used together for encoding texts. A markup language must specify what markup

continued on next page

controls, such as the ability to expand the relationship between the client and the server so that a Web page can change appearance randomly or in response to the type of user or even the date and time of day. The client computer could tell the server about itself and appropriate HTML code would respond, changing the appearance of the file on the client screen. Other document description languages such as PDF and VRML (which I'll talk about later) are competing with HTML, but at this point HTML rules.

HTML documents are viewed by a Web browsers, powerful viewing programs that interpret and apply the tags and links created in the original HTML

is allowed, what markup is required, how markup is to be distinguished from text, and what the markup means."
Electronic Text Center, University of Virginia,
TEI Guidelines for Electronic Text Encoding and Interchange, http://etext.virginia.edu/bin/tei-tocs?div=DIV1&id=SG

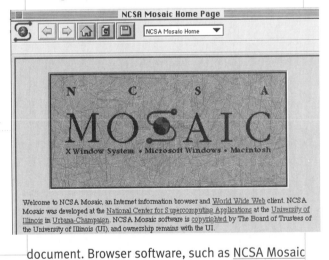

document. Browser software, such as <u>NCSA Mosaic</u> or <u>Netscape</u>, runs on the user's computer and is his

NCSA Mosaic

http://www.ncsa.uiuc.edu/SDG/Software/MacMosaic

http://www.ncsa.uiuc.edu/SDG/Software/WinMosaic

Netscape

http://home.netscape.com

or her functional interface to the Internet.

Browsers have different features. Some of the differences are operational, such as the ability to accept email or use different search engines, and some of the differences <u>affect the look</u> of a docu-

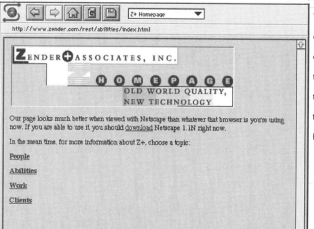

<u>affect the look</u>

The same document displays differently on Mosaic compared to Netscape. In this example, the document designer has anticipated this difference and encourages the Mosaic user to use Netscape to get the intended look of the page.

http://www.zender.com

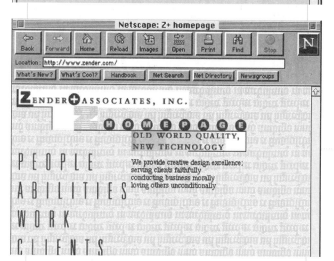

Netscape

ment. Cutting-edge browsers, such as Sun Microsystem's HotJava (http://java.sun.com), are demonstrating that it is possible to custom-program the browser on the fly. For example, HotJava, still under development as of this writing, will allow Web page designers to include animated graphics and other moving images on their pages with real-time interactivity. HotJava also supports real-time information updates in a Web document, such as the latest stock quotes or sports scores. The result is a communication environment more like an extremely dynamic cable television connection than a type-written page. Options such as Java (as well as Adobe's PDF format and the evolving VRML standard—which I'll discuss later) are still under de-velopment, so before visions of a wonderful new creative medium take hold, it's best to throw a little rain on the parade and tell you what's available *right now*.

HTML

Like the movie title *Back to the Future*, designers who set type on typesetting systems twenty years ago will have a twisted sense of déjà vu when they first use HyperText Markup Language. HTML pro-vides designers with a collection of markup styles, or tags, much like the markup tags used on 70s vin-tage typesetting systems. The tags give text format-ting and positioning information to a Web document. An HTML tag is identified by its enclo-sure in left and right angle brackets: < and >. This enables the HTML interpreter to distinguish be-tween copy to be displayed and HTML encoding in-structions. Information inside the brackets is HTML code; information outside is copy. For example, the HTML tag for a head is <H1>, and for a paragraph separator is <P>.

Tags are generally paired, with the first tag begin-ning the instruction and the last tag ending that in-struction (a computer is a literal device that often keeps right on doing what you command until you command it to stop, which can be quite a problem for those who don't always say exactly what they mean). Beginning tags are often differentiated from ending tags by the presence of a slash (/) at the start of the ending tag. For example, to label the word "Heading" as a level-one head, the designer

example

"Here is a bare-bones example of HTML tags

continued on next page

would type <H1>Heading</H1>.

As I said before, HTML's tags are embedded into the text of a document much the way typesetting commands were embedded into the text on proprietary typesetting systems, but with one major difference: HTML cannot control the font in which the document is displayed. The font is selected by the user as the default font for his or her browser. In fact, it is the HTML interpreter in the user's browser that controls all aspects of the form in which the document is displayed. Each HTML tag is decoded by the browser according to the browser's conventions. Depending on the particular browser, a level-one head <H1> might be 250 percent of the default/system font size and face, while another browser might define <H1> as 300 percent. It all depends on the browser used and the font selected by the client. Is "control" starting to sound less impressive? Well, read on!

applied:

<TITLE>The simplest HTML example</TITLE>

<H1>This is a level-one heading</H1>

Welcome to the world of HTML.

This is one paragraph.<P>

And this is a second.<P>"

National Center for Supercomputing Applications, A Beginners Guide to HTML, http://www.ncsa.uiuc.edu/General/Internet/WWW/HTMLPrimer.html

---

HTML

"The key to HTML is that it doesn't define formatting: although you can say that heading one is always bigger than heading two, for example, you can't specify either heading's point size or typeface. These, as well as window sizes, are determined by users in their browser. HTML just defines structure."

Anita Dennis, "Net Gains," *PUBLISH*, p. 51

---

level-one head

An example of heading sizes one through six. These heads would appear different depending on which browser you are using to display them.

Head 1
Head 2 sed diam
Head 3 elit aliquam erat
Head 4 lorem ipsum dolor sit amet
Head 5 vuis autem vel eum iriure
Head 6 velit esse molestie consequat.

Text 1onsectetuer adipiscing elit, sed diam nonummy nibh euismod tincidunt laoreet dolore magna aliquam erat volutpat. Ut wisi enim ad minim veniam, quis nostrud exerci tation ullamcorper suscipit lobortis nisl ut aliquip ex ea commodo consequat. Duis autem vel eum iriure dolor in hendrerit in vulputa velit esse molestie consequat, vel illum dolore eu feugiat nulla facilisis at vero eros et accumsan et iusto odio dignissim qui blandit praesent luptatum zzril delenit augue duis dolore te feugait nulla facilisi. Lorem ipsum dolor sit amet consectetuer adipiscing elit, sed diam nonummy nibh euismod tincidunt ut laoreet dolore magna aliquam erat volutpat. Ut wisi enim ad minim veniam, quis nostrud exerci tation ullamcorper suscipit lobortis nisl ut aliquip ex ea commodo consequat.

HTML is definitely evolving, and from the designer's viewpoint, getting better. HTML 3.0, the current version, provides more control over document appearance, page color for example, than HTML 2.0. More on this in chapter 12.

This book obviously isn't an in-depth HTML tutorial; there are plenty of other resources available that teach HTML perfectly well. Free HTML manuals describing the basics of the HTML language are available, such as <u>A Beginner's Guide to HTML</u>,

A Beginner's Guide to HTML

http://www.ncsa.uiuc.edu/General/
Internet/WWW/HTMLPrimer.html,
Illustration of page 1 and HTML tags for
page 1 .

Page 1

A Beginner's Guide to HTML

This is a primer for producing documents in HTML, the markup language used by the World Wide Web.

- <u>Acronym Expansion</u>
- <u>What This Primer Doesn't Cover</u>
- <u>Creating HTML Documents</u>
  - <u>The Minimal HTML Document</u>
  - <u>Basic Markup Tags</u>
    - <u>Titles</u>
    - <u>Headings</u>
    - <u>Paragraphs</u>
  - <u>Linking to Other Documents</u>
    - <u>Relative Links Versus Absolute Pathnames</u>
    - <u>Uniform Resource Locator</u>
    - <u>Anchors to Specific Sections in Other Documents</u>
    - <u>Anchors to Specific Sections Within the Current Document</u>
- <u>Additional Markup Tags</u>
  - <u>Lists</u>
    - <u>Unnumbered Lists</u>
    - <u>Numbered Lists</u>
    - <u>Definition Lists</u>
    - <u>Nested Lists</u>
  - <u>Preformatted Text</u>
  - <u>Extended Quotes</u>
  - <u>Addresses</u>
- <u>Character Formatting</u>
  - <u>Physical Versus Logical: Use Logical Tags When Possible</u>
    - <u>Logical Styles</u>
    - <u>Physical Styles</u>
  - <u>Using Character Tags</u>
  - <u>Special Characters</u>
    - <u>Escape Sequences</u>
    - <u>Forced Line Breaks</u>
    - <u>Horizontal Rules</u>
- <u>In-line Images</u>

HTML tags for Page 1

```
<html>
<base
href="http://pg3www.hv.boeing.com/web/webteam/docs/HTMLPrimer.html#A1.5.3.
2">
<HEAD>
<TITLE>A Beginner's Guide to HTML</TITLE>
</HEAD>

<H1>A Beginner's Guide to HTML</H1>

<P>
This is a primer for producing documents in HTML, the markup language
used by the World Wide Web.

<UL>
<LI><A HREF="#A1.1">Acronym Expansion</A>
<LI><A HREF="#A1.2">What This Primer Doesn't Cover</A>
<LI><A HREF="#A1.3">Creating HTML Documents</A>
  <UL>
  <LI><A HREF="#A1.3.1">The Minimal HTML Document</A>
  <LI><A HREF="#A1.3.2">Basic Markup Tags</A>
  <UL>
  <LI><A HREF="#A1.3.2.1">Titles</A>
  <LI><A HREF="#A1.3.2.2">Headings</A>
  <LI><A HREF="#A1.3.2.3">Paragraphs</A>
  </UL>
  <LI><A HREF="#A1.3.3">Linking to Other Documents</A>
  <UL>
  <LI><A HREF="#A1.3.3.1">Relative Links Versus Absolute Pathnames</A>
  <LI><A HREF="#A1.3.3.2">Uniform Resource Locator</A>
  <LI><A HREF="#A1.3.3.3">Anchors to Specific Sections in Other Documents</A>
  <LI><A HREF="#A1.3.3.4">Anchors to Specific Sections Within
```

which I used previously. Or, a quick query using <u>InfoSeek</u> (http://www2.infoseek.com) will locate several useful HTML resources.

There are also printed books available to help you

InfoSeek

List of HTML resources.

continued on next page

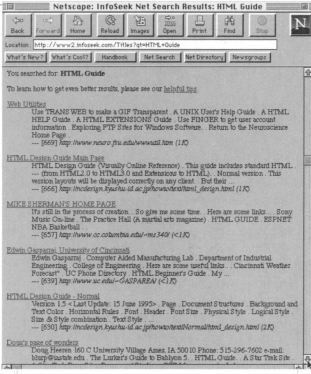

learn to use HTML tags, such as *Teach Yourself Web Publishing with HTML in a Week* (Sams Publishing; ISBN: 0-672-30667-0) and *Web Design Guide* (Hayden Books; ISBN: 1-56830-171-5). Like any programming tool, HTML takes some getting used to, but it is not especially difficult to learn. With just a basic understanding of HTML, you can successfully format Web documents.

There are other sources of help in formatting HTML documents. Because most Web browsers allow viewing the document in either its formatted form or as its HTML source code (in Netscape select Source in the View menu), it is easy to copy the HTML tags from other documents. You can read the tags of a particularly successful document and decipher how the page was formatted. Simple cutting and pasting copies the code from one document to another. So far there is nothing illegal about appropriating, or stealing, HTML code in this way. By doing this, you can accumulate a significant body of HTML code to use in formatting without doing a lot of original writ-ing. After all, it is still programming, and to most of us, it's not especially fun (though learning some skills and tricks from chapter 12 will help).

HTML Text Editors

HTML documents are written in plain text (ASCII) format and can be created using any text editor or word processing program, even the Mac's SimpleText. There are also specific HTML editors available to facilitate document creation, such as HoTMetaL for Sun Sparcstations, tkHTML for Windows, and HTML_Edit and BBEdit for Macintosh (see http://www.yahoo.com/Computers/World _Wide_Web/HTML_Editors for a good list of avail-able software). BBEdit, like more familiar word pro-cessing programs, has find/change, cut/paste, and change case functions, but in addition to these text editing tools, it has a palette of "Extensions" to au-tomatically create HTML tags. For example, typing Shift-Command-h, a command in the Extensions menu, creates a pair of Header tags with the cursor conveniently placed between them, ready to type the header copy. Or, you can highlight a text block and the same Shift-Command-h combination will place header tags around it. I hope you get the idea.

HTML Conversion Utilities

Fortunately, there are alternatives to writing actual HTML code. Utilities are available that convert exist-ing files, such as Microsoft Word 6 for Macintosh (http://www.netweb.com/cortex/content/software) or Windows (http://www.w3.org/hypertext/WWW/ Tools/HTML-Convertor.html), Excel for the Mac (http://www.rhodes.edu/software/ readme.html), Adobe PageMaker (http://www.bucknell. edu/ bucknellian/daveor http://www.iii. net/users

/mcohen/websucker.html), and QuarkXPress (see below) documents, into HTML format.

For example, HTML Xport, qt2www Perl script, and BeyondPress are HTML conversion utilities for QuarkXPress. One program, BeyondPress from Astrobyte (http://www.astrobyte.com), automates the conversion of Mac QuarkXPress documents into HTML format by establishing an editable Document Palette of icons that represent the content of the existing Quark document. These icons are the tools designers use to revise, edit, rearrange, and apply HTML tags to the Quark document contents. The changes made in this palette have no effect on the original Quark document—an important advantage. At the same time, any changes made to the original content of the Quark document will be evident in the HTML document. Options include the ability to revise and link original document elements: stories, headlines, and pictures. For example, to create linked text, you highlight the text you want to link, click on the linking icon in the Document Palette, and identify the item to form a link with in the dialog box that appears. BeyondPress's interface is familiar and easy to learn. The approach of altering an existing document accepts the fact that Internet documents should not necessarily duplicate their print-oriented cousins, but should maximize the linking and information structure of the Internet.

BeyondPress creates pointers to the text and image boxes of a Quark document to which it applies style and linking tags. The creation of pointers is what enables BeyondPress to permit changes made to the content of any box in the original Quark document to automatically update the HTML document as it is exported. The BeyondPress XTension, coupled with other XTensions to Quark that add interactivity and video file capability, make Quark a potent Web document design tool.

Other page creation programs, such as FrameMaker 5, have HTML conversion bundled as part of the functionality of the software, rather than offering it as an extension.

Either way, it's a great advantage as a designer to be able to work with a familiar page layout program to form the basis of a Web page. The software is comfortably familiar and productivity is immediately high. A disadvantage with a solution such as BeyondPress is that you must constantly switch back and forth between a Web browser and the Quark document to view the results of HTML formatting, since the Web document can't be viewed from within Quark.

HTML Document Layout Software

In response to the desire to immediately view the results of HTML encoding, there are several specific Web page authoring programs that function as both HTML editors and Web page viewer programs. WYSIWYG (What You See Is What You Get) programs such as Arachnid (http://sec-look.uiowa.edu/about/projects/arachnid-page.html) for the Mac and NaviPress (http://www.navisoft.com/homedoc/press/press.htm) for the Mac, Windows, or Unix enable you to see how the document will look onscreen as you are creating it.

Some of these programs employ the graphical user interface familiar to Mac users. Arachnid, from the University of Iowa, has a simple but functional palette for editing, linking, and adding objects such as buttons to create Web pages and documents. It works much like other document creation software. To import an image, you select Import Image in the File menu. As you are working, Arachnid offers help statements, such as "sorry, this file's name does not end with 'gif'," to help prevent simple mistakes.

Arachnid

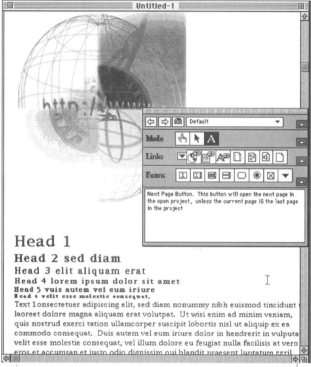

File Edit Format

While Arachnid offers WYSIWYG interaction, be warned that there is no guarantee that the appearance of your document in Arachnid is exactly the same as it will appear on a browser such as Netscape. Heads may not be the same size, for example. Even WYSIWYG isn't really WYSIWYG on the Net! To avoid unpleasant surprises, be sure to also view your Arachnid document on various popular browsers to see how it will look there. Oh, and one more thing: Arachnid, like most of the other products mentioned here, is still under development, so what you read here may change with future versions of the software!

In all of these WYSIWYG approaches, the HTML tags are automatically written into the Web document by the software as it is being designed, much the way PostScript formatting instructions are added unseen in page layout programs for print.

How each of these Web page creation options operate will have a dramatic effect on the process

change with future versions

"Thanks for you interest in Arachnid. Again, please remember that it is Beta software and will have some problems. We welcome any comments, feedback, problems, or ideas that you might have.

Subsequent versions of Arachnid can be accessed through the Internet by opening a connection from your browser to http://

continued on next page

designers use to design for the Internet. Using an extension to existing document creation software such as Quark necessitates the parallel use of a browser to view the HTML conversion results. This is an awkward process but has the advantage of beginning with an existing document that has already been designed. Using a WYSIWYG program obviously gives more direct feedback, but still is not an exact match of what users will see on their browsers.

None of the current Web design tools are excellent. With the state of the art, it makes sense to lay out a Web page using an existing software package with which the designer is already familiar, and use a conversion extension or filter to add the HTML tags. The alternatives are to learn HTML, which provides the most direct control, or to collaborate with an HTML programmer. Or, designers may simply refuse to use HTML and use an entirely different format, such as PDF (see the next section), to transfer formatted documents across the Internet. Designing for the Internet will continue to be problematic as a standard page description language emerges and evolves. This is similar to the way PostScript, now the dominant resolution-independent page description language for print publishing, revolutionized the printing industry. Until PostScript was adopted as the industry standard, it was difficult to make progress refining design tools.

PDF and Adobe Acrobat

Because the Internet is by definition a cross-platform environment, the design tools to create documents for it must address cross-platform issues. Adobe (http://www.adobe.com) created Adobe Acrobat software with its Portable Document Format (PDF) precisely to address these issues. While not specifically designed for the Internet and

sec look.uiowa.edu/ or http://sec-look. weeg.uiowa.edu/. There is a link on our Home Page to a page containing information on Arachnid and other projects we have developed or are currently developing."

http://sec-look.uiowa.edu/about/projects/ arachnid-page.html

Adobe Acrobat

"Adobe Acrobat software writes and reads (views) to a file format called Portable

continued on next page

Document Format (PDF). 'Portable' in this case means 'mobile' or able to be ported to different computer operating systems. The Portable Document Format is based on the PostScript programming language, also from Adobe Systems."

Patrick Ames, *Beyond Paper*, p. 26

not nearly as widely used as HTML right now, Adobe Acrobat has the potential to seriously challenge the dominance of HTML as the Internet standard page description language. Unlike HTML, Acrobat is proprietary software. Designers do not write PDF code. Adobe's Acrobat software converts PostScript files from any PostScript-compatible software into PDF, a form that can be viewed and edited on most any computer platform. Like HTML, the recipient must have the appropriate software—Acrobat Reader, Acrobat Exchange, or a browser (Netscape, soon) that incorporates them—to view the document.

Creating a PDF document is like sending a document to a printer. No tags to write or programming to do. Select Print from your document's menu and "print" it to PDF writer rather than to a printer. The result is a compressed electronic version of the original document with a .pdf suffix. As in printing, the original document is left unchanged. After the file is transmitted, it is viewed by the receiver using Acrobat Reader, a simple view- and print-only version of the application, or Acrobat Exchange, a fully functional browser-like software that not only permits document viewing but enables annotating, printing, searching/finding, and linking within files as well. Acrobat Exchange's features go well beyond those offered on most browsers, such as the ability to scan through a document in thumbnail view, create bookmarks within documents, move around a page in any direction, and zoom in or out on any portion of a page.

linking within files

"Another feature of Acrobat Exchange is its 'Link Tool.' With it a user creates 'link buttons' from one part of a document to another."

Patrick Ames, *Beyond Paper*, p. 53

And perhaps what is best for designers, Acrobat retains the layout of the original document, including text and pictures. And unlike HTML, Acrobat makes a close approximation of the type fonts selected for the original document. This means you can create documents using your favorite software and fonts, with the expectation that the recipient will see exactly what the designer intended. Well, almost exactly. Acrobat solves the type font problem by creating the PDF document using fonts that mimic the fonts used by the document designer. Carefully designed <u>multiple master fonts</u> in Acrobat Distiller, the

<u>multiple master fonts</u>

"When you create a PDF file...information about the font(s) that you use is included in that PDF file. When someone else opens your PDF file, Acrobat technology will substitute the Adobe Serif or the Adobe Sans typefaces (or both) for the original typefaces that you used. Multiple master typefaces can do this because they offer an unlimited palette of font variations as well as the ability to generate custom fonts on the fly. They do this by using a design matrix based on one or more variables: weight, width, size and style."

Patrick Ames, *Beyond Paper*, p. 90-91

original file

font substitution

software that translates PostScript to PDF, adapt themselves to simulate the original document fonts, avoiding <u>font substitution</u> problems. The multiple master interpretations are quite good in some cases, but they aren't the same as the originals.

font substitution

These illustrations show what often happens *without* PDF's multiple master font technology: font substitution.

Another format competing for cross-platform document exchange dominance is Lotus Notes. With a significant installed base and its acquisition by IBM, it has the potential to be a player on the Net. Although HTML is the current Internet standard, alternative document definitions such as PDF and Notes are moving aggressively to service the

Internet. Adobe's PDF position on the Internet is strengthened by its agreement with Netscape Communications, the leading browser company, to integrate the Acrobat Viewer into Netscape. Adobe has also created Acrobat Weblink as a plug-in for Netscape that will let users link Acrobat PDF documents to other documents on the Internet. If PDF documents can be viewed and linked on browsers much the way HTML documents can be, and if one looks at Acrobat's expanded viewing, browsing, and annotating functionality, one wonders if designers late to work on the Internet might not choose to never bother with HTML.

VRML and 3-D Web Software

Walking on the Web is also possible using 3-D viewers and authoring tools that are emerging. They will allow the construction and viewing of three-dimensional spaces that people can navigate through via the Internet. The Virtual Reality Modeling Language (VRML) promises to be the standard that will enable Internet clients to soar through 3-D worlds—cities, buildings, and anything else. VRML is written in Silicon Graphics' Open Inventor ASCII file format, much like HTML. This area is definitely under development. The best advice is to watch these sites and others for details as they unfold. Who knows what graphic designers might get into next....

Viewers can link through world after world and designers can use 3-D models to create and display information. A home builder might make model homes available on the Internet to workers transferring from other cities, providing each person with a virtual tour of a potential new home. VRML editors will enable 3-D content creation programs to convert 3-D images to HTML much the way BeyondPress converts Quark documents. A full 3-D room is reported to take no more than 100K. These

VRML

For information on VRML, see: http://vrml. wired.com

Internet clients

http://www.sgi.com/Products/WebFORCE/ WebSpace

http://www.hyperion.com/intervista/ technology.html

tools are evolving rapidly, making it too early to say much now.

Not only will browsers support VRML, but some Web browsers are promised that will utilize a 3-D model, rather than a text-based model, to link to documents on the Net. Stay tuned.

Graphics

In addition to the tools that directly design documents and links for the Net, a variety of more familiar design tools are important as well. Page layout and illustration programs are of course useful for creating images.

Web pages require images in GIF or JPEG format. Since these are not common formats for print publishing, most scanned images will require conversion using programs such as Photoshop, Fractal Painter, or a conversion utility such as GraphicConverter (see chapter 12 for tricks and skills).

For example, to convert an image to GIF in Photoshop, you open a file, either scanned or saved from a drawing program such as FreeHand or Illustrator, and make it RGB. Since computer monitors are lower resolution than image files created for print, it is often good to add a step to make sure the image is low resolution, only 72 dpi. Otherwise the resolution of the file will make it too large to download efficiently. Then change the RGB file to Indexed Color, which constrains it to 256 colors, and save it in the CompuServe GIF file format.

Newer versions of HTML support background transparency in GIF images. This is accomplished using applications such as Transparency (ftp://ftp.med. cornell.edu/pub/aarong/transparency). Just dragging your GIF file on top of the application icon launches Transparency; you click on the single color

---

conversion

An excellent shareware program for converting image file types on a Macintosh is Graphic-Converter, which is available from most large Macintosh FTP archives and also available at http://wwwhost.ots.utexas.edu/mac/ pub-mac -graphics.html. Of course, you can also save indexed color files in CompuServe GIF format in Photoshop.

Windows users can download LView Pro from ftp://oak.oakland.edu/SimTel/win3/graphics to accomplish the same thing.

(only one of the 256 can be transparent) in your image that you want to be transparent. Again, check out chapter 12 for transparency tricks.

Converting images to JPEG is equally as easy, but here, you may want to add a step to ensure that the image is RGB, not CMYK, because RGB is the only color space used by computer monitors and CMYK files are always larger than RGB. As I mention in chapter 12, there are specific times when GIF is preferable to JPEG and vice versa.

Audio

Listening to the Internet is as easy as one, two, three. Most Web browsers support the downloading of audio files. A site such as Perspective (http://jcomm.uoregon.edu/~perspect), a weekly radio journal of public affairs produced by students in the School of Journalism and Communication at the University of Oregon, has hot button links to audio files. Once downloaded, these audio documents (often several megabytes in size) can be played back. If you are using Netscape and a helper application is available on your computer, Netscape will automatically launch the helper, which will play back the file for you. Easy as, well, you know. Helper applications include SoundMachine (ftp://ftp.ncsa.uiuc.edu/Mosaic/Mac/Helpers) or SoundApp (ftp://sunsite.unc.edu/pub/multimedia/utilities/mac/audio) for the Mac, or Wham (ftp://gatekeeper.dec.com/pub/micro/msdos/win3/sounds), Wplany (ftp://ftp.cdrom.com/.5/cica/sounds), or Cool Edit (http://www.ep.se/cool) for Windows.

Audio files can also be heard on the Internet in real time using products such as RealAudio (http://www.realaudio.com). Like other helper applications, this software is able to play audio files; but unlike other programs, RealAudio files play in real time. This makes it easy to listen to past radio

SoundMachine

This program plays and records SND/AU (mu-law, A-law, linear) and AIFF/AIFC (MACE3, MACE6) sound files. There are a plethora of buttons during play to change speed, play backwards, loop sounds, switch formats, etc. And there's no restriction on file size; playing can take place in the background.

programs from National Public Radio (http://www.npr.org), for example. The RealAudio format allows the sound to play *while* it downloads, not after the whole file has been downloaded. When you have finished listening, the file disappears. RealAudio not only saves download time but also greatly enhances the Internet audio experience.

There are a variety of computer tools to record, edit, and convert sound files. Similar to the way images must be digitized, analog audio must be digitized to be used on the Internet. The Net supports WAV (.wav) (primarily for Windows) and AIFF (.au) audio file formats. Once digitized, editors such as SoundHack (http://hyperarchive.lcs.mit.edu/cgi-bin/NewSearch?key=SoundHack) or Sound Extractor (http://hyperarchive.lcs.mit.edu/cgibin/NewSearch?key=SoundExtractor) for the Mac, or Cool Edit (http://www.ep.se/cool) for Windows will help you get started with the editing process. This said, there are few graphic designers equipped to grapple with the intricacies of creating audio files, so this a likely area to consult with an expert.

And as always, the tools of choice are subject to evolve as quickly as everything else on the Internet, so these programs and URLs may disappear. Your best bet is to keep a constant eye on Yahoo (http://www.yahoo.com) for the latest and greatest in each category.

Video

Like audio, preparing video for the Internet requires an expert's knowledge and advice. For our purposes, let's just say that video tends to come in three formats on the Net: MPEG (.mpg), the most popular; QuickTime (.mov), still primarily Mac; and AVI (.avi), a Windows format.

For helper applications to play movie files on a Mac,

check out Sparkle (ftp://ftp.ncsa.uiuc.edu/ Mosaic/Mac/Helpers) for MPEG movies, MoviePlayer (which comes with QuickTime from Apple) for QuickTime movies, and AVI to QuickTime Converter (ftp://ftp.tidbits.com/pub/tidbits /tisk/util) for dealing with AVI files. For Windows, try MPEGplay (ftp://ftp.tidbits.com/pub/tiskwin) for MPEGs and Microsoft Video for Windows Runtime (ftp://ftp.eden.com/pub/pc/win/video) for AVIs. For QuickTime movies, you'll need QuickTime for Windows (ftp://ftp.ncsa.uiuc.edu/Mosaic/ Windows/viewers) and the Windows Media Player (ftp://ftp.tidbits.com/pub/tiskwin). Got all that? Good.

As you can imagine, movie files are huge and few people can afford the time to download them. So they're not that popular on the Net, though that could certainly change as bandwidth opens up in the future.

The Need for New Web Design Software

By now it should be glaringly obvious that better Internet design tools are needed. I believe that richer standard page description formats are required in order to develop the tools designers need. The situation is dynamic, with many potential standards in competition: HTML, Java, PDF, etc. It is not clear whether one standard, such as HTML or its successor, will emerge as dominant, or whether we'll have a suite of compatible standards. But standards will emerge or Internet design will languish in the design stone age.

As a powerful set of standards emerges, Internet design tools will be developed that move beyond the crude ones that now exist. Existing design tools are all unacceptable as final solutions, because they are based on document formats that are inadequate. Better design tools will enable designers to take full advantage of the Internet's amazing potential. The state of the art is plainly poor when it is heralded as a major new development that you can actually control the background color of your document (see chapter 12 on the differences between HTML 2.0 and 3.0). That is, you can control it on certain browsers! Of course, there are still browsers that don't even support images, so I guess color is a small worry!

Too much of the Web document is still beyond the control of the designer. This currently fits the idiosyncratic, democratic, individualistic personality of the Internet, but it does not contribute to good design. It is similar to writing with a keyboard that randomly substitutes a new letter for every fifth "e." The tools have potential, the emerging standards have potential, and the Internet has potential that is far from realized.

Potential is also the just the right word for design on the Internet. From a designer's perspective, the quality of visual design on the Net leaves a lot to be desired (see chapter 14). Someday soon the excitement will wear off and quality will have to replace enthusiasm as the driving force of design on the Internet. As tools improve and experience using them increases, it will happen. Soon.

Training and Education Needs

Of course, all of these new tools mean reeducation—not only once but continually, as new standards are proposed and tried and spawn new design tools based upon them. This era is similar to the early days of desktop design, when design firms frequently bought and tried both Illustrator and FreeHand before settling on a preferred drawing program. In the end, one tool sits on the shelf collecting dust and good people spent time learning a program that they will never use again. It is a wasteful and stressful thing to live on the bleeding edge. Until clear winners emerge in Internet design, the situation will remain somewhat chaotic and stressful.

Most designers enjoy learning—it seems to come with the profession: learning about new clients, new industries, new visual styles and trends. But forced learning is stressful. Designers are just assimilating into the desktop publishing revolution. Printers are just establishing smooth operations following the digital design revolution.

And now this. More equipment to figure out, new standard languages to learn, file transfer protocols to become familiar with—it's quite a stretch. And it's not really voluntary. The importance of the Internet will force itself on all of us, whether we want it to or not. Just try ordering type for a design project in hot metal. It isn't going to happen that way except in craft shops and museums. Begin training now, because the future is here.

Chapter 12

Developing New Skills

This chapter suggests some skills that need to be

developed to use the new tools effectively.

Act IV

Scene 3

SOS Design in the heat of Web page development.

Kit: "What the hey?! John, come here, look what happened to my type when it hits the browser…. It's got a halo or something."

John: "Whoa! Look at that. Wait a minute, I think I know what might be happening. Let me try something. I'll get back to you later."

Thirty minutes later.

John: "Hey Kit, I think I figured it out…. It was antialiasing that caused the halo. Look at this…."

Boundaries

Every tool has limits. Internet tools are no different. Creative people have long known that the tools' limits are the birthplace of skill and technique. The creative mind is stimulated by the challenge of finding a way to circumvent the boundaries. Often it is in the boundary between what is possible, what is desirable, and what is true to the medium that artistry happens. The tools and technologies necessary for designing on the Internet are no different. How can I design for multiple browsers, overcome bandwidth limitations, or overcome HTML's limits? The answers lie in the tools themselves. This chapter is about using those tools well.

Then again, the tools for designing for the Net are different. Maybe it's because the medium is so new and so complex that the design tools are so limiting. HTML, as discussed in chapter 11, has a limited ability to control document form, though its flexibility is increasing. What's more, the specifics of designing Internet documents are in constant flux because HTML is being extended officially—through standards committees—and unofficially—when new browsers add features that are unavailable on other browsers. Equipment will get better, and browsers more powerful. In the future, the specifics of designing documents will continue to change.

Now that the worst is out of the way, there is a lot designers *can* do with current versions of HTML and current browsers. This chapter approaches several underlying problems that are not likely to go away any time soon, and discusses solutions in terms of HTML, browsers, platforms, and Internet services as they typically exist in late 1995. This chapter does not pretend to be a comprehensive guide to HTML. There are many sources, both <u>online</u> and in <u>print</u>, that will answer this need.

online

A Beginner's Guide to HTML
http://www.ncsa.uiuc.edu/demoweb/html-primer.html

Netscape's Creating Net Sites
http://home.netscape.com/home/how-to-create-web-services.html
(This can also be reached under the Help menu in Netscape as How to Create Web Services.)

The Yale C/AIM WWW Style Manual
http://info.med.yale.edu/caim/Style Manual_Top.HTML

Also, see the HTML Glossary on the Designer's Guide to the Internet Web site with all tags currently available.

http://www.zender.com/designers-guide-net

continued on next page

print

Teach Yourself Web Publishing with HTML in a Week (Sams Publishing; ISBN: 0-672-30667-0).

Web Design Guide (Hayden Books; ISBN: 1-56830-171-5).

Netscape: Creating Net Sites

Back | Forward | Home | Reload | Images | Open | Print | Find | Stop

Netsite: http://home.netscape.com/home/how-to-create-web-services.html

What's New? | What's Cool? | Handbook | Net Search | Net Directory | Newsgroups

A S S I S T A N C E

CREATING NET SITES

So you've been wandering the Web for a while now, and you're ready to start contributing to the great flow of information on the Internet. The first thing to do is learn about HTML (HyperText Markup Language), the standard language used by Netscape Navigator and other browsers to bring documents to your screen. Next, you'll want to learn about adding on-line forms, graphics, sound, and video - taking advantage of the interactive and multimedia capabilities of the Web. And once you understand the basics and start coding pages like mad, you'll want to find some development tools to make your work easier.

And remember: You can always ask questions and swap stories in any of the NUGgies, Netscape's own on-line user groups or the comp.infosystems.www.* newsgroups.

The Viewing Environment

Every document that is part of the World Wide Web is viewed inside a "viewing environment." By this I mean the particular platform and type of browser

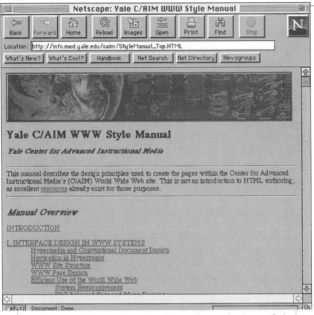

that is used, the color depth and resolution of the
monitor, and the speed of the Internet connection.
The viewing environment I am most accustomed to
is a Macintosh Quadra, with a 72 dpi monitor, running Netscape 1.1, with a 64 Kbps connection to the

Netscape 1.1 (Macintosh)

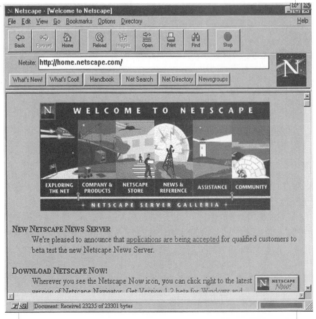

Internet. Another environment is a 486 Windows
clone running NCSA Mosaic with a 28.8 Kbps PPP

continued on next page

Netscape 1.1 (Windows)

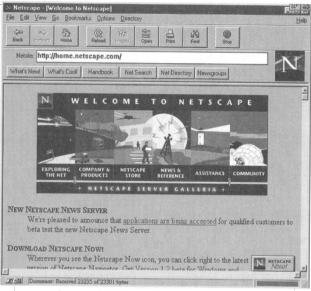

connection. Still another is a dial-in Unix shell, running Lynx, a common text-only browser.

Lynx

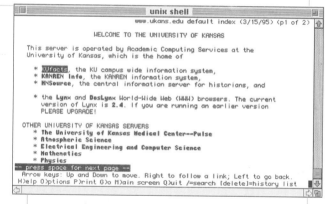

Referring to the viewing environment is a way to
sum up all of the possible variables that can affect
the way a document is viewed on the Web. Good design technique means creating documents that are
functional and aesthetic in most of these possible
environments.

The Document Creation Format

To be blunt, HTML as it currently exists can seem extremely limiting. Often, the lack of precise control
over how Web documents are going to look is disap-
pointing to experienced print designers. In a per-

verse way, HTML's limitations have actually helped the World Wide Web's early development by reducing visual noise. Most home pages look remarkably the same because what you can do is so limited.

The design tool is so limited that it has created its own distinctive visual form language. It's not a particularly good or interesting or beautiful language, but it's consistent. This has helped early adopters navigate from home page to home page with a sense of familiarity and without getting lost in the process. While creative people may be stimulated by the challenge of pushing a tool to its limits, to really push the edge of what is possible within HTML, designers need a certain degree of programming ability. This is likely to change as tools continue to evolve, but it is a fact of HTML life for now.

Of course there are those potential alternatives to HTML, such as Adobe's PDF format. As I said in chapter 11, PDF, if adopted widely on the Web, would be

PDF

PDF (Portable Document Format) attempts to include enough information to faithfully reproduce a document as it is designed. This means including every font and image with the document, which can result in very large files. Still, Acrobat isn't perfect. It often has to resort to approximations to allow a document to be viewed on different platforms. Since the Acrobat Viewer is available for free, PDF files are a good way to distribute large paper documents, such as manuals, over the Internet.

http://www.adobe.com/Acrobat

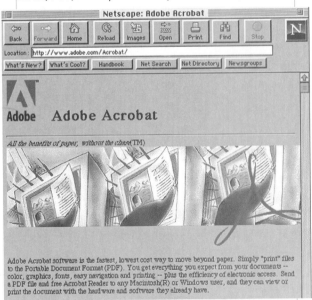

an easy solution for designers creating Web pages, since they could use familiar page layout and illustration software to create documents. And at this point, software programs such as QuarkXPress,

continued on next page

Acrobat Viewer on a Macintosh

PageMaker, FreeHand, and Illustrator have few of HTML's design limitation problems.

Others are aware of HTML's limitations. As I said previously, HTML is evolving to the point where two versions are available, 2.0 and 3.0, the latter still under development but prereleased with greatly expanded capability. One improvement in HTML 3.0 is the ability to control the background color of the browser. This is a small change, but significant for designers. Another is the use of table tags to define text areas. This allows for the vertical alignment of columns of text, whereas HTML 2.0 was limited to horizontal bands of text. More on this later.

HTML 2.0 can be properly interpreted by virtually every browser available, whereas 3.0 is still awaiting full adoption. The only exception to 2.0's acceptance would be viewers such as Lynx. Because Lynx presents documents inside of the standard text-only terminal screen, it preserves the structure of a document but does not allow images or different sizes and styles of text to be displayed.

What Can HTML Do?

Good books are available that teach HTML (see them listed a few pages back), but for your reference, a brief summary of <u>HTML</u> features follows.

HTML

Documents describing current proposed and finalized versions of HTML are available at http://www.w3.org/hypertext/WWW/MarkUp/MarkUp.html.

HTML 2.0 Control Tags

The **title** tags appear in the menu bar of most browsers.

Text **headings** can appear in one of six different sizes. They subdivide a Web page just like the headings and subheadings within this chapter.

Paragraphs and **line breaks** are significant because, with the exception of preformatted text (which I'll mention in a bit), any number of spaces are collapsed into a single space.

Links to other documents is probably the most important feature, making hypertext possible. A link can connect to other documents or to a different location in the same document. Links can also connect to completely different kinds of information, such as email addresses, Telnet terminals, Gopher sites, and Usenet newsgroups. Other file types, such as certain graphics, sound, and movie files that the browser can't display itself will be downloaded to the local disk drive so they can be viewed in another program. Most browsers keep a memory of traversed links (links that have been clicked on). Most often, untraversed links are displayed in blue and traversed links appear purple (though Netscape enables people to change these colors). This feature is a bit like leaving breadcrumbs behind as you explore the Web.

Lists can be bulleted (or unnumbered) or numbered, which replaces the bullets with numbers. Lists can be nested to create a complex, outline-style structure. A definition list is a less commonly used variant that allows text to be structured similarly to entries in a dictionary.

Preformatted text causes a block of text to be displayed exactly as it appears in a monospaced display, like a typewriter. One of the benefits of this is that all your spaces are left intact, not collapsed down to one space. This is often used for simple tables, for displaying a program listing, or for including text from other sources when you don't want to reformat it in HTML.

Blockquotes are indented quotation blocks.

Address blocks are a standard method of describing the author's email address. These references are often found at the bottom of a Web page.

There are several type styles possible, grouped into **Logical Styles** and **Physical Styles**. Logical Styles describe meaning, such as "emphasized" or "definition." The browser has considerable freedom to interpret these styles. For example, "emphasized" text might be displayed as bold, italics, or bold/italics, depending on the browser used. Physical Styles, on the other hand, describe direct type changes, such as "bold" or "italic."

Images can be included in-line—they can be inserted between any characters which may appear there. Like text, images can be used as links. A variant, the **imagemap**, enables different areas of an image to link to different documents. A text block can be provided as an alternative if users have a browser that cannot display images. There are several other variables that can also be controlled with images, such as aligning the top, bottom, or middle of the image with the line of text in which it appears. Newer extensions to HTML enable other variables to be controlled, such as the display area and the size of a border around the image.

Horizontal rules are thin lines stretching from the left margin to the right margin, often used to divide content.

Isindex search engine support provides a standard way for the user to input text into a single field. This text can be passed to external software by the server. The standard application for this feature is a search engine, enabling one to search directories, documents, and so on. A clever programmer can find many other uses for the feature. The tag has been effectively made obsolete by the more flexible **form** support that is standard in most browsers now.

Form elements enable the creation of complex forms within HTML documents. There are tags to describe text fields, checkboxes, radio buttons, pop-up menus, scrolling menus, and more. After people fill out the form, they click on a "submit" button to transmit the information to the server. At this point, there are no easy systems for nonprogrammers to create the external programs needed to interpret forms.

You may have noticed that many of these features, such as address blocks and logical styles, refer to the meaning of part of a document more than what it should actually look like. The idea, at least at the beginning, was that HTML should be used above all to describe the *structure* of a document, leaving the specific visual interpretation to the browser itself. This helped to keep pages consistent, provided a certain degree of machine readability (such as a program that automatically extracts definitions or author information), and encouraged the development of browsers by not placing many restrictions on their design.

HTML 3.0, which when this book was written was still officially only a draft standard, extends the functionality of HTML, making more precise visual control of documents possible. The only browser, at this time, to implement anything from HTML 3.0 is

Netscape 1.1. Netscape doesn't implement the whole specification, only a few important parts of it, such as tables. However, Netscape has been pushing the development of HTML by including its own extensions (or additions) to HTML. I would guess that, since most of these features are useful, most other browsers will eventually follow suit.

Netscape Tags

Netscape 1.1 supports an extended set of HTML tags which are, at the time this book was published, not available in any other browser. Most of these tags are proposed in the HTML 3.0 draft spec, but many of them are of Netscape Corporation's own devising.

The most significant new feature is the **table**, which enables the description of complex tables with variable numbers of rows and columns. The relative and absolute size of the table, the width of the border between cells, and the amount of white space between cells are all variable. Also, cells can cross more than one column or row, and the borders can be completely turned off if desired. Netscape 1.1 goes beyond the draft specifications, enabling you to nest tables inside of an individual cell in another table. Tables are significant because they allow objects to be placed more precisely within horizontal and vertical constraints. Information can be aligned in rows and columns instead of in just one long linear block.

No-break blocks of text can be defined to prevent text from word wrapping at the edge of the window.

Additional **image control** tags are provided that enable more precise control of alignment and enable you to modify the width of borders around images.

The thickness, width, and shading of **horizontal rules** can be defined.

> **extensions**
> Netscape's extensions are described at http://home.netscape.com/assist/net_sites/html_extensions.html, which can be reached through the How to Create Web Services option under the Help menu in Netscape.

The **size of text** can be modified within seven relative sizes.

Text and images can be **centered** on the page.

The **color of text** can be modified, including the three different colors that linked text can assume: traversed, untraversed, and active (the color a link takes on while your mouse is clicked down over it).

The **color of the background** can be modified.

A **background pattern** can be specified. A referenced image is tiled to cover the entire background.

Text can be assigned to **blink** on screen. This is usually annoying, but often useful to convey some urgent information.

Netscape also added a feature called dynamic documents, which includes **client pull** and **server push**. These enable a document to update itself without the user's intervention. The classic example is a stock quotes page, where the data is updated continuously. This feature will only be useful to people that are willing to do some programming.

All of these features are difficult to understand without seeing them in action. The best way to understand them, like most anything, is to experiment. Look at Web pages, view their source to see how they were created, and try to create your own using the same options. It doesn't take long to see what is possible.

Techniques and Tricks

Instead of my explaining what each of these tags can do on their own, we're going to make use of most of them to create a hypothetical site, Yoyodyne Juggling Equipment. As I mentioned before, we're not going to concentrate on learning HTML—there are plenty of good references for that. Instead, we will discuss the design of a simple page, using

dynamic documents
For more information, read about Netscape's Dynamic Document Features at http://home.netscape.com/assist/net_sites/dynamic_docs.html.

hypothetical   site
All of these example documents are available online at http://www.zender.com/designers-guide-net/yoyodyne. It will be easier to under-

continued on next page

this example to explain techniques for overcoming some of the problems you are likely to encounter designing any document for the Internet. The HTML code for these pages is included, with detailed comments, in appendix B and on the Designer's Guide to the Internet Web site.

stand these examples if you look at them on your computer rather than relying on the screen shots in this book.

First, some background information. Yoyodyne is a small retailer of juggling supplies and equipment. We have been contracted to design its home page. Yoyodyne has given us a simple description of its page. They want the company logo and options for Equipment Catalog, Equipment Ordering, Company Information, and Cool Juggling Links. They also want a short description of the company on this page. They were very clear about something else, though. They want as many people as possible to view their page, but they want it to look good by everyone who views it.

Problem: Designing for Multiple Browsers

Ideally, we'd all like to design simply for Netscape, since its extensions currently give the most design power. However, there is a decent chance our viewers will not be using Netscape to look at the document, especially if they are connected through one of the packaged online services such America Online or NetCruiser and are using their browsers.

The trick to successful design with these variables is creating documents that look good within any of the various Web browsers that are available. The browsers are given much freedom to decide exactly how to interpret most of these commands, so emphasis must be placed on the *structure* of your document, not its exact visual appearance. The earliest tags, such as title, heading, and author tags, attempted to actually describe the meaning of text, not simply the appearance of text. Each browser could interpret the tag as it wished, as long as it enforced the meaning.

Getting to know the ways different browsers interpret the same information is the only way to get really good at this. You shouldn't have to deliberately exclude browsers for most applications. Occasionally, you'll want to take advantage of special features of one browser, such as Netscape, but alternatives should almost always be provided for people with other systems. One thing is on our side: If a browser encounters an HTML tag it doesn't understand, it ignores it. There are many features of better browsers that you can take advantage of, knowing that the extra information will be ignored by older browsers.

yoyo-simple.html

yoyo-simple.html in Netscape

(Macintosh)

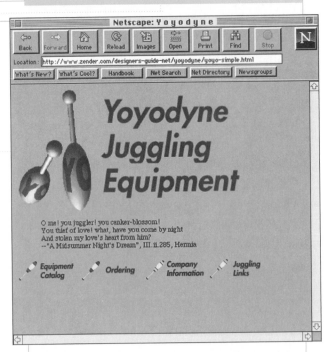

This Web page design was purposely kept simple to illustrate a few useful techniques which we'll look at separately: using horizontal default layout, using transparent color and other image-enhancing techniques, staying compatible with text-only browsers,

continued on next page

yoyo-simple.html in Netscape (Windows)

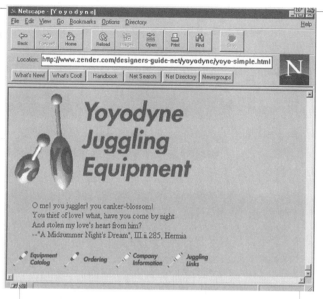

yoyo-simple.html in MacWeb

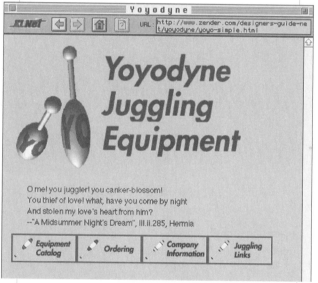

yoyo-simple.html in Lynx

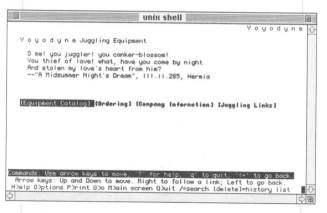

squeezing the best performance out of limited bandwidth, and dealing with the differences of the many different types of viewing environments your documents will encounter.

Take a moment to look at the screen shots and see how each browser interprets the same document differently. MacWeb looks very similar to Netscape except the font is different, and, since MacWeb doesn't understand the tag that removes the border around linked images, there are thick rectangles around the four options at the bottom of the screen. Lynx, a text-only browser, doesn't even display any of the images. In there places, however, you see alternate text that was included as part of the image description. Notice the more subtle differences between Windows and Macintosh Netscape. Because the screen resolution on a Windows machine is higher, images appear smaller while the text stays roughly the same size. Look at appendix B for a more detailed explanation.

Solution: Use a Horizontal Default Layout

The largely horizontal layout you see in MacWeb is a result of the difficulty MacWeb has in describing vertical screen elements in HTML 2.0. Keeping elements arranged in rows ensures that every browser will be able to interpret the page correctly.

Solution: Make GIFs with a Transparent Color

The nonrectangular picture elements at the bottom of the screen take advantage of a feature of GIF files that enables us to define a <u>transparent</u> color. Any one color in the file's color table can be marked as transparent. If a browser understands the transparent option, the background color will show through in any pixel of this marked color. Since there are still a few browsers that don't understand the transpar-

transparency

Transparency is a very simple shareware application for the Mac that enables you to assign transparent colors. It is available at ftp://ftp. med.cornell.edu/pub/aarong/transparency. There's also a useful plug-in for Photoshop

continued on next page

ent option, it's good to pick a nonobtrusive color, such as gray, as your transparent background.

Transparency also makes more precise font control possible, if you are willing to make the trade-off of increased file size. Right now, the only way to guarantee the font you select will be the font that arrives on users' browsers is to make your type a bitmapped image. This results in an often-unwanted rectangular color box around the type image, which can be eliminated by setting this color to transparent. Unless the type is exceedingly large, this can create its own problem, giving the type jagged edges that destroy readability.

By creating your type image in a program such as Photoshop, you can antialias the type edges. This too can create a new problem by making a <u>halo</u> or glow from the antialiasing. If when you make the type you are careful to make its background color the same as that specified for the background color of the browser, the halo will disappear, dramatically improving the text's appearance.

Solution: Maintain Compatibility with Text-Only Browsers

The ALT tag is best used to make the Web page viewable for those using Lynx, a text-only browser. The ALT tag enables you to specify a short text string that will be displayed if the image cannot be displayed. Netscape will display the string if the user has turned image loading off to reduce download time. For more information, see the code listings in appendix B.

Solution: Change Image Borders

The BORDER tag is used to turn off the link borders surrounding the images. Since our menu choice icons are irregularly shaped, the border interferes

called PhotoGIF (http://dezine.msg.net/ boxtop). Windows users might try WinGIF (ftp://ftp.best.com/pub/craig/windows_apps).

halo

If you use Adobe Photoshop to design images, it probably won't be long before you notice that there's an annoying band of color around some of your images after you define a background color. This is caused by Photoshop's antialiasing feature. In most cases, antialiasing is a good idea, since it effectively increases screen resolution, making images and text easier to see and read. Since antialiasing achieves its effect by fuzzing the edges of images with several shades of a color, but only a single color can be defined as transparent, some of the old color will inevitably be left behind. There are two good solutions to this problem:

1. Turn antialiasing off. This will result in a blockier edge, but this is more desirable than a halo.

2. Make your background color in Photoshop similar to the background color of your page (usually gray). The edge will be effectively antialiased to the background of your page. Not

continued on next page

with the page design. Unfortunately, not every browser understands this tag, as the MacWeb screen shot demonstrates.

Solution: Arrange with Tables

Netscape's table features give us considerably more design flexibility, as another possible Yoyodyne page shows. The code is listed in appendix B.

every color will be transparent, but the remaining colors will be so close to your background th at people won't notice. This enables you to stop blocky edges from appearing while still preventing the halos.

Yoyodyne page

yoyo-table.html in Netscape

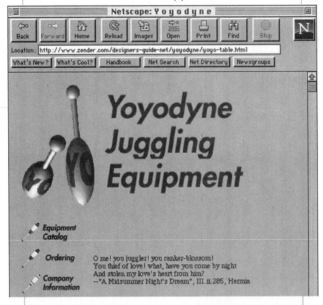

yoyo-table.html in Mosaic

continued on next page

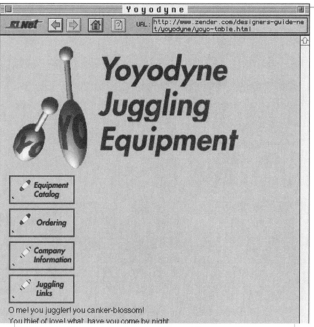

Because the table feature enables us to arrange elements vertically as well as horizontally, we can make our page design a bit more distinctive. Unfortunately, non-Netscape browsers won't be able to deal with these pages in the same way. Mosaic cannot control the table border, so thick lines appear between the elements. Other browsers can't even display the tables.

Solution: Use Alternate Document Branches

One common solution to the problem of varying browsers is to actually prompt users early on for the style of page they wish to view. One branch is lowest common denominator (text-only Lynx), and the other branch is for people with the most feature-rich browsers (Netscape). The same technique can be used to create branches for low- and high-bandwidth connections. A better solution is to create documents that react to the type of browser being used.

A better solution

When a browser contacts an HTTP server, it identifies itself with a unique identification string. Netscape 1.1N on a 68000 Mac identi-

continued on next page

Solution: Design Documents So Old Tags May Be Dropped

Remember that browsers simply ignore all tags that they do not understand. If you can design a page that still looks appropriate when all the table tags are removed, the document will be able to reach a wider audience. Obviously, this technique requires being very comfortable with HTML. In yoyo-table2.html, we moved the icon bar to the right side of the screen. See what this looks like in Netscape. This caused it to appear linearly in the code, after

yoyo-table2.html in Netscape

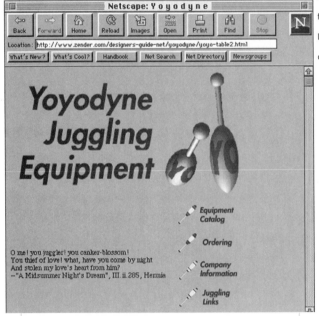

fies itself as "Mozilla/1.1N (Macintosh; I; 68K)." Other information is returned as well, such as the kinds of images that can be decoded and level of HTML that can be interpreted. By making use of CGI, the Common Gateway Interface, which allows external programs to be executed by an HTTP server, one can actually react to the type of browser a person is using. Check out http://www.zender.com/designers-guide-net/code for an example of a Perl script that does just this. For more information about coding CGIs, look at the listing in Yahoo at http://www.yahoo.com/Computers.

the text. A few extra BR tags caused line breaks to appear in the right places. The same document, when interpreted in Lynx or MacWeb looks like yoyo-simple.html. Some cleverness allows us to do what seems impossible. Create one document that takes advantage of a layout only possible with the new table tags, but still looks okay on an old browser. Again, check the code listing in appendix B for a detailed description of the changes.

yoyo-table2.html in Lynx

yoyo-table2.html in MacWeb

continued on next page

continued on next page

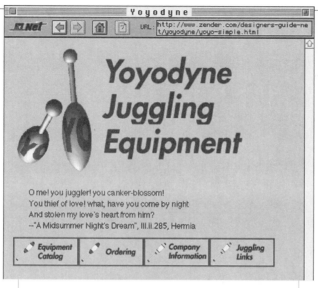

Solution: Check Macintosh vs. Windows

There are some more subtle differences between the same browsers on different platforms that one should keep in mind. Windows machines typically offer higher screen resolution (96 dpi) than Macintosh (which is almost always 72 dpi). This will cause images displayed on a Windows machine to be physically smaller on-screen than the same image on a Mac.

This wouldn't be a big deal, except that text on both machines appears roughly the same size despite the difference in resolution. If you design on a Mac, images will seem smaller and text relatively larger when you display it on a Windows machine.

Alternately, if you design on a Windows machine, large images that fit entirely within a default window on an average monitor may require scrolling to view on a Macintosh. You may not mind forcing users to widen the window, and this isn't a problem if they have a large monitor. However, people with entry-level machines will be unable to view the whole image at once. This is especially significant if you are designing a large graphical menu with choices that will appear horizontally across the screen. A good rule of thumb is to keep your pages about 470 pixels wide.

Problem: Dealing with Limited Bandwidth

At this time, the technical limitation that places the greatest restraint on design is certainly bandwidth. Bandwidth is measured in Kbs (kilobits per second) or Mbs (megabits per second) and is a dominating issue because it controls the rate of information flow. A 14.4 modem transfers data at an effective rate of about 1K per second. This means that a 10K file would cause someone to wait about ten seconds. This doesn't sound bad until you consider that a 500K photo, not very large by photo image standards, would require a wait of more than eight minutes, and a print-quality photo in the 20 MB range would tie up over 5.5 hours.

These times are totally unacceptable for a functional information source, not so much because of the cost of time online, but because of the sheer impatience of people. Instant access to information is possible, but it requires some skill to achieve. Careful document design will make files download faster or create the illusion of downloading faster. This is important since many users are via phone lines with relatively slow modem speeds. However, with the projected growth of the Internet, high-speed connections, even to average homes, are certainly possible within the decade.

The bulk of the total size of your Web page will always be image files, so it's a good place to start to develop skills. Compared to text, images are huge. To use a cliché, a picture is worth a thousand words. Actually, a 100K image file is worth around 17,000 words, in terms of memory usage. Most browsers can understand two main bitmapped file types: GIF and JPEG. Some browsers understand only GIF. Each of these types has its pros and cons, so there is no single correct choice for <u>converting</u> for every situation.

converting

An excellent shareware program for converting image file types on a Macintosh is GraphicConverter, which is available from most large Macintosh FTP archives and also available at http://wwwhost.ots. utexas.edu/ mac/pub-mac-graphics.html. Of course, you can also save indexed color files in CompuServeGIF format in Photoshop. Windows users can download LView Pro from ftp://oak.oakland.edu/SimTel/ win3/graphics to accomplish the same thing.

Solution: Use GIF Compression for Simple Images

GIF files describe images with a maximum of 256 colors. The 256 colors can be any colors out of the entire palette possible. GIF files will faithfully reproduce every pixel from your image when displayed on a browser. The only exception is when a color isn't possible to display on the hardware present in the viewing environment. In this case, browsers will make a best guess—usually the resulting change is difficult to notice, sometimes it is unacceptable.

GIF does offer some other advantages, such as transparency and interlacing. (It is not possible to describe a transparent color when using JPEG compression.) Interlacing causes an image to be displayed progressively during download, with detail added as new information arrives. I'll tell you more about interlacing later in this chapter.

GIF compresses very well when an image has large fields of solid color, such as the menu options in the Yoyodyne page. GIF doesn't compress nearly as well as JPEG with more complex images, but does guarantee that the image will be reproduced precisely, as long as its color palette is limited to 256 colors.

Solution: Use JPEG for More Complex Images

JPEG, on the other hand, is an approximate compression scheme. There are different levels of JPEG compression possible. You can give up some image detail in exchange for a smaller file, or keep as much detail as possible but end up with a large file. In most cases, close to maximum compression, which results in very small files, yields acceptable results. The best way to understand how JPEG works is to experiment with different compression results and view the output in a variety of situations, such as different color depth and different monitor hardware.

JPEG compresses much better than GIF with complex images such as photographs. Additionally, JPEG will reproduce more than 256 colors if the viewer's hardware allows it. When only 256 colors are available on the user's hardware, JPEG does a good job of dithering to approximate the original photo, something GIF is not nearly as good at. Unfortunately, sometimes only the precise color will do, such as when you want your image to match another image or a background color. Sometimes JPEG will modify a color just enough to create an unsatisfying result. Another problem: Not every browser can decode and display JPEG. The risk is usually worth the improvement in file size, since non-JPEG decoding browsers are definitely an endangered species.

Those of you trying to stay right on the edge should pay attention to the PNG, a proposed replacement for both these file types.

PNG

The Portable Network Graphics (PNG) specification effort, led by Thomas Boutell, promises to replace all these formats with a better, more flexible format. At this time, the specifications, in their tenth draft, are available at http://sunsite.unc.edu/boutell/png.html.

Solution: Place Many Small Images vs. One Big Image

Do you create your page with many small images or group as many images as possible together into one large image? As with all things, there is no definitive answer, but there are advantages and disadvantages to both options.

Many small images make it easier to create links inside of images, and will usually create a more flexible page design. Earlier, the second Yoyodyne table example wouldn't have been possible if we had grouped all the images together into one. Many images have another, not so obvious advantage: Most browsers cache—meaning that they store locally on your hard drive—all images that they have displayed on the screen during a session. If you create a group of pages using reusable, small image parts rather than whole new images every time, you will decrease the overall download time. As the viewer stores more and more of the images that appear in your group of pages, each page could load a bit more quickly.

On the other hand, many small images can be problematic, since each image has overhead associated with its download. By overhead, I mean the constant time that is needed to establish a connection and tear the connection down at the end of each download. If you have a lot of separate images, this overhead time will be a significant part of the total time needed to download a page. To reap the benefits of reusing images on many pages, your viewer may have to sit through a longer-than-normal download on the first page. Grouping images together into one larger block, then making use of imagemap techniques, provides an alternative, but will prevent the reuse of any smaller part of the image.

overhead

A proposed next generation version of HTTP, called HTTP-NG, would eliminate much of this overhead problem. To learn more about HTTP-NG, read about the specification at http://www.w3.org in the HTTP section.

Solution: Improve a User's Patience

Users, especially if they have a slow connection, will spend a lot of time waiting for images to download. Giving them little feedback as to what is going on will go a long way toward improving their patience. Good browsers such as Netscape inform users of

imagemap

Imagemaps are a way to define separate active regions within a larger image. Their use requires more interaction between the browser and the server than simple links, as well as some possible minor reconfiguration of the server, and setting everything up can be very difficult. WebMap for Macintosh (http://www.city.net/cnx/software/webmap.html) and

continued on next page

their current activity, providing progress meters at the bottom of the window. At minimum, if a file is large, you should give viewers the option to not download the image and warn them how large it is before they do choose to download it.

There are other things that can be done as well, such as GIF interlacing and low-res/high-res loading.

Solution: Make GIFs Interlaced

Interlacing was mentioned briefly earlier. When you convert a GIF file to interlaced, you reorder the information as it appears in the file. The beginning of the file has a very blocky, small description of the whole file. This description is loaded and displayed very quickly. Following this, the detail of the image is gradually filled in until every last pixel is properly colored. You have probably seen this happen if you have spent much time exploring the Web.

Converting GIFs to interlaced is easy and is more pleasing to see during download, so it should probably be done as much as possible. It also makes the image seem to load faster, enabling viewers to get a first look at it quickly and then decide if they want to wait around for the complete image. Beware, however: Occasionally one encounters a browser that doesn't deal properly with GIF interlacing.

Solution: Load Low-Res Then High-Res Images

Netscape has provided a new image tag: LOWSRC. LOWSRC lets you describe a small image to be loaded quickly, followed by a large image that will load more slowly. The LOWSRC gives the user something to look at while the full image is on its way.

The best way to understand LOWSRC is to see it in action. Check out http://www.zender.com/designers-guide-net/yoyodyne/lowsrc.html to see an example of usage in our Yoyodyne example. Or

MapEdit for Windows (http://sunsite.unc.edu/pub/packages/infosystems/WWW/tools/mapedit) speed up the creation of imagemaps. For more information on creating imagemaps, check out http://www.hway.com/ihip.

Converting GIFs

There are several good utilities for converting normal GIF files to interlaced. On the Macintosh, GIFConverter (http://wwwhost.ots.utexas.edu/mac/pub-mac-graphics.html) and Graphic Converter (ftp://sumex-aim.stanford.edu//info-mac/gst/grf) are good utilities. Windows users can use LView Pro (http://www.globalx.net/kerry/tbi.html) or VuePrint (http://www.primenet.com/~hamrick).

LOWSRC

A great description of how to implement LOWSRC is in the Yale C/AIM Style Manual. Check it out at http://info.med.yale.edu/caim/StyleManual_Top.HTML. The Style Manual also has many other useful tips.

look at screen shots of a page in two stages of loading. The one on the top shows only the <u>low-res image</u>.

low-res image

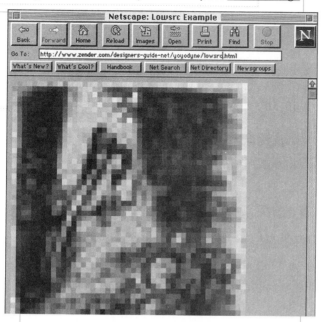

The one on the <u>bottom</u> shows how it looks once the rest of the information has been downloaded. As

high-res image

browsers become more sophisticated, techniques such as this should become more common and powerful, since most viewers will have to deal with a slow Internet connection for quite a while.

Solution: Try Some Tricks with the Page Title

There is one more trick that is even harder to demonstrate in print. If you're familiar with HTML or have been consulting the code examples, you know the TITLE tag usually appears at the top of the HTML document. While this is where it is supposed to appear, most browsers will interpret it even if it appears later in the document. Even better, if the browser encounters a TITLE tag more than once, it will interpret it each time, updating the information in the window title bar as each one is encountered. In a large document with lots of text, one could create 10 or even 20 title tags, each one displaying the amount of information loaded so far. The last tag would replace the status information with the real name of the page. To see this in action, check out http://www.zender.com/designers-guide-net/yoyodyne/longtxt.html.

Solution: Set Image Height and Width

A few browsers will interpret a WIDTH and HEIGHT tag used within an inline image tag. If you describe the exact size of the image in pixels using the tag, browsers will be able to format the rest of your page before any images have been downloaded. This is especially helpful if a user has turned off image loading to save time, since the layout of the rest of your page is preserved. Netscape will even display the contents of the ALT tag within the area used by the unloaded image. Setting the WIDTH and HEIGHT options to a size different from the actual size of the image also works, but some distortion will occur.

Problem: Designing a Beautiful, Functional Web Page

Despite the limited control that HTML provides and the primitive status of the software available for creating HTML documents, there is space to do quality work. HTML collapses white space, one of our favorite design tools, and HTML design tools are notably poor at sketching quickly and easily with good preview. This calls for good workarounds. In addition to the visual control, the design of the document's structure requires special attention. Large documents can force users to do an excessive amount of scrolling. With apology to Shakespeare: To scroll or not to scroll, that is the question.

Solution: Break Large Web Pages into Smaller Files

Should you group many files together into one single download or split up a large section into many separate, smaller Web pages? A large page can be convenient, with all information in one place. Separate parts of the page are accessible by using the scrollbar or by setting up internal links. Large files also tend to have large lists of choices, requiring users to scroll down to see every possible option. It's easy to miss something just because it appears just off-screen. In most cases, viewers shouldn't have to scroll to see important options.

Unfortunately, a large file can also take a long time to process. A smaller file will display more quickly, but will require many separate connections. Even so, this is often more desirable, especially in a large body of information, such as a hypertext version of this book, because the user may want only a portion of the information rather than the entire document. It is good to limit file size to no more than two or three 640 x 480 screens of information.

Solution: Control White Space

Since a browser will ignore any more than one space between characters when processing an HTML file, it can be difficult to control the blank space on a page. Usually, it is desirable to space visual elements out. There are a few ways to accomplish this.

Use the PRE tags, the preformatted text option. If you embed an image inside a large block of preformatted text, all spaces will be taken as significant. You can put in 20 spaces, an image, 10 more spaces, and another image and know all the spaces will be reproduced. Unfortunately, different browsers, and even the same browser between different platforms, will treat a single space differently. Depending on the choice of default type face and type size, your visual elements can end up in totally unintended places.

Use tables in Netscape. Tables will let you place an element nearly anywhere on the screen. There is a large tolerance to precisely where an element will be placed, but roughly the same relative placement will be preserved. Netscape's implementation of tables enables you to specify a relative size (when compared to the window size) or absolute size (in pixels) that the whole table object will assume. Again, browsers that don't support HTML 3.0 will simply ignore tables (see the previous section on designing for multiple browsers).

Use transparent GIFs. Using a 1 x 30 pixel GIF, with the entire image set to a transparent color, will let you specify a block of white space exactly 30 pixels wide. If you reuse the same spacer image multiple times, it will have to be loaded only once, so performance is not likely to be degraded significantly. In conjunction with tables, this technique can be very powerful.

Solution: Test Pattern Fills in Photoshop

Creating a pattern fill for a background is an efficient way to enhance a document's appearance, since only the small tile is downloaded—the client browser does the rest. Anticipating the exact appearance of a pattern fill is easy using Photoshop. Select or create an image, making sure the left and right, top and bottom edges are reflections of each other, copy using the Define Pattern command, open a new, larger document than the original file, and use the Pattern command in the Fill dialog box to fill the background of the new file with your sample tile. Repeating this operation until you identify the smallest tile that looks great will guarantee a tile that will work well in a browser.

Solution: Avoid Dithering

When you use GIF elements with large fields of a solid color, it's common for a certain degree of dithering to occur. The visual effect that comes across is a fuzzier, more mottled look to an area that you probably thought would be a solid color. Sometimes this is acceptable, but it would be better to be able to control precisely when it occurs. The dithering takes place because the exact color you described is not possible to display on the local monitor. This would occur on a Macintosh because an image was created in the "Millions of Colors" monitor setting but displayed in only 256 colors.

To prevent the dithering, you have to choose an exact color that will exist on a 256-color monitor. The easiest way to do this is to choose the closest matching System Color. This can be done inside Photoshop by manipulating the palette via the Indexed Color options. Other paint programs usually have similar options, or enable you to work in just a System Palette.

The biggest hurdle that experienced print designers will have to overcome is becoming comfortable with designing for pixels, not for paper. When one is working in only 72 dpi, not 1200 dpi, issues such as when to antialias, how to choose a color, and how to choose readable fonts become especially crucial.

Solution: Sketch in Familiar Page Layout Software

It's no shame on anyone that Web design tools are behind print design tools in their level of development. Web design tools are in their infancy by comparison. For now, initial sketching in a familiar illustration, design, or page layout program, such as PageMaker or QuarkXPress, will facilitate design exploration and free development from the cumbersome limitations of HTML.

This is a good way to start your design layout process, and I do mean *start*. As soon as the visual quality of your document begins to take shape, convert the elements to a form suitable for HTML and continue design development there. Otherwise you may create a document that is too large, too slow, or physically impossible to translate.

Solution: Use the Common Gateway Interface

The Common Gateway Interface, or CGI, offers functionality that designers can use to their advantage. A CGI is a script or program that an HTTP server calls for information. The program returns HTML code. Instead of being a static piece of information such as a file, the returned code can change based on any number of variables a programmer wants to take advantage of. Different documents can be returned based on what time of day it is, where the connection comes from, what type of computer the viewer is using—or it can change randomly.

The information in the document can be taken from directories, stock quoting services, information gathered from sensors, or any other piece of electronically accessible information. Images can be drawn in the fly, reacting to choices that the viewer makes. CGIs are required for some useful HTML options, such as searchable indices and forms. Really pushing the edge of what can be done in HTML requires doing some programming. This is probably never going to change. To learn more about creating CGIs, check out some of the links listed at http:// www.yahoo.com/Computers/Internet/World_Wide _Web/CGI___Common_Gateway_Interface.

Problem: Maintain Security

Operating a WWW server on the Internet requires that many complex security issues be addressed. Most of these, dealing with configuration of the server, should be handled by a skilled administrator. However, there are a few rules that we as designers of Web pages should follow.

Solution: Don't Ask Unless You Encrypt

When creating a form, never ask for sensitive information from a viewer, such as a credit card number, unless you are using Secure HTTP (http://home. netscape.com/newsref/ref/netscape-security.html). Because of the distributed nature of the Internet, there are too many ways that a malicious person's program could be listening for such information somewhere along the journey.

Solution: Keep Passwords Hard to Guess

Pick passwords that aren't easy to guess, unlike your name, your phone number, or other personal information. In an age of automatic password-cracking programs, this means not picking anything that appears in a standard dictionary. It's surprisingly easy to meet these criteria. One way is to pick two short words and stick them together with a number or punctuation mark, like "dog9cat" or "tree;frog." Another is to replace letters in a word with numbers, like "t1cktock."

Skill is a precious commodity because it costs so much. It doesn't cost in money—that would be too easy. Time, patient effort, hair-pulling frustration, and persistent learning are the price of purchase.

This chapter is a snapshot of some useful skills today. Tomorrow, with different tools, this chapter will be very different, so keep your eye on what's happening on the Net. Good luck!

Chapter 13

Refining Design Methods

This chapter takes a look at the nature of the new

medium of the Internet and suggests changes in

the design processes that should enable those

with good skills to produce excellent results.

Act IV

Scene 5

SOS Design, during the invoicing process for the BigCorp home page. In Bill's office, papers strewn all over his desk. (Bill is NOT smiling.)

Bill: "Kit, I need to ask you about the amount of time in this project. It looks like an awful lot of time in meetings with the programmer, and an awful lot of rework."

Kit: "Yeah, we're really gonna have to get together sooner next time to work out a better logic tree. For the first few weeks they just kept changing what was on the site and one thing changed another. I mean, John couldn't help redoing all those links…."

Bill: "I hate to say it, but the whole site still loses me sometimes. I don't think the logic is intuitive enough. It's still too complex, and the links get lost. Design is still design—our content and form have to reinforce each other."

Kit: "You know, I was thinking about that. I've got some ideas for next time…."

Bill: "Let's sit down with John and talk about what we can do next time to come up with a better site structure and be more efficient in the process. I'm not sure I can bill all this."

Kit: "You wanna meet today?"

As I mentioned before, the Internet makes no real impact on what design is. Creative thinking about the relationship between form and content is still essential to good visual communication. However, the Internet is a new medium, and the <u>process</u> of communicating on it is different from any previous medium. This calls for thinking about design <u>methodology</u> and making modifications in design <u>method</u>. We need to rethink our way of doing things not only for the sake of the quality of our work, but for the health of our bottom lines.

New Medium Requires New Processes

In recent years, the Total Quality movement has focused attention on the importance that process plays in the development of product. When a quilt is made by hand, the result is quite different than a blanket woven by machine. The gospel that TQM preaches is that process determines product.

By definition, design is both a verb and a noun, a process and a product. One of Steven Covey's Seven Habits is "Begin with the end in mind." This is another way of stating that design, as a verb, is the process of planning for a better outcome. If the desired product is Internet information, the design process must be tailored accordingly.

Communication design method has at least four phases:

1. Research content and audience

2. Strategize content and medium

Then...

3. Conceptualize communication message(s)

4. Produce communication message(s)

Communication messages generally include words and pictures. Internet messages can include much

---

process

A series of actions leading toward a result.

Derived from the Latin *procesus*, meaning advance or proceed, a process is a sequence of actions that lead to a result or a product. The process could be mechanical, organic, or outside of conscious control. For design, a series of process steps, performed routinely in a similar fashion, become a method.

---

methodology

The principles that guide the development and use of methods.

Compound of the words "method" and "logy" meaning study, the literal meaning would be *the study of methods*. A noun, a methodology is "a body of practices, procedures, and rules used by those who work in a discipline or engage in an inquiry…. But the misuse of methodology obscures an important conceptual distinction between the tools of scientific investigation (properly methods) and the principles that determine how such tools are deployed and interpreted—a distinction that the scientific and scholarly communities, if not the wider public, should be expected to maintain." Methodology is thinking about doing. Designers need to rethink how they do design for the Internet.

American Heritage Dictionary, Macintosh Edition 3.0

---

method

A systematic way of doing something, an organized process.

From the Greek roots *meta*, meaning with or beyond, and *hodos*, meaning way or journey, method is "a means or manner of procedure, especially a regular and systematic way of accomplishing something…. Orderly arrangement of parts or steps to accomplish an end."

continued on next page

more: hypertext, motion, and sound. Given the new medium, what new phases do designers need to develop to design effectively for the Internet? What modifications to familiar processes are desirable? The Internet is so new and still changing that the following answers are preliminary and tentative.

A method is more systematic than a process, method implies a conscious direction or design. Methods can be said to be the result of design of process. Design in turn can be a product of a method. After careful thought, designers will change their design method for the Internet.

1. Research

Research is the first phase of design method and the first one to need major revision to adapt design for the Internet. It's logical that the research phase of design deserves increased attention, because the original purpose for creating the Internet was to facilitate research. In modifying the research phase, we designers will likely spend more time in content research while also taking advantage of the Internet's capacity to gather information from and about the audience. This is what it means to adapt the process to match the medium.

Content Research

Designers use the Net to do research for their projects. The vast quantity of information on the Internet makes design research both easier and more daunting. Because of the Internet's complexity, designers need research skills that go far beyond those typical in current design practice.

Fortunately, the Internet facilitates this. A quick search on a single topic might easily reveal thousands of documents to choose from. When this happens, the difficult part is sorting, reviewing, and selecting the appropriate content. Designers who acquaint themselves with Boolean searches using "and/or" limiters and the various searching environments such as Gopher and Lycos will find the task easier. Netscape's Internet Search page links to several different search engines, including InfoSeek's commercial service, Lycos at Carnegie

Mellon University, WebCrawler at the University of Washington, and W3 at University of Geneva.

While writing chapter 10, I did a Lycos search for information about copyright issues. Entering the keywords "copyright fair use" located 19,203 documents, of which Lycos listed the first ten documents with the closest match to the three key words. One of the ten references was not to a document but to a site, the American Communication Association (http://cavern.uark.edu/comminfo/www/copyright.html) WWW site with over 60 separate articles, theses, books, and video tapes. I found several of interest both on the original Lycos list and on the Association site, did a quick read of each, copied the ones I wanted, and printed them out for further reference. The search was quick and rewarding. I got a quick education and valuable information for my client—you the reader!

As our research skills improve—our abilities to describe the information we want and the places to look for it—we will be able to focus and limit our searches to only the most appropriate areas, search engines, and indexing systems, reducing the volume of insignificant data.

Audience Research

The Internet also offers improved means of researching audience needs. The Internet's two-way communication gives designers the potential to interact directly with the audience. Informal market research and information gathering from customers is happening right now on the Net. Many sites require users to "register" to view their sites or gain access to certain levels of information. Nearly every server records the URL of every hit, automatically gathering, at a minimum, the electronic location of each user. The Internet has the potential to develop other means of expanding audience research and listen to the voice of the customer.

For here and now, you could easily post a question to a newsgroup and ask for the answers in quantitative form: "On a scale of 1 to 5, one being the dumbest, do you think bosses are smarter or dumber than their employees?" Ask visitors to fill out a registration form, similar to the one at HotWired http://www.hotwired.com, in order to have full use of your site. All of this, of course, should be done in such a way that your users clearly understand what exactly you are going to do with the information. People resent having their name given to junk mailing lists, printed or electronic.

Message testing and evaluation is another part of the design research process. This usually takes the extremely informal and unscientific form of passing the layout around the office, and eventually the client's office. A few high-budget projects may actually go to test market, but this has been the exception rather than the rule—until now.

The low cost of Internet publishing makes possible the testing of variations of the same message with direct consumer feedback. You might design two versions of the same site with every other visitor getting the alternate version; you can track which version holds viewers the longest. Sun tested the effectiveness of a change in the design of its navigational buttons by similarly tracking response. On the Net, responses can be gathered and a continuous process of design and content refinement can occur at minimal cost.

Sun tested

The people at Sun felt that their interactive buttons were not doing the job, so they redesigned them, making them more separate and more three-dimensional-looking. They report, "Changing the button design as illustrated above resulted in 416% increased use over a two-month period (January-March 1995). Considering that the use of the server in general increased by 'only' 48% in the same period, there can be no doubt that usability

As the Internet evolves, there is the potential to conduct more sophisticated audience research as well. One person's home page asks viewers to choose which color scheme they prefer for his house (http://www.mcp.com/cgi-bin/mulderpoll). This was a test market for a paint scheme, for free! As

continued on next page

engineering worked and resulted in a signifi-

cantly improved button design."

http://www.sun.com/cgi-bin/show?sun-

on-net/uidesign/usabilitytest.html

Internet research tools become more refined, designers will need to become sufficiently familiar with research methods to be able to understand and evaluate feedback. Methods such as QFD (Quality Function Deployment) have sophisticated statistical means to quantify and analyze information gathered, which is a perfect match for the natural information gathering capacity of the Net. This is a likely addition to an expanded design process.

Finally, as designers go through the Internet to gather research for their projects, they will be able to identify valuable information sources to which they can form links. This will bridge between the content they are developing for their client and appropriate content from other sources.

Research to Facilitate User Research

In addition to designers using the Net to research their projects, the projects that designers produce for the Net should facilitate research for their users. This means adding context to content via the power of hypertext linking. Good Web page design does not merely reproduce print files electronically. For example, *TIME* magazine (http://www.pathfinder.com/ time/timehomepage.html) on the Internet added a tool to its standard print magazine's political coverage enabling readers to learn how their representatives voted on an issue. This is taking good advantage of the Web's hypermedia linking capability (see chapter 9 for additional strategies).

An additional process step is required at the research phase of design practice to acquire the information needed for linking. This step involves anticipating questions readers will have and identifying links to answers. This is an important expansion of the standard research phase, which focused on understanding the clients' content and audience's needs.

Designers might anticipate users' questions by putting themselves in the users' position formally—through research studies and focus groups—or informally—through personal intuition, discussions, or Internet newsgroups. Designers also might identify desirable links through research into user needs by checking out lists of FAQs (Frequently Asked Questions) on other sites related topically to their own, or by adding a FAQ section to the project they are designing to collect questions. These questions could be sorted, links identified or answers generated, and the site modified at appropriate times. However it is done, the research phase in design needs to be expanded to develop extended content in areas that interest readers and to take advantage of the Internet's vast context.

Expanding the research phase in design practice might have an unanticipated benefit. The overall quality of graphic design might improve! The best design has always come not from copying design solutions from the latest Design Annuals, but from a vigorous investigation of both the conceptual and the visual content of a project. Fresh research and a broader data context should improve content and creativity in design.

2. Strategy

Strategy is not universally embraced as a design phase. Some prefer to limit phase two to concept development or creative thinking. Ongoing debate on the value of design to business hovers about this issue: Is design strategic planning or is it intuitive art? Without siding-up in the great debate, let's go with the dictionary definition of design, which includes the formation of a plan.

The Internet is arguably the most complex and dynamic information medium ever devised. In this complex, new medium, we need several new

copying

I do not see

that forced individualism

or forced exaltation

are the source

of convincing formulation

of lasting meaning

In my work

I am content to compete

with myself

and to search with simple palette

and with simple color

for manifold instrumentation

So I dare further variants

Josef Albers, *Josef Albers at The Metropolitan Museum of Art*, p.1

processes related to strategy in order to design effectively. We need to plan.

For starters, what information makes sense in this new interactive medium, the Internet? To answer this question, we would do well to first consider what is known as information processing theory in psychology. This widely accepted theory views those to whom we wish to communicate or educate as active investigators of their environment, people striving to make sense of the world around them. Communication strategies based on this theory require viewers to become active participants in the communication process. In this regard, effective Internet communication strategies ask viewers to observe, compare and contrast, and form concepts and generalizations based on their findings. Strategies to facilitate information processing and cognitive load will help give viewers the quantity and quality of information they need. Strategies to develop intuitive navigation, clear user interface, and logical information structure will enable users to find the information they want. The result will be informed, even pleased, viewers.

Information Processing Strategy

The Internet is an ideal medium to apply the information processing theory mentioned previously. And in fact, well-designed Web sites can be evaluated by a taxonomy of learning/communication. A typical Web presentation of content draws viewers in by first providing *data* that they interact with and process to become informed. Data processed by viewers is then combined into *information*. Further navigating through the site enables viewers to relate various pieces of information as they form *ideas* in their minds—concepts that help explain the subject at hand. Continued browsing may result in viewers combining these ideas to produce *wisdom* that

taxonomy of learning/communication

||

wisdom

||||||

ideas

|||||||||||

information

|||||||||||||||||||||||

data

|||||||||||||||||||||||||||||||||

takes on the why's and wherefore's of a subject, thereby resulting in very effective communication and fully leveraging the power of this new medium.

Graphic design, an enhancer of communication, supports this model by removing obstacles to this learning process, whether that means removing visual clutter for an urgent or direct message like a Stop sign or adding layers of information to enrich the context of an ambiguous message like a poem. Web designers confront both ends of the simple/complex continuum. The taxonomy can serve as a measuring rod to evaluate Web documents, which must be simple enough to enable intuitive navigation through a dense jungle of information.

Cognitive Load Strategy

Successfully structuring the exchange of information also requires designers to pay attention to two other important issues: cognitive load and navigation. Cognitive load involves this question: Just how much information can visitors to a Web site be expected to process, to read on the screen? Few are going to read *War and Peace* online. Large volumes of words are perhaps best made available to be downloaded and then printed and read at a later time.

Most Internet documents that are to be read on the screen, on the other hand, are brief, inviting a skim or "quick read" approach. This suggests that content specialists and designers place emphasis on careful information selection and presentation with a clear hierarchy. Each page should contain enough information to avoid <u>excessive scrolling</u> while providing sufficient data to avoid excessive navigation from page to page. A carefully developed logic tree, which I discuss under "Information Sequence"

excessive scrolling

"Determining the proper length for any particular World Wide Web (WWW) page requires balancing three main factors:

continued on next page

coming up, is the foundation of a carefully controlled cognitive load.

1. The relationship between the page and screen size.
2. The editorial demands of your content.
3. Modular design of online collections of WWW pages.

Many critics and designers of graphic user interfaces have noted the disorienting effect of scrolling on computer screens.... This argues for navigational WWW pages (home pages and menus in particular) that contain no more than about two to three 640 x 480 screens' worth of information...."

Patrick J. Lynch, Yale C/AIM WWW Style Manual, Page Length

Navigation Strategy

Content organization and searching strategies are intimately linked in the interactive presentation of information via the Web, a hypertextual environment that does not fully control what information viewers will begin with, visit along the way, and end with. Viewers of a Web site are free to navigate through the information space along the pathways created by the interactive designer. Once viewers select a link to a page outside a given Web site, they pass into the hands of another designer, hopefully on the same information trail.

Navigation, therefore, becomes a critical issue, requiring careful consideration during the formation of information strategies. Anticipating user need and designing appropriate means for interaction is a part of human interface design, and a topic of the book *The Psychology of Everyday Things* by D. A. Norman. An excellent Annotated Bibliography of Graphic Design for the User Interface is found at Patrick J. Lynch's Yale C/AIM WWW Style Manual (http://info.med.yale.edu/caim/Biblio_GUI.HTML) for further reading.

While it is beyond the scope of this book to discuss this topic in detail here, designers of Web documents will benefit from a solid understanding of this area. Several practical human interface design strategies follow.

Information Sequence

One of the first issues we should address as Web designers is the question of how sequential the information should be. For an author to anticipate strict sequential control is a denial of the medium, yet totally unstructured information is frustrating to users. Allowing viewers to visit multiple links within a site is powerful, yet it places a high degree of responsibility upon the designer, assuming the intent is clear communication leading to understanding. Designers must add a step to their method that evaluates the content in light of its complexity to determine just how structured it should be.

One helpful tool in properly organizing content to prevent cognitive overload and ensuring that viewers don't become lost is a "conceptual layout" or "conceptual architecture," often simply referred to as a "logic tree." A logic tree describes how an information space is organized and what types of pathways are used. Several standard conceptual architectures, first developed for other interactive communication media, can be easily adapted to the needs of the Internet. One method for designing information links is to sketch in thumbnail fashion the information structure, with linking arrows indicating the links between documents and information levels — two such examples are the Z+ Logic Tree

Z+ Logic Tree

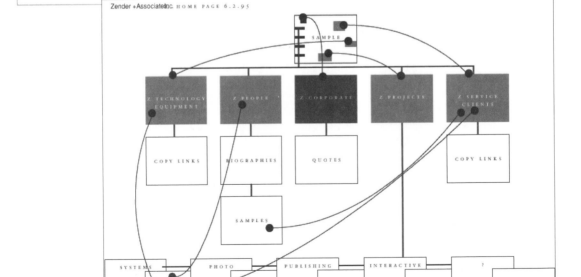

(which we used for designing our company Web site) and the <u>Birding Logic Tree</u>.

Birding Logic Tree

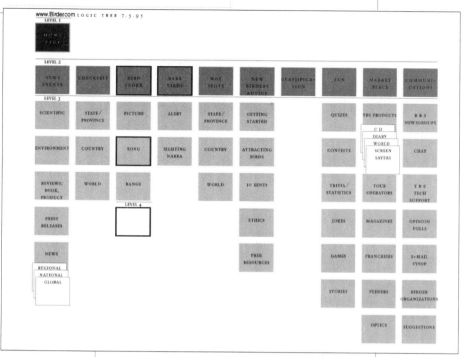

The designer needs to help Web visitors form a mental map of the information structure. Consciously or subconsciously, users need to grasp the logic tree to avoid frustrating confusion.

Experience has shown that information blocks in the three to seven range are easily retained by most people—witness the seven-digit phone number, subdivided into blocks of three and four. This suggests a basic information structure with between three and seven main categories or menus. The <u>number of subcategories</u> and links between categories should be similarly considered. Patrick J. Lynch suggests that the goal is an information hierarchy with a good balance between not too many information categories (too shallow a structure) nor too many nested menus (too deep a structure).

A simple but often overlooked navigation strategy is to provide "next page," "previous page," and

number of subcategories

"Menus lose their value if they don't carry at least four or five links; text or list-based menu pages can easily carry a dozen links without overwhelming the user or forcing users to scroll through long lists."

Patrick J. Lynch, Yale C/AIM WWW Style Manual

"home" buttons at both the beginning and end of each document page. These navigational aids supplement the browser's forward and back buttons by providing forward/backward navigation without forcing you to leave your document. Clicking on the browser's Back button may hop you to a site in Europe when all you wanted to do was back up a page on the site you were already on!

It is also helpful to provide visual clues that suggest how deep into a document a given page is. A visual trail of clues, like bread crumbs, can give users a sense of where they've been. On the Zender + Associates home page (http://www.zender.com), for example, previously selected typographic buttons are softened by blurring as you navigate successively deeper into the document, leaving a recognizable visual trail of where you've been.

A carefully developed logic tree and navigational structure are a dramatic contrast to the shovelware approach that throws everything but the kitchen sink onto the Net. While it might be tempting to neglect making a strategic decision about what to include on an Internet site because the storage space is inexpensive, not to decide is to decide badly in this case. The Net is complex enough without creating a weedpatch for users to hack through.

Designers should establish a process for working with content strategists from the client side to help make content and navigation decisions. Because the Net is a two-way communication medium, it is a good idea to draw upon strategists beyond the advertising, corporate communications, public relations, and marketing departments, and include customer service and technical support people as well. Their experience in gathering information from and responding to customers is important for Net communication. Interacting with customer service representatives about customer concerns and frequently asked questions will provide valuable insights. Their insights should help you make a Net site more user-friendly.

Interface Design Strategy

Interface design plays yet another significant role in the design of Web pages, even calling upon designers to formulate new interactive strategies. In her provocative book *Computers as Theatre*, Brenda Laurel notes how architects of public spaces first observe emergent footpaths on the grass before laying out sidewalks. She rightly advocates a democratic approach to information structure, giving the user control.

One means of granting control to Web navigators is to use graphic metaphors of familiar physical objects, such as push buttons and dials and slider bars (see the next chapter for examples out there on the Web).

These clichés grant a level of comfort to users of this unfamiliar medium. However, more exciting, entertaining, and meaningful metaphors are certainly possible, such as objects that become lighter to suggest distance, using what artists call atmospheric perspective to imply distance and push less important information to the background. One can use blurred images to suggest a change of focus as a metaphor of a change in interest from information past to information present.

Icons, or small graphic illustrations, are a navigational metaphor whose overuse is common on the WWW. They frequently occupy more space than a verbal descriptor, are often obscure in meaning, and take valuable download time. They are a new breed of what Edward Tufte coined chartjunk, Webjunk littering the Webscape.

We should include in our Web design method a time

---

democratic approach

"As long as designers see themselves as authors of one-to-many experiences, all of us will only be bottom-feeding on the fringes of fundamentally noninteractive forms. Neither participants nor authors have ultimate control over the shape of interactive experiences; form and structure emerge as artifacts of complex, asynchronous collaboration. Exploring the dynamics of emergent form will lead us to new, more appropriate ways to approach design."

p. 212

---

push buttons

"We are used to turning knobs, pushing buttons, and toggling switches, following directional arrows, stopping at red lights or changing gear, so it is natural that metaphors of all these familiar varieties of interface are used in hypermedia. We can control volume as well by turning a knob, as by pulling a slider up or down, whether the knob is real ('hard') or virtual ('soft')."

Bob Cotton & Richard Olive, *Understanding Hypermedia*, p. 44

---

chartjunk

"The interior decoration of graphics generates

continued on next page

to develop and evaluate apt navigational clues. Creative typography should be considered as a prime source of navigational aid. Words have been useful keys to information in the ancient past!

Hypertext and imagemapping on the Web make it so easy to build information-rich sites that it is amazing navigation works as well as it does. So far, the limited number of standard navigation tools have so few options that there is little diversity in navigational style. This gives Web users a familiar interface so they don't have to learn a new navigation scheme for each site. However, as the Web evolves, designers should conceive, design, and test more creative interface options that fit the content in both form and substance.

The process might involve prospective users who test trial navigational structures on the Web. The navigational structure and its visual form should be considered equally. An Internet site for an entertainment conglomerate might have a distinctive interface that is playful, even surprising, entertaining, and game-like, while an interface for a health care provider might have a much simpler, straightforward, even reassuring feel. In both instances, the interface needs to draw on familiar navigational methods to give users at all experience levels the keys to navigate successfully.

Nonlinear Strategy

As we go through the process of developing a site, we need to be constantly aware that linking and navigation are departures from the standard linear approach to information development. Some learners will be more comfortable with hypertext's nonlinear approach than others will. However, all rational thinkers depend to some extent on logical thought development. Lewis Carroll's menagerie of characters—the Caterpillar, the Tweedle brothers,

a lot of ink that does not tell the viewer anything new. The purpose of decoration varies— to make the graphic appear more scientific and precise, to enliven the display, to give the designer an opportunity to exercise artistic skills. Regardless of its cause, it is all non-data-ink or redundant data-ink, and it is often chartjunk. Graphical decoration, which prospers in technical publications as well as in commercial and media graphics, comes cheaper than the hard work required to produce intriguing numbers and secure evidence."
The Visual Display of Quantitative Information, p. 107

the Mad Hatter, and their friends—may be entertaining, even insightful, but a Web site designed by them would be a nightmare.

A Web site should blend departure from strict linear essay format with nonlinear but rational development of extensions and connections to related topics, media, and resources. Rather than a written listing of topics to explore, like a book, you might develop a visual display, a map or a floorplan, to display the contents of a document. This nonlinear strategy may be enhanced through the development of three-dimensional Internet displays (see VRML, chapter 11). It encourages exploration and supports a more intuitive, visual learning style. Taking appropriate advantage of the potential of the medium will support and encourage alternative learning styles, attention spans, and cognitive abilities, and enhance rather than inhibit learning.

3. Concept

A Web document calls for not only its own distinctive information structure, but its own distinctive conceptual approach and visual language as well. The concept phase is where the design fun really begins. Wild and crazy ideas are promoted, evaluated, and discarded. Here too, in the development of design concepts, changes in approach are called for. We designers need to adapt our approach to conceptualize apt visual systems, metaphors, and multimedia forms for the Internet. For example, a single Web document may contain hundreds of related pages navigated via menus and links. It is easy for users, who only view one page at a time, to get lost in a web of connections which cloud the perception of valuable information and block understanding. Good graphic design will provide visual and conceptual <u>consistency</u> for a Web document.

Depending on content, Web pages may be as similar

consistency

"Consistency and predictability are essential

continued on next page

as book pages or as distinctive as individual brochures from the same company. Either way, designers need to develop a distinctive visual language for their WWW site to unify, at whatever appropriate level, all the pages within a given document.

The best design method to accomplish this is a structured graphic design system. The system consists of a palette of visual components and rules for their use. Visual components may be functional, metaphoric, or abstract. They may rely on similar color, shape, texture, type style, movement, or content theme. Visual elements should suggest where the user is in the information hierarchy, who the owner of the document is, and how to navigate. As chapter 14 will show, when an effective design system is applied, users will notice immediately, by visual clue, when they have left one site and gone to another. This is helpful, since a mouse click might take you to the next page or to another site halfway around the world.

It is also important for us designers to develop models for conceptual sketching with time-based media, such as motion and sound. You might sketch in an authoring program such as Director to test animated typography and audio input. However, at this time, the only real-time motion on Web pages is blinking text (though there is some experimentation with very rough "animation"—see the Razorfish critique in chapter 14). While true real-time animation is still a promise in Web documents, it is so powerful that planning for it should not be neglected in today's conceptual development.

4. Production

Can we designers do all this alone? Are right-brain creative types the best candidates for information structure and analysis functions?

attributes of any well-designed information system, aiding users in identifying the origin and relationships of World Wide Web pages, providing consistent and predictable access to interface and page elements, and a consistent graphic design scheme. The design grid systems that underlie most well-designed paper publications are no less necessary in designing electronic documents and online publications, where the spatial relationships between on-screen elements is constantly shifting in response to user input and system activity."

Patrick J. Lynch, Yale C/AIM WWW Style Manual, WWW Page Design, http://info.med.yale.edu/caim/M_II_1.HTML

Revisions in design method in response to a new medium, new tools, and additional media options will, in most cases, necessitate collaboration between Web designers and other professionals. The Internet is a world dominated by information systems managers, typically programmers, who love writing code that does amazing things. On the other hand, few designers are enthusiastic about acquiring expertise in the left-hemisphere world of computer programming. This requires us to collaborate with programmers from the earliest stages of the design development process in order to ensure the viability of various concepts. Right now, universities are one of the best places to find talented Web programmers. The old hands at Web programming are mostly very young.

As the tools for designing Web pages become more sophisticated, this particular problem should diminish, but the need for collaboration will not. The Internet is increasingly an interactive hypertextual environment combining video, audio, and three-dimensional simulations. It is not likely that any designer can be an expert in all these areas. Extended training and collaboration are the answer.

Collaboration

Collaboration is not just a politically correct catch word. It is foreign to the individualistic spirit fostered in the very fabric of our educational system, and indeed our country. As a result, most designers are not natural collaborators. Skills that contribute to consensus-building are not taught in design school. For many, collaboration will be a totally new phase in design method. Maybe we so frequently share client horror stories because designers see clients more as adversaries than as partners. It doesn't have to be this way.

There are techniques that we can learn to facilitate collaboration. One is the ability to moderate a group discussion. Recording group ideas on a large white board or easel using pictures, symbols, and words is a very effective large group technique. Reporting the results of various inputs in the form of written project criteria or objectives and gaining group consensus are proven means of smoothing collaboration.

In addition, presenting visual concepts in a <u>matrix</u>

matrix

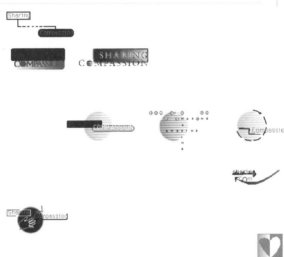

Fact /
Literal
Content

Feeling /
Metaphor

format is a powerful means of focusing on objective aspects of visual form and smoothing collaboration among visually and nonvisually oriented people. A matrix is a horizontal/vertical arrangement with a scale on each axis. Any design project can be placed on such a grid for evaluation. Labels appropriate for the parameters of the design project are given to each axis and potential solutions are arranged accordingly. The result is a remarkably concise evaluation of design solutions using objective criteria. The matrix is an effective means of negotiation because it focuses on objective criteria in a meaningful and understandable form. This promotes objective discussion without inhibiting spontaneity or creativity.

Servant leadership is always helpful in collaborative efforts. A leader with good personal communication skills and the humility to place the agenda of the group ahead of personal desires can really focus a collaborative effort. The result is a team all pulling the same direction, sharing the same vision, and being committed to making things work.

In-House Training and Team Building

At the conclusion of chapter 11, I said that it is a wasteful and stressful thing to live on the bleeding edge. One means of coping with this situation is to hold regular informal training sessions with peers. In an office, this might take the form of a regular staff lunch to discuss new technologies. For a free-lancer, this might mean getting together with friends who are more technically advanced or taking a formal class. An in-house design group might bring in a series of experts to hold training seminars. Or a firm could hire a summer intern who is a programmer to help the staff with technical aspects of programming. However you do it, the time should include both formal training and less formal team-building activities in order to build both knowledge and relationships.

Ramifications: Internet Thinking

Design method affects more than just design and designers; it affects culture, society, and how we learn and think and act. The Internet, and how designers help form it, will change the shape of society's way of thinking.

Cultural Impact

Since Marshall McLuhan described the impact that medium has on message, there has been a growing interest and concern over the impact of media, specifically television. Neil Postman's conclusion in television

"Television is culture's principal mode of knowing about itself. Therefore—and this is the critical point—how television stages the world becomes the model for how the world is properly to be staged. It is not merely that on the television screen entertainment is the metaphor for all discourse. It is that off the screen the same metaphor prevails.... In court-rooms, classrooms, operating rooms, board rooms, churches, and even airplanes, Americans no longer talk to each other, they entertain each other. They do not exchange ideas; they exchange images. They do not argue with propositions; they argue with good looks, celebrities, and commercials."

p. 92

Amusing Ourselves to Death is that television is a medium that is largely destructive to culture and thinking because, among other reasons, it is noninteractive and decontextualizing.

The Internet as a medium has the potential to help reverse these trends. Conceived as a tool to facilitate research, the Net has a designed-in research orientation. Its design is to facilitate the widest possible data gathering. This places the user in a much more healthy relationship to information than the images and sound bites offered by the evening news. The hypertextual experience facilitates and encourages exploration and consequently expands experience and context. The Internet's democracy of information empowers the reader to ask for more and get answers. This response ability places a higher level of responsibility on readers to become informed. It requires research skills to complement reading abilities. The definition of literacy may change over time from the ability to read to the ability to research and synthesize appropriately. How well designers structure Internet information can advance or hinder this change. If we fail to empower readers, we may well undermine society's ability to think.

In the past, the existence of formal publishers has served as a control on information quality. The reputation of the publisher was an incentive that served to ensure high quality of scholarship and commitment to the truth. The extreme democracy, even info anarchy, of the Internet might erode this. Coupled with the general yet pervasive slip of belief in objective truth, this could result in a society in which all information is little more than gossip and people are unsure when they are reading factual information or info-fiction. Fiction posing as fact already exists on the Internet. Not all Internet information is equally reliable. We as designers have a role to play in committing to the truthfulness and reliability of the information we help put on the Net.

It is also possible that the Net could contribute to the illusion of being informed if users draw wrong conclusions due to ineffective research and analytic skills that arm them with unbalanced or incomplete data. It is important to know your limits. It is the most dangerous type of foolishness to inflate your own expertise. Designers and Internet users alike will need an accurate understanding of their own critical thinking skills and the information humility to effectively analyze the information experience and recognize when they are in over their heads.

Future Impact

Chapter 1 called on no less authority than God in recognizing the power of global communication. The tower of Babel, a story of humankind's attempt to breech heaven with technological products spawned from universal communication, demonstrated that the ability to communicate is one of the most powerful and profoundly human of attributes.

Even so, overstatement of the power of the Internet is rampant. Many seem to envision an electronic Babel reaching to conquer ignorance, want, and greed. The globe is *not* unified by the Internet. Information is dispersed—that is all. Exchanging information is not the same as communication. We can talk, but no one is obligated to listen or understand. Understanding, though founded upon information, is a matter of the heart more than of the mind. Raw information has no soul, solves no real need, adds nothing to life or living.

The Internet , powerful as it is, is not the answer to all our problems. It will not bring about global communication. Only people communicate, and people are flawed communicators. No matter how much the

Babel
"Now the world had one language and one common speech…. If as one people speaking the same language they have begun to do this, then nothing they plan to do will be impossible for them…."
Genesis 11:1-7, New International Version

Internet helps, we are still, as Pogo says, our own worst enemy. We need to recognize communication's limits. Designers of all people must avoid being blinded by information mania.

Yet the Internet is a product, perhaps an inevitable product, of our age, the information age. The designer/author is an information assembler. Designers gather and organize information into a meaningful and expressive form to address an audience's specific needs. The flood of information available will increase the value of those who are skilled at adding relevance and meaning to the flood. Designers have a dynamic and profoundly significant role to play in the information age, not as saviors, but as servants.

Chapter 14

Web Page Design Case Studies

This chapter shows some actual samples of work

done on the Internet. It examines several current

Web documents and offers an instructive critique.

Act IV

Scene 6

SOS Design conference room, a meeting to critique the recently completed BigCorp Web site.

Bill: "It wasn't easy, but overall I am pleased with the site. It's easy to navigate from page to page and the links are meaningful."

Kit: "Yeah, I like how the background kind of fades in there; it goes with the blurry type thing. It's pretty c o o l . My friend Steve, who works with Casey in a little two-person firm, well, he's on the Net all the time and he said he thought ours is one of the best sites he's seen."

John: "Hey, it's pretty functional. We got it to look good on pretty nearly every browser, which took some programming. Look here...."

Bill: "Before we get too far, we've had several other calls about Web sites and we are going to need to hire more Web designers. Do you two know anyone...."

Firms are looking for experienced Internet designers. Why not?! The Web hasn't been around long enough to generate that much experience! Requests for Web site designers, called variously Web-spinners, Web-weavers, programmers, and worse, frequently include a preference for competency in HTML, Perl, C, C++, and Lingo programming. If you have to ask what those are, don't. Most of us designers are not likely to trade in our drawing tools for a pocket protector and programmer's guide. It's partly because so much of what's been done on the Web has been done by nondesigners and programmers that designers are needed. Designers experienced on the Web are sought; the issue is how to get experience when you have none.

That's the purpose behind this last chapter. It is designed to instruct and inspire aspiring Web designers in what goes into a good Web document by reviewing existing Web documents. Without doubt one of the best ways to learn design is by critical evaluation of what works and what doesn't. Critiques can be polite or vicious, but schools have proven the value of the crit as an instructional tool for centuries. The Internet is a new medium, but there is no reason a proven method, appropriately modified, can't serve well.

One Web critic referred to most Web pages as one-joke sitcoms that give no reason to tune in next week. This insight raises the critical issue of information dynamics on Web pages. It's a topic not normally part of the traditional design critique. In fact, the critique process has become so routine in many forums that criteria are more assumed than discussed. The Internet is so new and different that appropriate criteria need to be debated and defined.

For example, take the information dynamics issue just mentioned. The Internet is a dynamic, changing medium, with new items added and deleted every moment. Frequent Net users become accustomed to change—they anticipate it. Should we designers supply it in our Web document? Should a benchmark for a successful Web site be some accommodation for regular visual and content change? If so, how much and how often should the change occur: monthly, weekly, daily, hourly? What is good change and what is senseless change?

Any crit will be only as good as the criteria that

guide it. Exactly what criteria should we use to judge <u>Web documents</u>? How do the criteria differ from those for print design? According to Patrick J. Lynch's Yale C/AIM Style Manual, there are two primary considerations in designing WWW pages: interface design and page design. I assume that in page design Patrick includes the interaction of all the pages in a document, not just a single page.

Others have developed Web evaluation criteria as well. In selecting its top 100 Web pages, Interactive Age (http://techweb.cmp.com/techweb/ia), used this criteria: design (I assume that means visual form), ease of use, linking, and content. I find these criteria less satisfying because they imply some questionable dichotomies—design as opposed to content, for example—and they use blurry terminology—ease of use compared to linking, for example. A Web site by David Siegel called High Five (http://www.best.com/~dsiegel/high_five/high_five.html) features a best Web site each week. David selects winners "on the basis of design, conception, execution, and content, with an emphasis on clear information design and visual aesthetics." Again, good criteria, but a little more precision on what those terms mean for the Web would be helpful.

As you might expect with an entirely new medium, the initial criteria to evaluate it are diverse and the language imprecise. Given the uncertainty, it seems best to use an expanded version of proven, existing design criteria. Graphic design is defined broadly as the relationship between content and visual form that enables users to discover meaning. Given that as the task, the measure for success is therefore how effective the marriage of content and form is. Interactive, multimedia Web documents, as suggested by Lynch, have two related design components: the interface and the information. Each of these components has content and form. It is on

Web documents

Only Web documents created using HTML, as opposed to other Internet documents such as Acrobat PDF files or file transfer-only (FTP) documents, are being critiqued here, in an attempt to make fair comparisons. Other Internet documents are either much more limited in design flexibility (see chapter 11) or are based on a design tool sufficiently different that it makes for an unfair comparison.

this structure that the following criteria for evaluating Web sites have been developed.

Interface Design

Navigational Structure: How effective and appropriate are the navigational tools and how well do they support content?

Design System: How inventive, appropriate, and informational are the visual components of the navigational system? How effectively does it support the information?

Content Design

Information: How usable, relevant, and well written is the content, and how effectively does it use the dynamic, hypertextual environment?

Visual Form: How inventive, appropriate, and aesthetic is the visual form of the content? Does it enhance both the content and the user's experience?

There are hosts of issues that this list does not address, such as the loss of tactile quality inherent in electronic documents and the cultural stratification encouraged by an information system limited to those privileged with computers. These critiques of the medium itself are not addressed here (see chapters 1, 10, and 13 for discussions of these issues). Rather, the focus of this chapter is the successes and failures of existing Web pages.

It is in the spirit of appreciation for the hard and innovative effort expended by each of these Web page designers that the following critiques are offered.

existing Web pages

Warning: The Internet and the documents on it are transient. The document appearance and structure will almost certainly be different when you visit these sites yourself. These critiques are snapshots (literally and figuratively, since they are all screen grabs) of documents on the Net. The fact that the documents are changing in no way changes the lessons that can be drawn from them.

How to Join:
Register Now
Unguided Tour
Need Help?

Members Only:
Overview
What's New
Your View

H O T W I R E D

HotWired

http://www.hotwired.com

HotWired 1

The HotWired Web site, the online version of *Wired* magazine, gets points immediately for variety in both form and in content. The list of feature articles is updated daily, or nearly so, and a more novel visual feature is the background "page color," which changes nearly every time you connect: lime green Thursday afternoon, bright yellow Friday morning. The navigational tools are simple and meaningful, since they are typographic. There are three kinds of tools, with a different category of information presented with a different visual form: Articles have editorial images as their navigational icons, site categories have typographic descriptors, and the staff has the HotWired logo.

HOTWIRED

SIGNAL

Flux
Fetish
Net Surf
Net Soup
DaveNet
BBF!!!
Market
 Forces
Muckraker
Intelligent
 Agent

**WORLD
BEAT**

On the Road
Planet Wired
Deductible
 Junkets

PIAZZA

Club Wired
Rants &
 Raves
Threads
Ask Allison

**RENAIS-
SANCE 2.0**

Retina
Kino
Soundz
Twain
Serial

COIN

Uncommon
 Market
Window
 Shopping
Library
Sponsors

WIRED

Back Issues
Subscribe
WiredWare
Privacy
Archive

OVERVIEW:

FRONT DOOR · WHAT'S NEW · YOUR VIEW · SEARCH · HELP

HotWired 2

The site is not as visually connected as it should be when I move from page to page. Here, at the first level past the home page (in this case the Overview page, only available to registered subscribers—registration is free), there is a change in visual feel. The background changes color, which isn't too bad, but the icons have changed as well. Gone are the Courier typographic descriptors; they're replaced by cool but nearly meaningless drawn icons with lists in a different sans-serif font. Not only are the look and feel of the navigational tools different, but the structure is different: an image followed by a typographic list followed by a row of buttons. A small point: The list is unclearly organized, not alphabetical, and the meaning of the labels is obscure (though the terms are explained lower on this page—in some cases, much lower).

While obscure titles may be fun in a print document, in a Web document, which may well have a time penalty for each new click of the mouse, they lose some of their charm. In a Web document, it is helpful to have some clear idea of where you are going and whether it will be worth the wait. And while a different feel for each section may be suitable for print *Wired*, it hurts the Web site. My rationale is that a magazine, being a physical object, cannot be immediately confused with some other magazine—you know what you are holding in your hands. A Web document, on the other hand, can immediately go to any other document or site, making the need for a consistent visual presence more pressing. This is a classic case of too heavy a reliance on past print experience, too much preconception of what a magazine should be.

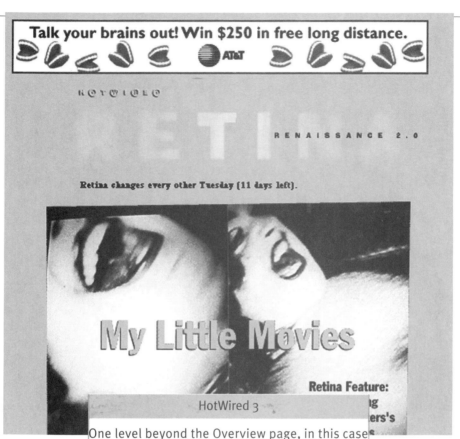

HotWired 3

One level beyond the Overview page, in this case
Retina, the look switches back to something more
like the home page. The page color is an immediate,
strong connection that even the AT&T ad doesn't destroy. The centered photographic image is reminiscent of the home page as well, and an excellent
visual counterpoint to the soft "RETINA" type above
it. Small details here are very well considered, like
the mention of how often the content of the page
changes and how many days are left before the
change: a content calendar. Also, listing the sizes of
downloadable files is a much-appreciated courtesy
to readers with slow connections. These are very
helpful and kind navigational tools on a different
order than those previously encountered. They help
a viewer decide what to visit when, whether to read
this today or over the weekend, and what to download
today or when the Net is less busy; they help one
navigate between this visit and a subsequent visit.

Retina Feature:
The Unveiling
of John Waters's
Photographs

Filmmaker <u>John Waters</u> has been secretly taking photos for
years, but he's only recently shown them to the public.

`YOUR VIEW`   `WHAT'S NEW`   `OVERVIEW`   `SEARCH`   `HELP`

S P E C I A L   R E P O R T
Is Christo's wrapping of the Reichstag an ego-driven
carnival or a great excuse for a picnic?

G A L L E R Y
Art crimes are taking over walls from Los Angeles to Amsterdam.

S U R F
Hundreds of sex-drenched pictures ... of flowers.

R E V I E W
Electronic artists embrace biological metaphors and flick the triggers
of hope and paranoia - a report from the Interactive Media Festival.

T H R E A D S
Add to the 6 topics or the 42 links currently in Threads.

And they encourage repeat visits. That's a lot of
mileage from a simple little line of copy.

HotWired 4

Here, the lower portion of the same Retina page, are
the contents of the feature area. Again, this is clearly related to the original home page, using Courier
as the font for the navigational buttons and pho-
tos/illustrations as informative teaser "buttons."
Here, at the contents level, the nature of Retina becomes clearer: It's an area devoted to arts. One
thing missing from this page is a navigational button to return to the home page.

s the story goes, an American citizen living in Berlin sent a postcard of the Reichstag building to Christo, mentioning that it would be a good idea to wrap it. Christo, being the artist that he is, said yes, and here we are, 24 years later, witnesses to th...

HotWired 5

O The next level, in this case the Special Report page it was within Retina, is (when I was there) an article on the wrapping of the Reichstag by Christo. For those who count, that's four levels so far, and in, out, and back in through three navigational styles to reach our first real article. However, this particular article was also available at the second level (Overview) as the feature article under the Retina selection, but only this particular article—the other Retina articles were not mentioned there.

The background change here is strong but arguably appropriate, taking the form of wrinkled cloth. The navigational tool is the minimal but familiar button bar, found only at the bottom of the screen. The content is well written and illustrated acceptably, although the type on the wrapped building raises the question of whether there was type on the actual building wrapping.

THREAD: Retina
TOPICS: 6

1. **The wrapped Reichstag**
   Manuel Chakravarty (torun) on Wed, 5 Jul 95 03:36 PST
   Posts 0 - Add a Post

   I really like the article about the wrapped Reichstag. Here at the University of Berlin, there is a WWW-server, called KULTURBOX, which is the official WWW-server about the Wrapping. Have a look...

   Manuel

   POSTS-FIRST-PREVIOUS-NEXT-SINCE-INDEX-TOPICS

2. **Wanted: A Collection of Rave Art**
   Wesley Golby (wgolby) on Thu, 15 Jun 95 05:13 PST
   Posts 1 - Last Post: Thu, 15 Jun 95 17:41 PST

   Are there any Printed Collections ?

   Since 1990, I have collected rave flyers - as many as
   I could get my hands on in Denver, San Diego & New York. But those
   that I have collected are just the tip of the iceberg, both in number and geography.
   Does anyone know of a coffee-table art book that has a couple thousand (or more)
   of these flyers ? Is there a gallery that collects and perhaps catalogs them ? Does anyone want to do
   this project (perhaps with me ?)

   Any information appreciated: wgolby2@ibm.net....Thanks !

   POSTS-FIRST-PREVIOUS-NEXT-SINCE-INDEX-TOPICS

3. **How do I submit drawings into Gallery?**
   Ofer LaOr (olaor) on Sun, 4 Jun 95 10:55 PST
   Posts 1 - Last Post: Wed, 7 Jun 95 13:44 PST

   I've been
   virtual G

While there are no hotlinks in the copy, there is a slightly less convenient THREADS hotlink reference at the bottom of the page. This navigational tool has no visual relationship with any previous navigational tool, unfortunately, and it wastes the wonderfully relevant hypertext capacity of placing links conveniently within the relevant text. This THREADS category, which appears at the bottom of each Retina article, reverse-engineers hotlinks into yet another contents list, quite a step backwards in design sophistication.

HotWired 6

A next level within the HotWired site, Threads: Retina in this case, is completely different in appearance from anything seen previously. It first appears to be a text-only document. No logo, font, or other navigational tool gives an immediate visual indication that this is still HotWired. Only at the bottom of the page are the familiar button bars and

HotWired logo. The immediate feeling is that I have just switched sites. I feel adrift on the Net, unsure where I have just landed apart from the Location indicator on my Netscape browser.

HotWired 7

The next level is not part of the HotWired site at all, but a new site, in Germany in this case (though fortunately with English text). The site is reached by selecting the Wrapping link within a message that a reader posted to the Threads: Retina page. This linking is part of why the Net is so thrilling. I am digging deeper and deeper into a topic of interest. I can compare the HotWired article with information from another source and begin to evaluate the author's observations. Here I discover that the wrap did not include typographic elements. From this site I can look at several different views of the project, selecting one for viewing at a larger size.

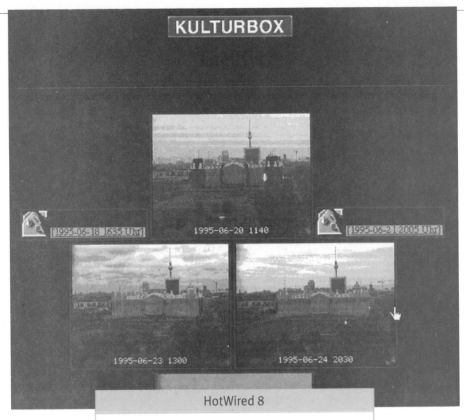

HotWired 8

Continuation of the KULTURBOX site.

HotWired 9

Continuation of the KULTURBOX site.

Parting Shots

Overall, the HotWired site is one of the best on the Net. It makes excellent use of the Net's changing nature (content changes), gives ample incentive to visit frequently (content calendar), reinforces the verbal incentives with visual cues (changing page color), uses appropriate visual forms connected to content (button styles, background textures), is well written, and provides excellent links to other sites containing relevant information.

Where HotWired falls short is in the lack of consistency of visual appearance (icon styles and text-only-looking pages) and in an over-reliance on print magazine design principles (obscure copy). It was easy to lose a sense of where I was as I navigated through the document. Not only did I have difficulty forming a mental map of where I was, but I often lacked the ability to jump to where I thought I wanted to go. Different levels and branches within the document have not only different visual appearances but different navigational schemes. This may be an intentional mime of the discontinuity experienced while traveling on the Net. If it is, it is using a nondesign situation, the unrelated documents on the Net, as the model for a document design — using chaos to build order. This is conceptually intriguing, perhaps, but not a good recipe for effective Web design.

One thing defending HotWired in particular, and a special challenge for Web designers in general, is the evolving nature of Web sites. The patchwork appearance may be the natural consequence of a site that is constantly changing and adapting to new needs. This ability to change constantly is a dangerous thing. It promotes fixes and changes that over time don't relate to each other and erode the original concept of the site.

Yale C/AIM WWW Style Manual

Yale Center for Advanced Instructional Media

This manual describes the design principles used to create the pages within the Center for Advanced Instructional Media's (C/AIM) World Wide Web site. This is not an introduction to HTML authoring, as excellent resources already exist for those purposes.

Manual Overview

INTRODUCTION

I. INTERFACE DESIGN IN WWW SYSTEMS
　　Hypermedia and Conventional Document Design
　　Navigation in Hyperspace
　　WWW Site Structure
　　WWW Page Design
　　Efficient Use of the World Wide Web
　　　　System Responsiveness
　　　　Well-balanced Page and Menu Designs

II. WWW PAGE DESIGN
　　Design Integrity in WWW Systems
　　Essential Elements of WWW Pages
　　Page Length
　　Design Grids for HTML
　　Sample Ter
　　Local Links

Yale C/AIM WWW Style Manual

http://info.med.yale.edu/caim/StyleManual_Top.HTML

Yale 1

The Yale WWW Style Manual's first visual impression is of a table of contents. This immediately suggests that the document is based on a book metaphor, which proves to be true. These Web pages, part of a larger site, appear to be an electronic manual, perhaps intended for use by other designers at Yale C/AIM. The simple, no-nonsense information presented is a brief abstract describing the Manual, followed by contents consisting almost entirely of links. The content descriptions are clear, making it easy to identify what content I want to explore further. The illustration, a globe and circuit board collage, serves as an effective visual anchor while adding little to the message. By relying predominantly on links for navigation, the document takes excellent advantage of the hypertextual nature of the Web.

At the bottom of the page are helpful navigational buttons along with much-appreciated author, ownership, revision date, and URL information. It is surprising how few Web pages include their URL as part of the document, a little like printing a brochure and forgetting to include the client's address. The revision date suggests that the information changes periodically, giving viewers both a sense of how frequently the site is updated and incentive to revisit the site.

◀ Prev Page   Next Page ▶   Manual To ⊼   Home Page ⊼

Yale C/AIM WWW Style Manual: *Design Integrity*

II. WORLD WIDE WEB PAGE DESIGN

Design Integrity in WWW Systems

Consistency and predictability are essential attributes of any well-designed information system, aiding users in identifying the origin and relationships of World wide Web pages, providing consistent and predictable access to interface and page elements, and a consistent graphic design scheme (Norman, 1993). The design grid systems that underlie most well-designed paper publications are no less necessary in designing electronic documents and on-line publications, where the spatial relationships between on-screen elements is constantly shifting in response to user input and system activity (Hurlburt, 1978; Marcus, 1992).

Clown's Pants

Current implementations of the Hypertext Markup Language (HTML) do not allow the flexibility or control that graphic designers routinely expect from page layout software or conventional multimedia authoring tools. However, the HTML markup language can be used to create complex and highly functional information systems if it is used carefully. When used inappropriately or inconsistently the typographic controls and inlined graphics of World Wide Web (WWW) pages may result in a patchy, confusing jumble, without any apparent visual hierarchy of importance. This unfortunate "clown's pants" effect of haphazardly mixed graphics and text results in decreased usability and legibility, just as it does in paper pages:

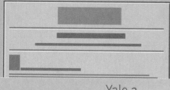

Yale 2

The next level, if we follow the II. WWW Page Design link in this case, is distinguished by a smaller version of the opening page collage. While it's not impressive at all visually, the reduced size of the repeated image clearly and intuitively suggests that I've moved down a level in the information hierarchy. Added to the header area are a set of handy navigational buttons: Prev Page, Next Page, Manual Top (the contents page), and the site Home Page. The Manual Top button is bordered by a different color, indicating that I have already visited that location.

The Clown's Pants illustration is instructive if uninspired. For all of its excellent qualities, the advice in this case is primitive and somewhat misleading. The Clown's Pants "bad" example is not demonstrably inferior design to the preferred example. This flaw is easy to overlook since the author clearly addresses

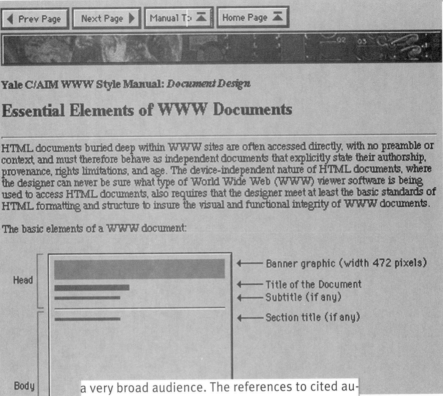

◄ Prev Page   Next Page ►   Manual To ⤒   Home Page ⤒

Yale C/AIM WWW Style Manual: *Document Design*

Essential Elements of WWW Documents

HTML documents buried deep within WWW sites are often accessed directly, with no preamble or context, and must therefore behave as independent documents that explicitly state their authorship, provenance, rights limitations, and age. The device-independent nature of HTML documents, where the designer can never be sure what type of World Wide Web (WWW) viewer software is being used to access HTML documents, also requires that the designer meet at least the basic standards of HTML formatting and structure to insure the visual and functional integrity of WWW documents.

The basic elements of a WWW document:

Head

← Banner graphic (width 472 pixels)

← Title of the Document
← Subtitle (if any)

← Section title (if any)

Body

a very broad audience. The references to cited authors at the bottom of the page added to both the scholarly quality and the book feel of the document.

Yale 3

The next level, Essential Elements of WWW Documents (click on Next Page to get there), is visually indistinguishable in format; only the Manual Top and Prev Page buttons have changed color, indicating that they are previously visited pages. This may appear to be a boring similarity compared to other documents, but the net result of this approach is that the content screams to the front while the navigational environment plays a purely supporting role. One missed opportunity is the lack of hypertext links to either the excellent glossary or bibliography of this Style Manual.

Manual To ⤒   Home Page ⤒

Yale C/AIM WWW Style Manual

Glossary of Graphic User Interface Elements

Buttons
A rectangular graphic that is usually labeled with text to indicate its function. Buttons usually perform an instantaneous action to initiate or conclude a process.

    [OK   ]
    [Cancel]

Check boxes
Used when alternatives are not mutually exclusive, or may be applied simultaneously, such as type styles: type can be both bold and italic at the same time. Check boxes never initiate or conclude an action, they are only used to set choices.

    ☐ Bold
    ☐ Italic
    ☐ Outline

Cursors (or pointers)
An extremely important but often overlooked component of graphic interfaces. Cursors indicate the point of action or insertion o   g and editing
on-screen objects. C   ss cursors indicate

Yale 4

The last level I visit is the Glossary (I have to click on the Manual Top button and return to the main page to find Appendix: Graphic Interface Glossary). Again the overall feel is identical to previous pages except for the content. This reinforces the book look and feel and the clear mental map of the site. The simple but effective illustrations are especially effective because the white/black of them contrasts so well with the gray background.

Parting Shots

The Yale C/AIM WWW Style Manual is perhaps the best large site I've seen on the Net in terms of being easy to navigate and understand. It also makes quiet use of illustrations, is very well written with an excellent annotated bibliography, and contains mostly solid advice. Perhaps the Style Manual's most endearing feature is its structure. My mental map of the document was clear from the start so that I not only had the tools available to go where I wanted, but I actually knew where I wanted to go.

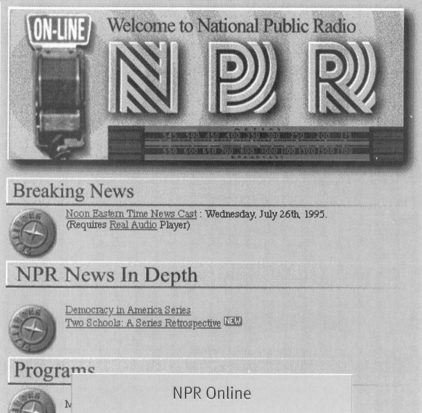

Welcome to National Public Radio

Breaking News

Noon Eastern Time News Cast : Wednesday, July 26th, 1995.
(Requires Real Audio Player)

NPR News In Depth

Democracy in America Series
Two Schools: A Series Retrospective NEW

Programs

NPR Online

http://www.npr.org

NPR 1

The first impression of the NPR (National Public Radio) site is the pleasant and unusual greenish-tan page color. The impression is sophisticated, educated, scholarly, reminiscent of old books or newspapers—all good impressions for public radio, which is often affiliated with universities and classical music.

The document is headed with an apt illustration done in a horizontal masthead format typical of most Web home pages. The illustration wisely incorporates the radiating lines of the typographic NPR symbol combined with photographs of an old-looking radio dial and microphone. This nostalgic approach adds a familiar, comfortable quality to this document on a cutting-edge medium.

Welcome to National Public Radio
NPR

Breaking News

Noon Eastern Time News Cast : Wednesday, July 26th, 1995.

RealAudio Player

Title: 12:01 ET News Cast
Author: National Public Radio
Copyright: Copyright 1995

Playing network stream   1:06.5 / 4:59.7

The information structure is clear but requires some scrolling to see the entire list—a small disadvantage. The navigational bars are easy to understand because the labels are clearly descriptive words in a large type font free of confusing icons. Unfortunately, the round navigational buttons beneath the bars are nearly useless other than as decoration, since they are all identical and unreadable.

NPR 1a

The next "level" in this document, Breaking News in this case, shows the real strength of this site and is a premier example of the Internet's multimedia capability: real-time audio from NPR's broadcasts. Clicking on Breaking News or Noon Eastern Time News Cast starts a RealAudio document that immediately plays a recording of the previous weekday's afternoon broadcast through my computer's speaker (this happens because I have visited NPR before and have copied RealAudio's player onto my hard drive; see chapter 11 on RealAudio, or visit RealAudio at http://www.realaudio.com). The controls of the sound file are effective, giving fast-forward, reverse, and pause capability along with volume control via a simple tape recorder button metaphor. The time length of the audio program and its progress are displayed. I find this helpful in deciding whether to continue listening or move on. It would be more helpful if the length of each story within the newscast were given, or the listener were given the ability to skip forward or back to the next selection like on an audio CD. The audio quality is not high, but the benefit of live sound in real time, without the hassle of first waiting to download a multimegabyte file then launching a sound player to listen to it, far outweighs any loss in sound quality.

The NPR Web site's presentation of radio broadcast information on demand is an excellent use of the Internet. It makes this kind of information much more accessible than ever before. Elsewhere on this site I find the full All Things Considered programs for the past several months, available story by story (gopher://gopher.npr.org:70/11/NPR_Online/ Programs/All_Things_Considered/ATC_Rundowns). This makes it possible to review a previously heard program or one that was interrupted, or to share a favorite program with a friend.

Democracy In America

An NPR special series exploring America's relationship with democracy and community.

Democracy Series Information

NPR AUDIO: NPR's Elizabeth Arnold reports on New Technology and Direct Democracy (Requires Real Audio player.)

Frances Moore Lappe Comments on Democracy

Dr. Amitai Etzione Comments on Democracy

Related Online Resources

Related Organizations Not Online

Bibliography

NPR 2

From the home page, the Democracy in America Series link takes us down a level. It has an illustration similar in style to the initial one, with radiating lines in the background and an old radio photo. This forms an effective identity system, since the radiating lines originate from the NPR logo. The use of visual elements related to the logo as a way to build other images is an inventive extension of the visual language of the logo. It expands the identity to more of the page, enhances the overall organization image, and unifies the document. The horizontal band orientation of the illustration relates to the first illustration, but it has a reduced vertical dimension, suggesting the change in information level. In addition, this page features some nice content such as a bibliography, a discussion group, and direct email capability.

Democracy Series Information

NPR AUDIO: NPR's Elizabeth Arnold reports on New Technology and Direct Democracy (Requires Real Audio player.)

Frances Moore Lappe Comments on Democracy

Dr. Amitai Etzione Comments on Democracy

Related Online Resources

Related Organizations Not Online

Bibliography

Democracy in America On-Line Discussion Group -- Enter "subscribe" or "info" in the Subject line.

NPR's Member Stations

E-mail us with comments or suggestions.

How to order Transcripts and Tapes

This page, and all   NPR 2a   Washington, D.C.

An additional navigational icon is added to the bottom of the document at this level. The form is an appropriate metaphor of a radio dial. The content is a restatement of the original contents listing on the first page, granting easy access to the second information levels without traveling all the way back to the home page.

Here, finally, the meaning of the round navigational buttons on the first level becomes clear: They are tiny radio dials. I thought they were compasses to suggest navigation! The use of the metaphor is interesting and effective; I wonder why it was not introduced earlier? Its position at the end of the document is a bit unexpected and could be missed entirely if I hadn't scrolled down sufficiently.

About Democracy in America

Story List

During the month of July, before the country again launches into its quandrennial excersize of electing the nation's leader, NPR News and member stations will explore the question that lurks behind political events: What about democracy? With all the technological changes in our lives, how has the process of transmitting power between the people and the government changed?

Democracy in America will be the sixth NPR Specials series to focus NPR and local station programming and outreach on a single topic of vital social concern. Are "we the people" still in charge? Are enough of us participating in the political process for our elected leaders to truly exercise their power "with the consent of the governed?" Or does an increasing body of Americans perceive the political process as meaningless? And what of the suspicion and intolerence that appear to have led, in the name of hatred of government, to the horror of Oklahoma City?

All Things Considered, Morning Edition, and Talk of the Nation will look at such questions in July. We will present stories that probe new challenges to the traditional political process: immigration and xenophobia; "shadow governments"; group rights vs. individual rights vs. the "common good"; the underclass of people marginalized from the mainstream of work, family values, and civic life.

Local stations will design companion reports, forums, and call-ins to create a connection between public radio and the community.

The NPR Specials are supported by funding from the Corporation for Public Broadca
AMERICA.

NPR 3

The next level, Democracy Series Information, is nicely connected by the page color to the rest of the site. There is no illustration heading this level, but the color works efficiently as a navigational clue that I am now at the third level in the information structure. The content is well written and clearly arranged, though there could be more links to other documents. The visual layout at this level is simple, even boring.

The next level isn't a level of the NPR site at all, but a link to a new site, the Corporation for Public Broadcasting's site in this case. Here the effectiveness of the distinctive page color as a unifier of the NPR document becomes immediately apparent. The CPB site is clearly a new location, with a gray textured background. Of course, the new logo and visual layout are also different, but the first and simplest indicator is page color, since that is what Netscape a la HTML loads first. Moreover, color is one of the most significant elements of the visual language used by designers, a fact often overlooked on Web documents, especially those created prior to newer versions of HTML and Netscape that give Web page designers the ability to control page and type color.

Parting Shots

The NPR site's navigational tools are simple and effective. There are subtle but effective visual clues that suggest where you are in the information hierarchy, effectively forming a mental map of the document's structure. It uses color to build a strong visual identity that connects one page to another, making it abundantly clear when linking to a new site. Much over-reliance on page color could present a problem on browsers that don't allow show page color, but the NPR site has sufficient other visual consistencies to avoid this pitfall.

The overall design system is effective at building the organization's identity through the use of repeated references to the visual language of the logo. Some branches in the site, however, use an amazing green texture pattern in the background. Not only is this a powerful and unwanted departure from the dominant design system, but the type is almost illegible (and I have good eyes). I assume this is a holdover from a previous version of the site design. The best part of the site is its exemplary use of multiple media to grant greater access to NPR's wealth of audio information. The number of links was paltry in some areas—a place for improvement.

Welcome to vivid studios' website

Wouldn't want to be the last on your block to know what's going on in the ever-trendy world of multimedia, now would you? Entangle yourself in our website and find out more:

- Check out our latest masterpieces in idea mill.
- Visit paparazzi to see what is being said about **vivid**.
- Sign up on our mailing list in the visitors center.
- **Make a bookmark** of the site so you can stay on top of the latest gulch happenings.

Want to work with us? Talk to our beloved leader, Henri Poole for details. Want to work *for* us? Then check out these job postings for our wish list of colleagues -- you may be one of us and not even realize it yet. And if you've got a great idea for an online program, send it to acquisitions@vivid.com and we'll do lunch.

About vivid

Located at the epice... ...ative online studio
that is redefining e... ...velopment **vivid**

vivid studios

http://www.vivid.com

vivid 1

The vivid studios Web site makes a solid first impression with the company name and with illustrative icons forming the table of contents of the site. It immediately suggests this is a site about a firm, which it is. The name and icons form a solid information structure that looks good. The massive size of the company name is mediated by the soft color value, a lavender to pale yellow blend. The small icons illustrate clever verbal descriptors that are explained by the less-creative but more meaningful words in the dark bar below. The result is a nice combination of clear information and creative copy.

The content is sparse, but substantial enough to provide guidance on what the document is and what information it provides. Ample hypertext links are provided, mostly linking to other pages within the site—a slight disadvantage for the inquisitive reader, but an advantage if the intent is to keep a reader interested in this site. The page color is standard gray and the illustration is carefully controlled to blend with it. The address, additional navigational tools, copyright, owner, and webmaster information at the bottom of the page are all good additions, though they lack distinguishing visual qualities that reinforce the visual or navigational tools at the top of the page.

The document is a little flat, relying too heavily on proven Web conventions: horizontal header band, illustration icons, and gray page color. This suggests sparse creativity for a design firm. In addition, the page is remarkably void of references to the high technology that is the organization's business staple. The overall impression is of a modest, traditional art studio.

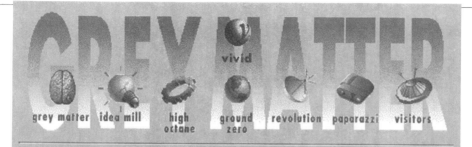

Meet the vividians!

vivid is a studio: a dynamic gathering place where schedules and situations flow as freely as ideas. We try to be as flexible as possible in adapting to people's creative needs and schedules. vividians are nine-to-fivers (well, more like nine-to-midnighters), part-time staffers, and contractors. Below you'll meet **vivid**'s founders, plus the members of Team **vivid**, our core group of brilliant-minds-in-residence, and Regular Contributors, close associates who make frequent appearances on project teams when a little extra brilliance is needed.

Founders

- Henri Poole, Founder and President
- Nathan Shedroff, Founder and Creative Director
- Ken Fromm, Founder and Producer

Team vivid

- AnnD Canavan, VP of Production
- Pamela "Bondy" Bondurant, QE Lead Engineer
- Drue Miller, Wordsmith and Webweaver
- Eric Watt
- Eric Fran
- Jonas Du

vivid 2

On another level, Grey Matter, makes a nice visual transition by replacing the word "vivid" in the header with the words "grey matter" done in the same font and visual gradation as the previous page. In addition, the icons are still present but have changed from color to monochrome (lavender for all but the current selection, which is gray), giving me an effective visual clue that I'm a level removed from home base.

Again, the content is brief but to the point. The copy style is informal and appropriately creative. The main content is a list of vivid workers, all hotlinks to the next level.

Henri Poole, Founder and President

Henri grew up in Oklahoma and began his software career at age 16 by founding a company. Although he was also an active artist at the time, he did not yet link the two passions. After attending the University of Science and Arts of Oklahoma and working in sales for several years, Henri moved to Silicon Valley and in 1988 began developing multimedia technology at Apple Computer.

In 1990 Henri four   vivid 3   r merged with **vivid publishing**.

The next pages, such as Henri Poole's, has an identical header to the previous page. The biography is again brief but informative. A few copy links add interest, again all within the site.

A little intuitive exploration of the header illustration at this level reveals that each monochromatic icon is still a hotlink to that area. This makes navigation within the site intuitive and remarkably easy. Even the small vivid logo at the top center serves as a link back to the home page. A click on the ground zero icon takes me to another content area.

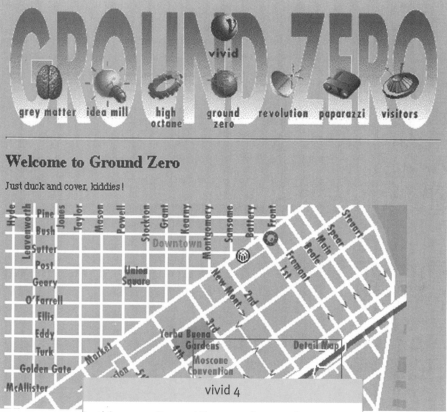

vivid 4

In this area, Ground Zero, an interactive map appears. The header is a logical extension of the previous ones, with all icons but the current selection rendered monochrome. Within the wide map are several darker icons. Clicking on one of them takes me to a new site, a store that sells design books in vivid's neighborhood, for example. This use of multimedia is an excellent example of the Web's potential. The exploration is informative and fun. The broad overview map invites exploration in a way that straight copy does not.

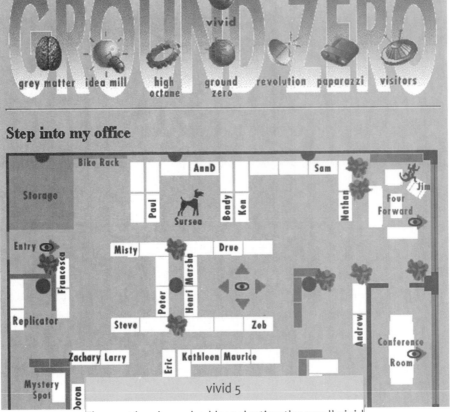

grey matter   idea mill   high octane   ground zero   revolution   paparazzi   visitors

Step into my office

vivid 5

The next level, reached by selecting the small vivid icon on the map, retains the header from the previous page. Although the header itself is a large image, the download time is not long, since the image has apparently been cached on my computer, evidence of smart document design. Though this is functionally smart, the large image is already becoming old, and more importantly, since it is so large it requires scrolling to move it up the page so that the entire floor plan image, the real content of the page, can be viewed.

The floor plan has names of workers, which link to their biography pages in the grey matter area. It also has small eye and arrow icons that are links to photographic views of the office. Selecting the icon in the conference room on the right side links to a new page.

grey matter   idea mill   high   ground   revolution   paparazzi   visitors
                            octane   zero

Deja View

vivid 6

You are standing in   n the main office.

Again, the same header occupies space, which necessitates scrolling to view the photo of the city below. In spite of this, the entire experience has been easy and enjoyable, giving an entirely different level of information about the firm than that received in the Grey Matter section.

Parting Shots

The vivid site is a superior example of user interface, navigation, and multimedia experience. This may explain why it falls a bit short on innovation. This is a dilemma for a designer working in any new medium: how far to stray from convention, avoiding cliché while retaining communication. vivid strikes a reasonable but safe balance, while making a blatantly self-promotional site fun to explore. One oversight: The site gave no indication whether the content would change or not, missing the opportunity to encourage repeat visits.

The White House

http://www.whitehouse.gov

White House 1

The White House Web pages open appropriately with a large, if not expected and uninspired, photograph of the White House. This centered photo is surrounded by Presidential seals that serve, with their typographic labels, as navigational buttons. The buttons' functions are clearly labeled and easy to recognize. Two of the buttons are symbolic of their function, the podiums for the Presidential messages, and one of the buttons is a literal expression of its function, the guest book for Guest Book. The others are not symbolic of the button's function at all. This mixed level of sign function is inconsistent at best. The clear implication is that some kinds of information are more important than others, which is not born out by the content (unless the main function of the page is to gather guest names). The impression left by the visual quality of the buttons ranges from comic (the cute little podiums) to solemn (the seals). The entire mass is surrounded by a blue and gold border, apparently in a lame attempt to unify the various visual forms: photo, symbol, and icon.

The contents are logical and useful, but the description "An Interactive Citizens' Handbook" is redundant, useless, and even poorly written. "Interactive" seems to describe "citizen" rather than the intended "handbook." The type fonts, a script and a serif similar to Times, set a formal tone, as does the small plaque at the top. The visual interaction of the two fonts is dissatisfactory, however, being too similar in size and texture. The overall impression, from the images used as well as the borders, colors, type fonts, and centered organizational structure, is formal but disjointed.

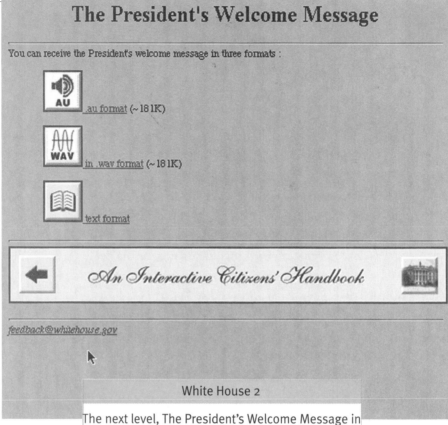

The President's Welcome Message

You can receive the President's welcome message in three formats :

.au format (~ 181K)

in .wav format (~ 181K)

text format

An Interactive Citizens' Handbook

feedback@whitehouse.gov

White House 2

The next level, The President's Welcome Message in this case, is another list of content choices, with no real additional information. This indicates an ill-considered information hierarchy that is unnecessarily deep, requiring the user to navigate through level after level to reach the desired information. The navigational buttons are a new style (square graphic icons) and the page color has changed from white to gray, creating the impression that I have just linked to a new site rather than moved from one level to another within the same document. Only the large navigational bar at the bottom suggests continuity with the first level through its use of the original words and script type font. The navigational bar, however, is unnecessarily large for the amount of content and function; it only does one thing. Moreover, it repeats the unfortunate descriptive statement from the previous level. The result is a huge indicator that suggests that I have left the

President's Welcome

"Welcome to the White House -- our first on-line citizen's handbook. I hope you find this a useful way to find answers to your questions, a better way to let me know what you think, and a powerful way to find information you can use --- whether you are in Nome, Alaska or right down Pennsylvania Avenue. Please don't forget to sign the guest book and let us know what you think of this new service."

 An Interactive Citizens' Handbook

To comment on this service: *feedback@www.whitehouse.gov*

Interactive Handbook, which, appearances to the contrary, I have not.

This level takes advantage of the Internet's multimedia capability by offering the message in audio as well as text formats. Unfortunately, nothing is really gained in this case by my having the same message in two forms, unless I am desperate to hear the sound of the President's voice, which I am not. Like most Americans, I am familiar with it already.

White House 3

The next level, the text version of the President's Welcome Message, is a brief statement with no hypertext links. The same navigational bar as the previous level is the only visual link to the style of the home page. The content itself is redundant: The President's Welcome begins with "Welcome to the White House," the same thing I have been reading since page one. The cumulative effect is a lot of navigational work and Internet time spent for nothing.

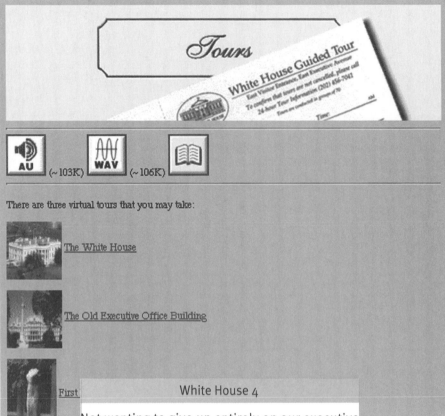

There are three virtual tours that you may take:

The White House

The Old Executive Office Building

First

White House 4

Not wanting to give up entirely on our executive branch's site, I try another option from the home page, this time Tours. The illustration this time is a nice connection to the home page look and feel; it uses not only the script font but the plaque border and white background as well. Added to these familiar elements is an image of a tour book. This creates a pleasant and meaningful visual system that relates to the home page while adding information relevant to this specific topic. The square button icons are a familiar aberration. Again, the primary purpose of this level is an additional contents listing, creating the same navigational awkwardness as before.

Twentieth Century American Sculpture at the White House

The twelve works of art selected from American art museums for this special exhibition span over seventy years of the 20th century, and represent a diverse and vital aspect of our cultural heritage. Conceived by Mrs. Clinton and drawn from public collections in the heartland of the nation and installed in the First Ladies' Garden of the White House, the exhibition has been organized under the auspices of the Association of Art Museum Directors.

Over half of the inclusions in this exhibition are by living American artists. Diverse in their ideas, idioms, and chosen medium, they span several artistic generations. Divided almost equally between figuration and abstraction, all evoke references to nature and the human figure. We hope you enjoy the following virtual tour of the exhibit.

"Observer" by Louise Bourgeois.
On loan from Sheldon Memorial Art Gallery, University of Nebraska at Lincoln.

"Five Rudders" by [...]
On loan from the W[...] [...]is, Missouri.

White House 5

The First Ladies' Garden page, one of the tours I can take, offers a brief overview of the garden contents with a hypertext link and a list of images for viewing. Potential links to information about the artists or the contributing museums would have been nice, and would have given me the opportunity to easily expand my knowledge and those gracious enough to contribute their works the opportunity to promote their contribution. The overall visual impact of the page is generic, a simple gray background without any visual clue to connect it with previous pages, apart from the familiar navigational bar at the very bottom of this long page.

White House 6

The next level is reached via a clicked link to an image file, "Walking Man" by George Segal. While the photo is less than ideal (part of the artwork, the man's foot, is cropped off), it does give me some idea of not only the First Ladies' Garden but of George Segal's work. This is a good use of multimedia that would be much better if the designer had included the name of the sculpture on the page with the image. Also missing are navigational links, copyright information, ownership information, and anything that indicates what this is, where it came from, or how to move elsewhere. Simply downloading a GIF image in this case, without creating a page that contains supporting information, can disrupt the entire document design and completely lose the user. This is poor document design at its best. I am at this point totally disconnected from the original document, lost in cyberspace, with only my browser to guide me.

Executive Branch

| White House | The President's Cabinet | Independent Federal Agencies & Commissions |

There are four ways to use this service to look for government information:

- By selecting a government agency from one of the categories in the image above.
- By agency using a map of Washington, D.C.
- By a subject index to government information online, which is provided by FedWorld.
- By a government information locator service (GILS), which is an index being built to all government information.

Find Information from Other Branches of the Government

Choose this for a te:

White House 7

One more try yields much more substantial content. The Executive Branch option on the home page takes me to a header image with the familiar plaque and script visual forms. This time these familiar forms are joined by a new button type, three rectangular boxes, each containing a color seal. Why the seal alone wasn't used with type over it, giving it continuity with the home page, is beyond me. And why the four types of information offered are navigated in different ways, one through the already described icons and the others through hypertext links, is a mystery. While this page is similar to others at this level, being primarily another contents listing, it is at least rich in hypertext linking options.

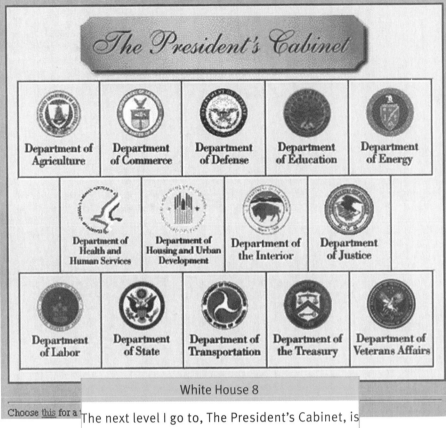

Choose this for a

White House 8

The next level I go to, The President's Cabinet, is nice in its consistency with the previous level through use of the plaque and script type, while the increased size and number of navigation button options (14) suggests a whole new level of information. While the consistency is strong and builds a nicely unified document, the result is a somewhat confusing mental map of this site. In some cases on this site, navigational options take me to finer levels of detail (such as the First Ladies' Garden); but this one takes me to a much greater range of opportunities. I am now unsure when I select a navigational option whether I am going toward greater detail or toward broader topics. This suggests insufficient time spent by the designers developing an information logic tree and user interface appropriate for the obvious depth and complexity of the content.

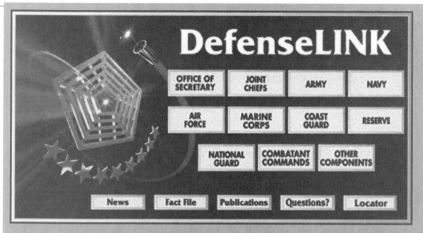

Secretary of Defense <u>William Perry</u> would like to <u>welcome you</u> to DefenseLINK, the <u>World-Wide Web</u> <u>Information Service from the Department of Defense</u>.

The **Department of Defense** is responsible for providing the military forces needed to deter war and protect the security of our country. The department's headquarters is at the <u>Pentagon</u>.

Under the <u>President</u> who is also Commander in Chief, the Secretary of Defense exercises the authority, direction, and control over the department, which includes:

- The <u>Office of the Secretary</u>
- The <u>Joint Chiefs of Staff</u>
- The <u>Army</u>
- The <u>Navy</u>
- The <u>Air Force</u>
- The <u>Marin</u>
- The <u>Coast</u>
- The <u>Reser</u>
- The National

White House 9

The Department of Defense link unexpectedly takes me not to a new page in White House site, but to a site at the Department of Defense. The visual images and icons are all new: a new illustration style, new navigational button format, and new information structure. There are just enough visual similarities to the White House home page (the blue and gold border and gray page color) to stimulate confusion about whether I have really joined a new site or not. The DoD site is rich in content and hypertext links.

Parting Shots

The White House site is commendable simply because it exists—admittedly that's not very high praise, but attempting to be online suggests an unusual forward-thinking attitude for our government and I applaud it. The site suffers tremendously from inadequate attention to information structure and user interface. The result is a missed opportunity to not only communicate effectively about the executive branch but to clarify the structure of the entire government. Instead, a tour of the White House unexpectedly turns into an advertisement for the U.S. Marines, making for an interesting if not mind-wrenching visit.

The visual forms are appropriate but stale and uninteresting. They are unified nicely at times yet dramatically different at others. The content quality varies widely also, from mind-yawning shallowness to mind-boggling complexity. The White House page is simply a nice attempt that falls apart. Better luck next time.

Features

Apple Computer

http://www.apple.com

Apple 1

The first impression of the Apple site is its speed: *slow*. This is not a good first impression for a computer company, yet it seems to be something of a trend for the sites of computer manufacturers. Apple is not the only one to use very large illustrations/images that take a lot of time to download. Perhaps Apple assumes that most of its audience is high tech enough to have high-speed connections— I don't know. But I am not impressed. It takes little skill to build a slow Web page.

The image already mentioned is a bizarre screen, vaguely like a computer, with three image areas that serve as hot buttons. It is only obvious that these are buttons because the screen includes copy telling me to "click on any selection above"—a clear admission of navigational failure. The best navigation empowers me react to visual clues without reading a list of instructions. A vertical row of navigation buttons on the left side and a horizontal button bar across the bottom form the rest of the navigational tools. While all of the buttons have clear typographic descriptors, it isn't clear why there are three different kinds of navigational buttons: a screen, a bar, and a row of buttons. The remainder of the page is a poorly organized table of contents. One category, Features, is arbitrarily subdivided and almost alphabetically listed. One nice linking touch, About this server, gives a little technical information about the server hardware, highly appropriate for a computer maker.

Apple Computer

Information about Apple

HotNews
Daily summaries of computer industry news items and Apple press releases
Apple press releases
Full text of Apple press releases. Older press releases are archived by month.
Apple Announcements and Events
Selected seminars and events with descriptions and schedules
Employment Opportunities
Investor Information
Apple phone numbers
For contacting Apple Computer in North America and Europe, including numbers for Educational and Government customers.
Apple Sales Offices
Contact information for sales offices worldwide
Corporate Fact Sheet
Apple History

 | Apple Internet Servers | What's New | Index | Feedback |

Apple | **Servers** | **What's New** | **Index** | **Feedback** | **Help**

Copyright 1995 Apple Computer, Inc.
Send any questions
last modified by W[...]

Apple 2

I move to the next level by clicking on About Apple. This page introduces a new header bar: a simple white rectangle containing the Apple logo. Gone are the vertical buttons, gone is the bizarre screen with its icons—in fact, gone are images of any kind beyond the logo and the horizontal button bar toward the bottom of the screen. And that bar is duplicated by a text-only list of links. The interface design becomes disconnected and confusing because so much has changed. Visual clues do not suggest where I am or help me form a mental map of the document. They aren't particularly inventive or appropriate for the topics or the company. The overall visual quality is staid and not at all appropriate for either the company or the products it produces. The content is very brief, almost an annotated table of contents, but with numerous links. That being perhaps the best that can be said for this page, the overall result is a shabby page with poor navigation.

Apple Computer

HotNews

for Thursday, July 27, 1995

copyright 1995, Apple Computer, Inc.

Top of the HotNews

- Fifteen companies, including Apple, Compaq, and IBM, have teamed up with Oracle as part of the Object Definition Alliance, to support an open cross-platform standard for multimedia objects. Microsoft's competing multimedia standards are closed and proprietary, which worries some developers. --Knight-Ridder

The Marketplace

- Hewlett-Packard is making a strong push into the home PC market, expanding its retail outlet presence beyond its current exclusive arrangement with Circuit City. H-P will sell systems through eight additional national retail chains, including Office Max, CompUSA, and Incredible Universe. --Knight-Ridder

The Industry

- To meet the increasing demands of faster computer processors, Texas Instruments has announced the development of SDRAM (synchronous dynamic random access memory) chips, capable of matching their speed to match their environment. TI says the new chips will cost about as much as regular D[...]

- Akai has a[...] ony's, and plans to introduce [...]es, primarily in

Apple 3

At the next level, HotNews, I was immediately impressed by a change in page color, from gray to white. The overall light field is more compatible with the original home page than the level I just left, making for a disconcerting transition. The now familiar Apple logo, minus the white box, is at the top of the page, joined by another header bar containing a HotNews logo. This logo, the first appearance of this kind of typographic illustration or header bar, is a rather predictable color blend from red to orange on a black field. The only navigational tools, besides a few text links, are at the bottom of the page. The content is appropriately brief and informative, but the links are sparse; I certainly wish for more. The page includes a nice reference to date, giving the information not only an appropriate sense of urgency but a hint that it will change again tomorrow, encouraging repeat visits.

Apple Computer

Apple Product Information and Product Support

Hardware I Software I Recently in the News I Customer Support I Service Providers

Hardware Products

APPLE PRODUCT LIST
Looking for a specific product? This list of all currently shipping products offers part numbers and brief product descriptions.

PRODUCT INFORMATION SHEETS
To browse a product group in more detail, try our Information Sheets covering the following product lines: Macintosh Performa, Macintosh Servers, Macintosh Desktop Computers, Monitors, Newton, Peripherals, PowerBooks, Printers, and Software.

APPLE COMPETITIVE INFORMATION
Read the most recent competitive analysis studies from Apple's Competitive Analysis Group. Compare Macintosh and Power Macintosh computers with other personal computers.

APPLE INTERNET SERVER SOLUTION
The Apple Internet Server Solution is the easy and affordable way to establish an Internet server using the MacOS. To see what the Workgroup Server 9150 can do, read the About this server message from www.apple.com.
For examples of Apple customers running Internet servers using the Apple Internet Server Solution, visit the Useful Internet Server Information page.

POWER MACINTOSH AND POWERPC
Visit the Power Macintosh - PowerPC home page for product information, white papers, and a list of PowerPC n:

APPLE NEWTON

Apple 4

Not wanting to give up yet (I am using a Macintosh to do this, after all), I try another option from the home page, Product & Support. Here I am back to a gray background and the Apple logo in a white box. The text is another semiorganized contents list.

Apple Software

Desktop Computer Systems

Apple Peripherals

Apple Monitors

Portable Computers

Printers & Imaging

Newton

Networking & Connectivity

Welcome to AppleFacts Online — a concise electronic guide to Apple products. AppleFacts Online is intended as a convenient, computer-based, one-stop reference for basic product information, such as U.S. data sheets, descriptions and specifications, upgrades, and accessories. Because product availability, configurations, and part numbers vary worldwide, we suggest that you contact your local Apple reseller or Apple office for this information.

Apple 5

Selecting Product Information Sheets takes me not to what I expected, Product Information Sheets, but to something that looks and feels like a new site, Apple Facts Online. The background has changed back to white and the familiar Apple logo is here, but a new and different contents list/navigational button type appears on the left-hand side. This page turns out to be a long contents list, five or six full screens' worth.

Desktop Computer Systems

1. The Macintosh Advantage
2. The Power Macintosh Advantage
3. Macintosh LC 475
4. Macintosh LC 580
5. Macintosh LC 630
6. Macintosh LC 630 DOS Compatible
7. Macintosh Performa 580
8. Macintosh Performa 630 and Performa 630 CD
9. Macintosh Performa 631 CD
10. Macintosh Performa 636 CD
11. Macintosh Performa 630 DOSCompatible
12. Performa 640 CD DOS Compatible
13. Macintosh Performa 5200CD
14. Macintosh Performa 5215CD
15. Macintosh Performa 6100 Series
16. Macintosh Performa 6116CD
17. Macintosh Performa 6200CD
18. Macintosh Performa 6216CD
19. Macintosh Performa 6218CD
20. Macintosh Performa 6220CD
21. Macintosh Performa 6230CD
22. Macintosh Quadra 630
23. Macintosh Quadra 950
24. Power Macintosh 5200/75 LC
25. Power Macintosh 6100/66 and 6100/66 AV
26. Power Macintosh 6100/66 DOS Compatible
27. Power Macintosh 6200/75 (outside U.S. only)
28. Power Macintosh 7100/80
29. Power Macintosh 8100/110, Power Macintosh 8100/100AV, and Power Macintosh 8100/100
30. Power Macintosh 9500
31. Desktop System Upgrades
32. Desktop System Accessories
33. DOS Compatibility Card for Power Macintosh 6100

Apple Periph

Apple 5a

Selecting Desktop Computer Systems links me to a point further down the same page. A long contents list with navigational links is not uncommon on Web sites, where the navigational buttons do not take me to a new document, or even to another page, but simply serve to hop down this page to the area selected. The result of all these changes noted here and above is an unsettling feeling of being jerked around. A new look, a new navigation button format, a new linking concept from page to page... Is this how they design computers?

 **Apple Computer**

Macintosh Quadra 630 Product Shot

Macintosh Quadra 630

Features

Power and speed

- 66/33-MHz 68040 microprocessor with 32-bit data bus
- Integrated math coprocessor
- 4MB of RAM, expandable to 36MB

Display support

- 1MB of video memory supports Apple displays of up to 15 inches
- Works with a wide range of VGA and SVGA monitors

Expansion

- Can be upgraded to PowerPC
- Comes with built-in ports for hard drives, printers, scanners, and modems
- Supports most processor-direct cards compatible with Macintosh Quadra 605 and Macintosh LC series of computers via an internal expansion slot
- Includes a communications slot for an Ethernet connection or 14.4-baud fax/data modem
- Has video slot for NTSC, PAL, and SECAM video-input card
- Includes expansion bay for television tuner
- External drop box provides expansion for NTSC or PAL video output
- Includes bay for CD-ROM player

Convenience

Apple 6
Bingo! I finally get my product information when I select Quadra 630, an actual product page. Here's a nice layout that's nicely related to the previous page, except that even after several tries, the image fails to download. Now I'm sorry I wrote down that server information back on the home page—this thing isn't working right.

Apple Computer

Data Sheet

Macintosh Quadra 630

Features

Power and speed

- 66/33-MHz 68040 microprocessor with 32-bit data bus
- Integrated math coprocessor
- 4MB of RAM, expandable to 36MB

Display support

- 1MB of video memory supports Apple displays of up to 15 inches
- Works with a wide range of VGA and SVGA monitors

Expansion

- Can be upgraded to PowerPC
- Comes with built-in ports for hard drives, printers, scanners, and modems
- Supports most processor-direct cards compatible with Macintosh Quadra 605 and Macintosh LC series of computers via an internal expansion slot
- Includes a communications slot for an Ethernet connection or 14.4-baud fax/data modem
- Has video slot for NTSC, PAL, and SECAM video-input card
- Includes expan
- External drop

Apple 7

Another try gets it done.

This page, packed full with six or seven screens' worth of information, has no contents list or navigational tools to help locate what I want. The page makes good use of the Apple company type face reversed out of a black rectangle to structure the space. The reference to a printable Adobe Acrobat version of the data sheet makes a nice touch at the very bottom of the page.

Parting Shots

The Apple site could be much better. It is visually uninteresting with a disjointed user interface. Where there are attempts at visual quality, such as the bizarre screen image on the home page, Apple creates a mixed impression of an unfamiliar technology. The screen isn't exactly futuristic, or retro, or computer, or video game; it isn't anything really. The result is a subtle disorientation that is distracting and unfortunately symbolic of the entire site.

Where the White House is commendable simply because it exists, the Apple site fails in part because it is for a company that should do so much better. Apple should be leading the way in quality use of the Web instead of trailing the pack.

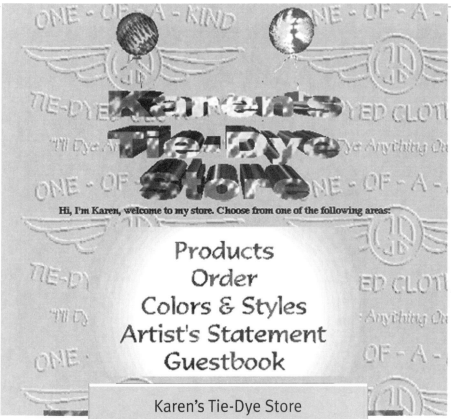

Karen's Tie-Dye Store

http://www.tie-dye.com

Karen's Tie-Dye 1

Karen's Tie-Dye Store is an example of a simple electronic storefront. As the file loads, the page color on my Netscape browser flashes a series of colors, making a tie-dye-like special visual effect, a nice use of the medium to project an image appropriate to the product. The general impression, largely based on the embroidered-looking background that loads after the initial color flashes, is of quality clothing. The multicolored lettering is appropriate to the subject, although the three-dimensional zoom is an obvious computer trick that flies in the face of the otherwise personal, hand-made quality of Karen's store.

The navigational structure is simple and clear, and

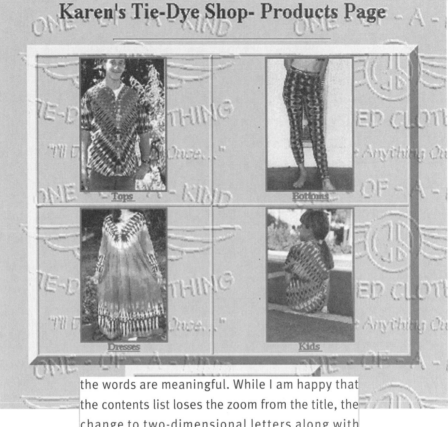

the words are meaningful. While I am happy that the contents list loses the zoom from the title, the change to two-dimensional letters along with the change in font style disconnects the navigation from the title. The glow behind the contents list is simply a cliché. The small teaser at the bottom for Netscape users is not fun. It causes several reconnects, takes forever (well, seems to), and is unspectacular. Just some HTML 3.0 fireworks.

Karen's Tie-Dye 2

Moving to the next page, Products in this case, reveals an illustrated product listing by type. The background remains consistent with the home page, as does the no-nonsense writing. I mean, "Karen's Tie-Dye Shop Products Page" is pretty hard to argue with! A new three-dimensional effect makes its appearance—not lettering, but a border around the photos. It isn't any more appropriate than the first three-dimensional computer trick. I

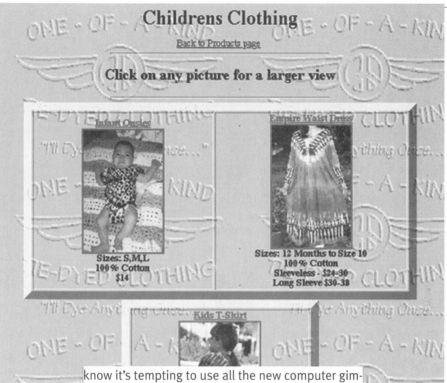

Childrens Clothing

Back to Products page

Click on any picture for a larger view

Infant Onsies
Sizes: S,M,L
100% Cotton
$14

Empire Waist Dress
Sizes: 12 Months to Size 10
100% Cotton
Sleeveless - $24-30
Long Sleeve $30-38

Kids T-Shirt

know it's tempting to use all the new computer gimmicks after going to all the trouble to figure out how to pull them off, but it really is better to design with visual tricks that *support* content, rather than using the new skill for the skill's own sake. This is a very typical and understandable failing in a new medium, but it is bad design.

Karen's Tie-Dye 3

Selecting Kids takes me to—where else—children's clothing! This site isn't as deep as something like Apple's site, but it gets me where I want, and expect, to go.

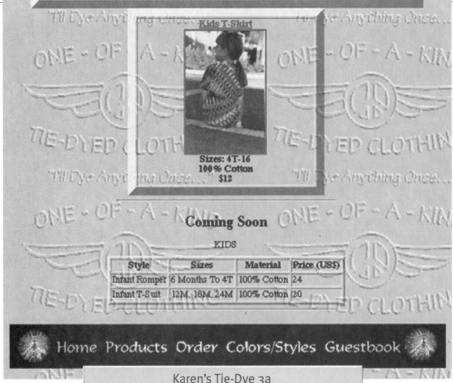

Karen's Tie-Dye 3a

Scrolling to the bottom of the page reveals that all along my Netscape window has been set too narrow—the navigational toolbar runs right off my screen. The issue of page size is a problem on Web documents: The designer doesn't really know the proportion of the page being designed. In this case the flaw isn't fatal—I didn't miss any vital information or get lost. The navigational bar at the bottom is an unattractive but functional repetition of the original content list. The page is way short of capitalizing on the Internet: nothing concrete that would encourage a repeat visit, no URL to help me find my way back if I want to return, no copyright protection (is there such a thing?), no author or owner name other than Karen, no multiple-media options, no links to speak of.

Karen's Order form

Check out the products and colors and styles then fill out the form and then push submit. Please allow 4-6 weeks for delivery

[Submit Form]   [Clear Form]

Personal Information

[ ]	- Name
[ ]	- E-Mail
[ ]	- Street address
[ ]	- Address 2
[ ]	- City, State and ZIP
[ ]	- Phone number

Payment Preference

There is a 4 dollar shipping charge on domestic orders, 1 dollar per additional item

- ○ - I will send a check or money order (We won't start work till the check arrives). Mail to:
    - o Karen Ferguson
    - o 41 Homer Lane
    - o Menlo Park, CA 94025
    - o 415-854-9370
- ○ - COD (extra)
- ○ - I would like to be called for my credit card number

Karen's Tie-Dye 4

Being a good consumer, I want to order something to reward Karen for her Net ambition. The form is simple and easily maneuvers around the credit card issue by her offer to call me and get my number. The colors and options are clear and easy to navigate.

Parting Shots

Karen deserves all the credit in the world for putting a solid and functional document up on the Web. The site overcomes several Web design problems: navigation, information structure, and cohesive design system. While not all the visual content is appropriate for the subject matter, it is remarkably consistent. The document also has a functional process for taking orders and arranging for payment for merchandise over unsecured Net lines. All in all, this site is as good, in some ways better, than sites for much bigger companies.

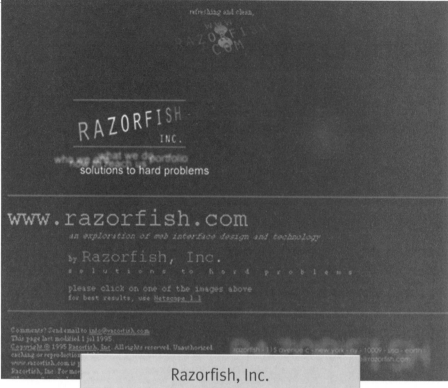

Razorfish, Inc.

http://www.razorfish.com

Razorfish 1

The Razorfish site, from a New York interactive design firm, takes full advantage of the Net to make an animated statement. The blue dot on the right spins and dissolves, and the type that makes up the navigation and content structure flashes and blurs, making for quite an impressive display of not only animation but bandwidth consumption. I stay actively connected to the site as long as I leave the home page on my screen. This isn't exactly the most polite use of crowded Internet lines, but many feel that (overcrowding or courtesy, I'm not sure which) is becoming irrelevant. I was fascinated and waited for more to happen, but the animation loops just played over and over again, leaving me unamused and uninformed. Perhaps a simple statement, such as "You've seen it all now, stupid," would encourage stupid visitors like me to move on after a repetition or two, freeing up a lane on the highway. Animation is a very powerful communicator. Animated typography can be unbelievably expressive (see chapter 10). Unfortunately, this animation was a brief but meaningless adventure into the potential of live movement on the Internet.

Razorfish 2

Clicking on the animated content list on the home page takes me to a nonanimated content list for the document. The visual language is consistent from one page to another, though the striking animation is gone (but not forgotten). The Razorfish logo is repeated larger and in a different color. A bit of content, ownership, and URL information is thoughtfully provided at the bottom of the page.

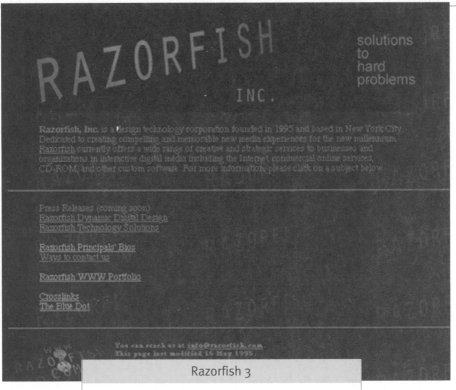

Razorfish, Inc. is a design technology corporation founded in 1995 and based in New York City. Dedicated to creating compelling and memorable new media experiences for the new millennium, Razorfish currently offers a wide range of creative and strategic services to businesses and organizations in interactive digital media including the Internet commercial online services, CD-ROM, and other custom software. For more information, please click on a subject below.

Press Releases (coming soon)
Razorfish Dynamic Digital Design
Razorfish Technology Solutions

Razorfish Principals' Bios
Ways to contact us

Razorfish WWW Portfolio

Crosslinks
The Blue Dot

You can reach us at info@razorfish.com.
This page last modified 16 May 1995.

Razorfish 3

Selecting Coming Soon moves me to a text-heavy page stating the company's beliefs about several related topics. The copy size and color are unusual and handsome, but make reading difficult for such a large body of copy, a trade-off that would be more justifiable if it added something to the meaning. There are few links in the copy—an unfortunate omission, since the content is interesting.

Parting Shot

The site is a great adventure. Other branches within the document reconnect to the animation. But the animation is so commanding, yet so pointless, that it dominates the site, becoming the most remarkable feature on, or missing from, each page. I am sure that in time Razorfish will find something important to say on its site using animated typography, something worth the bandwidth, something that animation can say that static type can not. For now, it's a nice site that pushes the technical envelope, but not design. Someone has to do it. Thanks!

Appendix A

Essential
Internet
Resources

What follows is a brief listing of valuable online resources. Most of these were given throughout the book, but we thought that compiling them all together would be useful. Keep in mind that these URLs may change, as the Internet continues to evolve and change at an astonishing rate.

Your best bet for finding online resources is the Designer's Guide to the Internet Web site, which has up-to-date links to all sorts of design-related Internet resources. Check it out at http://www.zender.com/designers-guide-net!

Internet Resources

General Internet Information

Adam Engst's Internet Starter Kit Resources
http://www.mcp.com/hayden/iskm

BBS Page
http://mail.eskimo.com/~future/bbs.htm

Beginner's Guide to URLs
http:www.ncsa.uiuc.edu/demoweb/url-primer.html

Vicious Book of BBSs
http://www.dsv.su.se/~mats-bjo/bbslist.html

VRML
http://vrml.wired.com

Winsock
http://www.yahoo.com/Computers_and_Internet/Software/Protocols/Winsock

The World Wide Web Initiative: The Project
http://www.w3.org

WWW Names and Addressing
http://www.w3.org/hypertext/WWW/Addressing

Zender + Associates, Inc.
http://www.zender.com/designers-guide-net

IRC/Chat

Homer
ftp://ftp.utexas.edu/pub/mac/tcpip

IRC-Related Resources on the Internet
http://urth.acsu.buffalo.edu/irc/WWW/ircdocs.html

A short IRC primer
http://mistral.enst.fr/~pioch/IRC/IRCprimer/IRCprimer1.1/IRCprimer1.1.html

WS-IRC for Windows
ftp://cs.bu.eu/irc/clients/pc/windows

Newsgroups/Mailing Lists

DTP Internet Jumplist—Discussion Groups
http://www.cs.purdue.edu/homes/gwp/dtp/groups.html

Mailing Lists of Interest to Macintosh Users
http://rever.nmsu.edu/~elharo/faq/mailinglists.html

Newsreader Archive (Windows)
http://uts.cc.utexas.edu/~neuroses/snews.html

Usenet FAQ Archive
ftp://rtfm.mit.edu/pub/usenetUsenet FAQs
http://www.cis.ohio-state.edu/hypertext/faq/usenet

Other Net Services

MacWAIS
http://www.wais.com/newhomepages/surf.html

MUDs
http://www.yahoo.com/Entertainment/Games/Internet_Games/MUDs__MUSHes
__MUSEs__MOOs__etc_
http://www.pitt.edu/~jrgst7/MOOcentral.html

WinWAIS
ftp://ftp.einet.net/einet/pc

WS Gopher
ftp://dewey.tis.inel.gov/pub/wsgopher

Research Tools

AT&T Internet Toll Free 800 Directory
http://www.tollfree.att.net/dir800

Archie search
http://www-ns.rutgers.edu/htbin/archie
http://cuiwww.unige.ch/archieplexform.html
http://www.sura.net/archie/Archie-Usage.html

CUI W3 Catalog
http://cuiwww.unige.ch/w3catalog
http://cuiwww.unige.ch/meta-index.html

Digital Planet Netcount
http://www.digiplanet.com/DP1/netcount.html

EINet Galaxy
http://galaxy.einet.net/galaxy.html

Email Address-Finding Tools
http://twod.med.harvard.edu/labgc/roth/Emailsearch.html

Email Addresses
http://www.cis.ohiostate.edu/hypertext/faq/usenet/finding-addresses/faq.html

Florida Law Weekly
http://www.polaris.net/~flw/flw.htm

Gopher search
gopher://info.psi.net:2347/7
gopher://veronica.utdallas.edu:2348/7
gopher://gopher.scs.unr.edu/00/veronica/veronica-faq

GNN Whole Earth Catalog
http://gnn.com/gnn/wic/index.html

GVU Center's WWW User Survey Home Page
http://www.cc.gatech.edu/gvu/user_surveys

InfoSeek
http://www.infoseek.com

Interest Groups Finder
http://www.nova.edu/Inter-Links/cgi-bin/news-lists.pl

Internet Audit Bureau
http://www.iaudit.com

I/PRO Internet Profiles Corporation
http://www.ipro.com

Lycos
http://lycos.cs.smu.edu

Medline Guide
http://www.sils.umich.edu/~nscherer/Medline/MedlineGuide.html

Money & Investing Update
http://update.wsj.com

Mr. Bad Advice
http://www.echonyc.com/~spingo/Mr.BA

NCSA What's New
http://www.ncsa.uiuc.edu/SDG/Software/Mosaic/Docs/Docs/whats-new-
form.html

NewsPage Home Page
http://www.newspage.com

NewsLink registration
http://www.newslink.org

Open Market Home Page
http://www.openmarket.com

Planet Earth's Home Page Virtual Library
http://godric.nose.mil/planet_earth/ info.html

Security APL Quote Server
http://www.secapl.com/cgi-bin/qs

WebCrawler
http://webcrawler.sc.washington.edu/WebCrawler/WebQuery.html

Web search engine
http://www.opentext.com:8080/omw.html

WebTrack
http://www.webtrack.com

The World Wide Web Virtual Library
http://www.theworld.com/SUBJECTS.HTM

The World Wide Web Worm
http://www.cs.colorado.edu/home/mcbryan/WWWW.html

The WWW Virtual Library
http://www.w3.org/hypertext.DataSources/by Subject/Overview.html

Weather Information Server
http://acro.harvard.edu/GA/weather.html or http://life.anu.edu.au/weather.html

Yahoo
http://www.yahoo.com

Yahoo: News
http://www.yahoo.com/News

Security

Netscape Data Security
http://home.netscape.com/newsref/ref/netscape-security.html

Service Providers

America Online
http://www.aol.com

CommerceNet Service
http://www.commerce.net/directories/products/isp

CompuServe
http://compuserve.com

designOnline
http://www.dol.com

eWorld
http://www.eworld.com

Evaluation of Providers
http://web.cnam.fr/Network/Internet-access/how_to_select.html

Microsoft Network
http://www.msn.net

Performance Systems International (PSI)
http://www.psi.com/indivservices/interramp

Prodigy
http://www.prodigy.com

Productivity OnLine
http://www.pol.com

Yahoo: Business and Economy: Companies: Internet Access Providers
http://www.yahoo.com/Business_and_Economy/Companies/Internet_Access_
Providers

Shopping

Access Market Square Internet Shopping Mall
http://www.icw.com/ams.html

The Branch Mall
http://branch.com

eMall's Home Page
http://eMall.Com/Home.html

Electronic Auction
http://www.primenet.com/~auction

MarketNet: The Electronic Marketplace
http://mkn.co.uk

The Internet Mall
http://www.mecklerweb.com/imall

The Super Mall
http://supermall.com

Downtown Anywhere
http://awa.com

Software via the Internet

California State University at San Marcos Windows Shareware Archive
http://coyote.csusm.edu/cwis/winworld/winworld.html

The Center for Innovative Computer Applications at Indiana University:
PC/Windows FTP Archive
http://www.cica.indiana.edu/cgi-bin/checkftp

Info-Mac Archive
ftp://sumex.stanford.edu/pub/info-mac

Mirror Archives (America Online)
ftp://mirrors.aol.com

Search Info-Mac
http://www.msc.wku.edu/Dept/Support/MSC/Macintosh/search_infomac.html

Search UMich
http://www.msc.wku.edu/Dept.Support/MSC/Macintosh/search.umich.html

University of Michigan Mac Archive
ftp://mac.archive.umich.edu

Windows TCP/IP directory
ftp://ftp.execpc.com/pub/windows/winsock

Yahoo's shareware listings
http:// www.yahoo.com/Computers/Software/Shareware

Videoconferencing

Avistar Systems
http://www.siren.com/avistar

Desktop Videoconferencing Product Survey
http;//www2.ncsu.edu/eos/service/ece/project/succeed_info/dtvc_survey/
survey.html

White Pine Software
http://www.wpine.com/cu-seeme.html

Web Browsers

Intervista (VRML)
http://www.hyperion.com/intervista/technology.html

Java/HotJava
http://java.sun.com/mail.html

Mosaic
http://www.ncsa.uiuc.edu/SDG/Software/MacMosaic
http://www.ncsa.uiuc.edu/SDG/Software/WinMosaic

MacWeb
http://galaxy.einet.net/EINet/MacWeb/MacWebHome.html

Netscape
http://home.netscape.com

WebSpace (VRML)
http://www.sgi.com/Products/WebFORCE/WebSpace

WinWeb
http://galaxy.einet.net/EINet/WinWeb/WinWebHome.html

Design Resources

Design Organizations and Information

AIGAlink
http://www.dol.com/AIGA

BusinessGraphics
http://www.busgrfx.com/busgrfx/bushome.html

DCI Events by Technology
http://www.DCIexpo.com

DESIGNLINK
http://www.designlink.com

designOnline
http://www.dol.com

design resumes
http://www.dol.com:80/Root/people/resumes/resumes.html

Desktop Publishing/Printing GS Home Page
http://degaulle.hil.unb.ca/UNB_G_Services/GSHomePage.html

DTP Jumplist
http://www.cs.purdue.edu/homes/gwp/dtp/dtp.html

Graphic Arts Technology at Royal Institute of Technology
http://www.gt.kth.se/info/GT.info.eng.html#100

High Five
http://www.best.com/~dsiegel/high_five/high_five.html

NCD
http://ncdesign.kyushu-id.ac.jp

OnLine Design Homepage
http://www.cea.edu/online.design

Online Prepress Service, Postscript to Film Output
http://www.wco.com/~billn

PrePRESS Main Street
http://www2.prepress.pps.com

SIGGRAPH
http://siggraph.org

The Graphix Exchange
http://www.rust.net/TGX_WWW_pgs/TGX.html

University of Tampere in Finland
http://www.uta.fi/~samu/graphic_design_books.html

Yahoo: Business and Economy: Companies: Communications and Media Services:
Graphic Design
www.yahoo.com/Business_and_Economy/Companies/Communications_and_
Media_Services/Graphic_Design

The World Wide Web Virtual Library on Design
http://www.dh.umu.se/vlib.html

Prepress Online
http://www.mindspring.com/~sledet/po

Designers' Sites

Clement Mok Designs
http://www.cmdesigns.com

Razorfish, Inc.
http://www.razorfish.com

vivid studios
http://www.vivid.com

Zender + Associates, Inc.
http://www.zender.com

Fonts

Font Archive
http://jasper.ora.com/comp.fonts/Internet-Font-Archive/mac.archive.umich.edu/ index.html

fontsOnline
http://www.dol.com/fontsOnline

Graphion's Online type Museum
http://www.slip.net/~graphion/museum.html

Internet Font Archive
http://jasper.ora.com/comp.fonts/Internet-Font-Archive

Internet Font Browser
http://cuiwww.unige.ch/InternetFontBrowser.html

Letraset
http://www.letraset.com/letraset

TypeLab
http://www.dol.com:8o/TypeLab

Will-Harris House
http://www.will-harris.com

Galleries and Image Archives

AIGAlink virtual gallery
http://www.dol.com/AIGA/door.html

A Global Canvas: The Museum Book of Digital Fine Art
http://www.mcp.com/hayden/museum-book

Electric Magic
http://www.emagic.com

freeSpace
http://www.rca.ac.uk/freespace

Graphica Obscura
http://www.sgi.com/grafica

Graphics on Call
http://www.pacific-coast.com/GOCDemo.html

PhotoDisc
http://www.photodisc.com

The Place
http://gertrude.art.uiuc.edu/ludgate/the/place/place2

Sandra's Clip Art Server
http://www.cs.yale.edu/homes/sjl/clipart.html

The Stock Solution
http://www.xmission.com/~tssphoto/tssphoto.html

Tony Stone Images
http://www.tonystone.com

WebLouvre
http://mistral.enst.fr/louvre

HTML Help

A Beginner's Guide to HTML
http://www.ncsa.uiuc.edu/General/Internet/WWW/HTMLPrimer.html

Dynamic Documents
http://home.netscape.com/assist/net_sites/dynamic_docs.html

Extensions to HTML
http://home.netscape.com/assist/net_sites/html_extensions.html

TEI Guidelines for Electronic Text Encoding and Interchange
http://etext.virginia.edu/bin/tei-tocs?div=DIV1&id=SG

Yale C/AIM WWW Style Manual
http://info.med.yale.edu/caim

Hardware and Software Information

PageMaker FAQ
http://www.cs.purdue.edu/homes/gwp/pm/pmstation.html

Photoshop
http://www.adobe.com/Apps/Photoshop.html

Hardware and Software Providers

Adobe
http://www.adobe.com

Apple
http://www.apple.com

Canon
http://www.canon.com

Corel Corporation
http://www.corel.ca

Father of Shareware
http://www.halcyon.com/knopf/jim

Hewlett Packard
http://www.hp.com

HSC Software
http://the-tech.mit.edu/KPT/contact.html

IBM
http://www.ibm.com

Macromedia
http://www.macromedia.com

Microsoft
http://www.microsoft.com

NEC
http://www.nec.com

Qualcomm
http://qualcomm.com

Shareware Central
http://www.intac.com/~dversch/swc.html

Sun Computer
http://www.sun.com

Virtus
http://www.virtus.com

WordPerfect
http://www.wordperfect.com

Helper Applications and Converters

AVI to QuickTime Converter (video)
ftp://ftp.tidbits.com/pub/tidbits/tisk/util

Cool Edit (audio)
http://www.ep.se/cool

GraphicConverter (graphics)
http://wwwhost.ots.utexas.edu/mac/pub-mac-graphics.html

LView Pro for Windows (graphics)
ftp://oak.oakland.edu/SimTel/win3/graphics

Macintosh applications
http://wwwhost.ots.utexas.edu/mac

MPEGplay (video)
ftp://ftp.tidbits.com/pub/tiskwin

Microsoft Video for Windows Runtime (video)
ftp://ftp.eden.com/pub/pc/win/video

PNG (Portable Network Graphics) Specification, Tenth Draft
http://sunsite.unc.edu/boutell/png.html

QuickTime for Windows (video)
ftp://ftp.ncsa.uiuc.edu/Mosaic/Windows/viewers

RealAudio (audio)
http://www.realaudio.com

SoundApp (audio)
ftp://sunsite.unc.edu/pub/multimedia/utilities/mac/audio

SoundExtractor (audio)
http://hyperarchive.lcs.mit.edu/cgibin/NewSearch?key=SoundExtractor

SoundHack (audio)
http://hyperarchive.lcs.mit.edu/cgi-bin/NewSearch?key=SoundHack

SoundMachine (audio)
ftp://ftp.ncsa.uiuc.edu/Mosaic/Mac/Helpers

Sparkle (video)
ftp://ftp.ncsa.uiuc.edu/Mosaic/Mac/Helpers

Transparency (graphics)
ftp://ftp.med.cornell.edu/pub/aarong/transparency

Wham (audio)
ftp://gatekeeper.dec.com/pub/micro/msdos/win3/sounds

Windows applications
ftp://bitsy.mit.edu/pub/dos/utils

Windows Media Player (video)
ftp://ftp.tidbits.com/pub/tiskwin

Wplany (audio)
ftp://ftp.cdrom.com/.5/cica/sounds

Web Design Tools

Arachnid
http://sec-look.uiowa.edu/about/projects/arachnid-page.html

HTML Editor for Excel for the Mac
http://www.rhodes.edu/software/readme.html

HTML Editor for Word (Mac)
http://www.netweb.com/cortex/content/software

HTML Editor for Word (Windows)
http://www.w3.org/hypertext/WWW/Tools/HTML-Convertor.html

HTML Editor for Adobe PageMaker
http://www.bucknell.edu/bucknellian/dave

HTML Editor for QuarkXPress
http://www.astrobyte.com

List of HTML Editors
http://www.yahoo.com/Computers/World_Wide_Web/HTML_Editors

NaviPress
http://www.navisoft.com/homedoc/press/press.htm

WebMap for the Macintosh
http://www.city.net/cnx/software/webmap.html

Other Sites Mentioned

1996 Olympic Games
ttp://www.atlanta.olympic.org

Antiques World
http://www.webcom.com/~antiques

BarclaySquare
http://www.itl.net/barclaysquare

Buena Vista MoviePlex
http://www.disney.com

CDnow
http://www.cdnow.com

ESPNET SportsZone
http://espnet.sportszone.com

FedEx
http://www.fedex.com

First Virtual InfoHaus!
http://www.infohaus.com

HotWired
http://www.hotwired.com

IUMA
http://www.iuma.com

Interactive Age
http://techweb.cmp.com/techweb/ia

Karen's Tie-Dye Store
http://www.tie-dye.com

Lands' End, Inc.
http://www.landsend.com

Macmillan Bookstore
http://www.mcp.com/cgi-bin/do-bookstore.cgi

MCI
http://www.internetmci.com

Mercury Center Home Page
http://www.sjmercury.com

Mountain Travel*Sobek
http://mtsobek.com/mts

National Public Radio
http://www.npr.org

Network Wizards World Wide Web site
http://www.nw.com

Perspective
http://jcomm.uoregon.edu/~perspect

Pizza Hut
http://www.pizzahut.com

Project 2000
http://www2000.ogsm.vanderbilt.edu

SandCastle Magic!
http://www.sandcastlemagic.com

Sony Online
http://www.sony.com

Steve Mulder
http://www.mcp.com/cgi-bin/mulderpoll

Time
http://pathfinder.com

UPS
http://www.ups.com

The White House
http://www.whitehouse.gov

Appendix B

HTML for Yoyo

This appendix consists of the HTML code (and comments on it) that is referred to in chapter 12.

Please note that tabs have been used to format these documents visually so they are easier to read. Remember that the visual layout of the text has no bearing on the browser's interpretation of the document. All of the extra tabs and spaces between the words and tags could be removed and the documents would still be displayed in the same way.

yoyo-simple.html

This HTML document is designed to work on virtually every browser. It uses a simple horizontal layout, but still makes use of newer tags, like ALT, HEIGHT, and WIDTH, that will improve performance on newer browsers. You can view this document online at

http://www.zender.com/designers-guide-net/yoyodyne/yoyo-simple.html.

Extra Space in Title

An extra space between every character in the title spreads the letters out, making it look a bit more distinctive. Any more than one space will be ignored by the browser.

```
<head>
<title>Y o y o d y n e</title>
</head>
```

WIDTH and HEIGHT Tags

WIDTH and HEIGHT tags allow a browser to display the document's overall layout before the images are loaded. All text will be displayed quickly, then the space left for the images filled in. Right now, only Netscape understands these tags.

```
<body><img src="yoyo-head.gif" width=373 height=192 alt=
"Y o y o d y n e Juggling Equipment"><br><br>
```

ALT Tag

Setting an ALT string in an inline image allows text-only browsers, like Lynx, to display something in place of the image. Other browsers will display this string if image loading is turned off.

BLOCKQUOTE Tag

Browsers have quite a bit of liberty regarding how to interpret the BLOCKQUOTE tag, but usually they will indent a block of text.

```
<blockquote>
O me! you juggler! you canker-blossom!<br>
You thief of love! what, have you come by night<br>
And stolen my love's heart from him?<br>
—"A Midsummer Night's Dream," III.ii.285, Hermia
</blockquote>

<p>
        <a href="catalog.html">
        <img src="catalog.gif"
            alt="[Catalog]"
            width=100
            height=40
            border=0></a><br>

        <a href="ordering.html">
        <img src="ordering.gif"
            alt="[Ordering]"
            width=100
            height=40
            border=0></a><br>

        <a href="info.html">
        <img src="info.gif"
            alt="[Company
            Information]"
            width=100
            height=40
            border=0></a><br>

        <a href="links.html">
        <img src="links.gif"
```

```
                    alt="[Juggling Links]"
                    width=100
                    height=40
                    border=0></a><br>
</body>
```

yoyo-table.html

This HTML document makes use of the newer table tags to make a more vertical layout possible. Unfortunately, at this point only Netscape and Mosaic are able to interpret tables. On other browsers this design will not work very well. You can view it
online at http://www.zender.com/designers-guide-net/yoyodyne/yoyo-table.html.

```
<head>
<title>Y o y o d y n e</title>
</head>
<body>
```

TABLE Tag

The TABLE tag marks the beginning of a table. The border, cellspacing, and cell-
padding options control the size of the border, as well as white space between cells.
At this point, only Netscape understands these controls. Mosaic will always display
the same size border.

```
<tableborder=0
          cellspacing=0
          cellpadding=10>
```

TR Tag

The TR tag marks the beginning of a row in the table.

```
<tr>
          <td colspan=2><img src="yoyo-head.gif"
          width=373 height=192
          alt="Y o y o d y n e Juggling Equipment"><br>
</td>
```

TD Tag

The TD tag, which stands for table data, marks the beginning of an individual cell.
The COLSPAN tag defines the number of columns this particular cell will span. A similar tag, ROWSPAN, does the same for rows.

```
</tr>
<tr>
     <td align=left>
```

ALIGN Tag

The ALIGN tag, which can appear in either TD or TR tags, controls the horizontal justification of a cell's contents. Possible values are left, right, and center. A similar tag,
VALIGN, controls the vertical justification of a cell's contents.

```
          <a href="catalog.html">
          <img src="catalog.gif"
               alt=" [Catalog] "
               width=100
               height=40
               border=0></a><br>

          <a href="ordering.html">
          <img src="ordering.gif"
               alt=" [Ordering] "
               width=100
               height=40
               border=0></a><br>

          <a href="info.html">
          <img src="info.gif"
               alt=" [Company Information] "
               width=100
               height=40
               border=0></a><br>

          <a href="links.html">
          <img src="links.gif"
               alt=" [Juggling Links] "
               width=100
```

```
                    height=40
                    border=0></a><br>
</td>
        <td align=left>
            O me! you juggler! you canker-blossom!<br>
            You thief of love! what,
            have you come by night<br>
            And stolen my love's heart from him?<br>
            —"A Midsummer Night's Dream,"
            III.ii.285, Hermia
        </td>
</tr>
</table>
</body>
```

yoyo-table2.html

The last document, yoyo-table.html, looked great in Netscape, but in older browsers, the layout left quite a bit to be desired. Since a browser simply ignores a tag when it doesn't understand its meaning, if one can create a document that still looks good when all newer tags are removed, it will display adequately on any browser. In this case, the information was rearranged so when all table-related tags are removed, the document ends up looking remarkably similar to our first example, yoyo-simple.html. You can view this document online at http://www.zender.com/ designers-guide-net/yoyodyne/yoyo-table2.html.

A Block of White Space

The PRE tag is used to define a long row of spaces. Any text that is within the PRE tags is displayed on-screen exactly as it appears in the file. This extra white space makes sure that this column appears at the correct width on-screen. To understand the effect it has, try loading this document and removing this line. The difference is greatest in Mosaic 2.0.

```
<head>
<title>Y o y o d y n e</title>
</head>
<body>

<tableborder=0
        cellspacing=0
```

```
                cellpadding=0>
        <tr>
            <td colspan=2><img
            src="yoyo-head2.gif"
            alt="Y o y o d y n e Juggling Equipment">
            <br><br></td>
        </tr>
        <tr>
            <td>
            <pre>                    </pre>
```

Nested Table

This document makes use of "nested tables." This means that the contents of one of the cells in a table is actually another table. This feature allows for very complex layouts to be designed. Remember to keep it as simple as possible, though. It's easy to make mistakes that are difficult to find if one uses a lot of table nesting.

```
            O me! you juggler! you canker-blossom!<br>
            You thief of love! what,have you come by night<br>
            And stolen my love's heart from him?<br>
        -"A Midsummer Night's Dream,"
        III.ii.285, Hermia<br><br>
        </td>
        <td align=right>
            <table   border=0
                  cellspacing=0
                  cellpadding=0>

            <tr>
                <td>
                <a href="catalog.html">
                <img src="catalog.gif"
                    alt="[Catalog]"
                    width=100
                    height=40
                    border=0></a>
            </td>
          </tr>
          <tr>
            <td>
```

```
                    <a href="ordering.html">
                    <img src="ordering.gif"
                        alt="[Ordering]"
                        width=100
                        height=40
                        border=0></a>
                    </td>
                </tr>
                <tr>
                    <td>
                        <a href="info.html">
                        <img src="info.gif"
                            alt="[Company Information]"
                            width=100
                            height=40
                            border=0></a>
                    </td>
                </tr>
                <tr>
                    <td>
                        <a href="links.html">
                        <img src="links.gif"
                            alt="[Juggling Links]"
                            width=100
                            height=40
                            border=0></a>
                    </td>
                </tr>
            </table>
        </td>
</tr>
</table>
</body>
```

The following document is what yoyo-table2.html looks like if you remove all of the table-related tags. Notice that this document is virtually identical to yoyo-simple.html.

```
<head>
<title>Y o y o d y n e</title>
```

```
</head>
<body>


<img  src="yoyo-head2.gif" alt="Y o y o d y n e Juggling
Equipment"><br><br>
<pre>                    </pre>
O me! you juggler! you canker-blossom!<br>
You thief of love! what, have you come by night<br>
And stolen my love's heart from him?<br>
—"A Midsummer Night's Dream," III.ii.285, Hermia<br><br>


<p>
          <a href="catalog.html">
          <img src="catalog.gif"
             alt="[Catalog]"
             width=100
             height=40
             border=0></a><br>

          <a href="ordering.html">
          <img src="ordering.gif"
             alt="[Ordering]"
             width=100
             height=40
             border=0></a><br>

          <a href="info.html">
          <img src="info.gif"
             alt="[Company Information]"
             width=100
             height=40
             border=0></a><br>

          <a href="links.html">
          <img src="links.gif"
             alt="[Juggling Links]"
             width=100
             height=40
             border=0></a><br>
</body>
```

Appendix C

Bibliography

Albers, Josef. *Josef Albers at The Metropolitan Museum of Art*. New York: The Metropolitan Museum of Art, 1971.

Ames, Patrick. *Beyond Paper*. Mountain View, CA: Adobe Press, 1993.

Cotton, Bob and Richard Oliver. *The Cyberspace Lexicon*. London: Phaidon Press Limited, 1994.

Cotton, Bob and Richard Oliver. *Understanding Hypermedia*. London: Phaidon Press Limited, 1994.

Dennis, Anita. "Net Gains." *PUBLISH* 1. 3 (March 1995): 51.

Engst, Adam C. *Internet Starter Kit for Macintosh, Third Edition*. Indianapolis: Hayden Books, 1995.

Engst, Adam C. *Internet Starter Kit for Windows, Second Edition*. Indianapolis: Hayden Books, 1995.

Fahey, Tom. *net.speak: the internet dictionary*. Indianapolis: Hayden Books, 1994.

Foucault, Michel. "What Is an Author?" *Bulletin de la Societe française de Philosophie* 63.3 (1969): 73-104.

Gilster, Paul A. "The Internet Made Easy." *CompuServe Magazine* 14.6 (June 1995): 14.

Holy Bible, New International Version. New York: New York International Bible Society, 1978.

Laurel, Brenda. *Computers as Theatre*. Redding, MA: Addison-Wesley Publishing Co., 1993

Lynch, Patrick J. Yale C/AIM WWW Style Manual. Yale Center for Advanced Instructional Media: http://info.med.yale.edu/caim/StyleManual_Top.HTML, 1995.

Postman, Neil. *Amusing Ourselves to Death*. New York, NY: Viking Penguin, 1985.

Reid, Elizabeth M. *Electropolis: Communication and Community on Internet Relay Chat*. Honours thesis. University of Melbourne, Australia, 1991.

Ruder, Emil. *Typography: A Manual of Design*. Switzerland: Arthur Niggli, Ltd., 1967.

Schweikart, Karl. "Head Farming." *AIGA Minnesota Newsletter*. AIGA Minnesota.

Tufte, Edward. *The Visual Display of Quantitative Information*. Cheshire, CT: Edward R. Tufte, 1983.

Zender, Mike. *Getting Unlimited Impact with Limited Color*. Cincinnati: North Light Books, 1994.

INDEX

A

access providers, 27, 34
　listing, 32
　rates, 29
　redundancy, 31
　speed, 31
Adobe Acrobat, 250
　multiple master fonts, 252
Adobe Acrobat PDF, 131
America Online, 19, 22
Anarchie, 82
antialiasing, 275
Apple (eWorld), 23
Apple Computer site, 365
Arachnid (HTML), 248
Archie, 82, 85, 170
ARPAnet, 7
article delivery service, 200
ASCII
　FTP, 61
　encoding, 43
　　btoa, 44
　text, 237
audience, 297
audio (WWW), 255
　see also sound
Avistar Systems, 67

B

backbones, 17
backgrounds (WWW pages), 288
bandwidths, 17, 280
BBSs (Bulletin Board Systems), 35
binary files (FTP), 61
BinHex files, 43
BITNET, 7
borders, 275
bps (modems), 17
browsers, 40, 59
　HotJava, 241
　Mosaic, 240, 262
　Netscape, 240, 262
　portability, 271
　text-only, 237
　　HTML, 275
btoa (ASCII encoding), 44
bugs (tech support), 173
Bulletin board systems, 35
bulletin boards, 11
business
　article delivery service, 200
　authentication techniques, 213
　combination models, 216
　CommerceNet, 196
　demographics, 208

Library model, 185
netiquette, 181
Netscape, 198
Open Market, 198
Quote.Com, 199
salt lick strategy, 184
selling, 206
soft selling, 179
Sponsorship model, 187
storefronts, 207, 210-212
subscription services, 200
Time Warner, 202
virtual malls, 212-214
catalogs, 40
home pages, 122
searching, 72
Yahoo, 73
CDnow (storefront), 209
CGI (Common Gateway Interface), 290
chatting, *see* IRC
clients, 116
communication, 128
market research, 126
phoning, 129
videoconferencing, 128
clip art, 135
collaborating, 110, 311
color, transparent (GIFs), 274
combination model sites, 216
combining graphics, 282
CommerceNet, 196-197
communication
clients, 128
dialogue, 231
speed, 162
community, 97
compression
GIFs, 281
PKZIP, 44

CompuServe, 19, 21, 172
connections
direct, 37
Internet, 18
online services, 19
PPP, 25
SLIP, 25
consistency of design, 309
context (hypertext), 227
conversion utilities (HTML), 246
Creative Labs, 67
CU-SeeMe (videoconferencing), 65
culture, 313
future, 315
customer service, 177
repetitive requests, 178
soft sell, 179
Cyberspace, 6

D

demographics, 208
design
collaboration, 110
consistency, 309
information sequence, 303
interface, 307
networking, 103
production, 311
tech support, 97
design community, 97
DesignLink site, 104
desktop publishing (WWW), 150
digital printing presses, 154
direct connections (Internet), 37
directories (WWW), 170
dithering (GIFs), 289
dividing files (WWW), 287
documents (HTML), 264

downloading
  freeware, 145
  shareware, 145
  software, 144
DTP Jumplist, 92

E

e-mail, 47, 161
  flaming, 190
  MIME, 49
  multimedia, 49
education, 258, 313
electronic bulletin boards, 11
encryption (WWW), 291
eWorld, 19, 23
exchanging files, 131

F

FAQs, 48, 92-93
  Usenet FAQ archive, 93
file formats, 45
  ASCII encoding, 43
  uucode, 43
files
  BinHex, 43
  compressing, 44
  exchanging, 131
  prepress, 152
  WWW, 287
flaming (e-mail), 190
Florida Law Weekly, 204
fonts, 139, 141
  multiple master (Acrobat), 252
  type, 237
  forms
  HTML, 268
  WWW, 163
free samples, 182-184
freespace (galleries), 107
freeware, 49, 145

FTP, 60
  ASCII files, 61
  binary files, 61
future (culture), 315

G

galleries (freespace), 107
gateways, 25-26
Gibson, William, 6
GIF(graphics), 254
  compression, 281
  dithering, 289
  interlaced, 284
  transparent color, 274
  Gopher, 62
  graphics
  antialiasing, 275
  borders, 275
  clip art, 136
  combining, 282
  GIFs
    compression, 281
    dithering, 289
    interlaced, 284
    transparent color, 274
  height, 286
  high-resolution, 284
  JPEG, 282
  low-resolution, 284
  stock photos, 136
  width, 286
  WWW, 254
groupware, 165

H

head farming, 97
height (graphics), 286
high-resolution graphics, 284
history of Internet, 7
hits (sites), 188

home pages, 12, 116
  catalogs, 122
  HTML, 119
  links, 125
  search engines, 119
  What's New lists, 123
host computers, 8
HotJava, 241
HotWired, 322
  site, 216
HTML (Hypertext Markup Language),
59, 239, 242, 278
  Arachnid, 248
  backgrounds, 288
  conversion utilities, 246
  documents, 264
  forms, 268
  home pages, 119
  imagemaps, 267
  Isindex, 268
  layout software, 248
  links, 266
  portability, 271
  tables, 276
  tags, 266
    Netscape, 269
  text editors, 246
  text-only browsers, 275
  title, 286
  versions, 265
  whitespace, 287
http (hypertext transfer protocol), 41
hypertext, 5, 224-225
  context, 227
hypertext links (WWW), 57

I

imagemaps (HTML), 267
Indexes, 73-74
information processing, 301

information sequence, 303
InfoSeek, 120
interactivity, 231
interfaces, 307
interlaced GIFs, 284
Internet
  ARPAnet, 7
  backbones, 17
  bandwidths, 17
  BITNET, 7
  connections, 18
  culture, 313
  direct connection, 37
  gateways, 25-26
  history, 7
  ISDN lines, 18
  news, 171
  online services, 19
  packets, 25
  PPP accounts, 25
  searching, 72
  SLIP accounts, 25
  TCP/IP, 8
IP (Interent Protocol), 26
IRC (Internet Relay Chat), 68-69
ISDN lines, 18
Isindex (HTML), 268

J-K

JPEG graphics, 254, 282
Jughead, 82, 85

Karen's Tie-Dye Store, 375

L

Land's End (storefront), 207
layout (HTML), 248
library model, 185
links
  home pages, 125
  HTML, 266

LISTSERVs, 55
loading graphics, 284
local access providers, 34
Lotus Notes, 166
low-resolution graphics, 284
lurking, 181
Lycos (search engine), 78, 120, 169

M

Macintosh (WWW), 279
MacTCP, 26
mailing lists, 53-54, 56
   LISTSERVs, 55
   tech suport, 149
malls (virtual), 212, 214
market research, 126
McLuhan, Marshall, 13, 313
MEDLINE database, 205
Microsoft Network, 19, 24
MIME (Multipurpose Internet Mail Extensions), 49
modems, 17
   bps, 17
   PPP, 27
   SLIP, 27
   MOOs (MUD Object-Oriented), 70
   Mosaic, 240, 262
MUDs (Multi-User Dungeons), 70-71
   collaboration, 112
multimedia, 229
   e-mail, 49
multiple master fonts, 252
museums, 107
MUSHs (Multi-User Simultaneous Hallucinations), 71

N

navigating
   researching strategies, 303
   strategies, 305

Netiquette, 92
   business, 181
NetPhone, 111, 128
Netscape, 59, 240, 262
   business, 198
   HTML tags, 269
Network Wizards site, 8
networking, 103
   DesignLink, 103-104
Neuromancer (William Gibson), 6
news (Internet), 171
newsgroups, 7, 50, 53
   tech support, 101, 149
newspapers, 201
   San Jose Mercury News, 203
   Wall Street Journal, 203
   USA Today, 201
NPR (National Public Radio), 339
NSFN (National Science Foundation Network), 8

O

on-line research, 167
Online services, 19, 172
   America Online, 22
   CompuServe, 21
   eWorld, 23
   Microsoft Network, 24
   Prodigy, 23
Open Market, 198
   Time Warner, 202

P

packets, 25
paperless office, 163
PDF (portable document format), 264
   WWW, 250
phoning clients, 129
pipeline (video), 67
PKZIP, 44

POP (Points of Presence), 28
portability (browsers), 271
ports, 72
PPP accounts, 25, 27
prepress files, 152
printing (digital presses), 154
Prodigy, 19, 23
production, 311
protocols
    IP(Internet Protocol), 26
    MacTCP, 26
    TCP/IP, 8
public domain software, 49
public relations, 178-180, 191
    markets, 189
publishing, 205
    newspapers, 201
        San Jose Mercury News, 203
        Wall Street Journal, 203
        USA Today, 201
    subscription services, 200
        MEDLINE, 205
        Florida Law Weekly, 204

Q-R

Quote.Com (business), 199

rates (access providers), 29
Razorfish site, 380
redundancy (access providers), 31
registering home pages
    catalogs, 122
    search engines, 119
repetitive requests, 178
research, 296
    audience, 297
    information processing, 301
    navigation, 303
    on-line, 167
    users, 299

S

salt lick strategy (business), 184
San Jose Mercury News, 203
SandCastle Magic (storefront), 211
search engines, 40, 72, 77, 168
    Anarchie , 82
    Archie, 82, 85
    home page registration, 119
    InfoSeek, 120
    Jughead, 82, 85
    Lycos, 78, 120
    Submit It!, 121
    Veronica, 82, 85
    WebCrawler, 120
    WWW, 169
searching, 72
    catalogs, 72
    indexes, 73
security (WWW), 291
selling, 206
    Library model, 185
    salt lick strategy, 184
    Sponsorship model, 187
sending prepress files, 152
    servers
    WAIS, 63
    WWW, 57
shareware, 7, 49, 145
    free samples, 182
sites
    Apple Computer, 365
    combination models, 216
    hits, 188
    HotWired, 322
    Karen's Tie-Dye Store, 375
    Network Wizards, 8
    NPR(National Public Radio), 339
    Razorfish, 380
    vivid studios, 347

White House, 354
Yale C/AIM WWW Style Manual, 333
SLIP accounts, 25, 27
soft selling, 179
software
  downloading, 144
  free samples, 182
  public domain, 49
software manufacturers
(tech support), 95
Software.net (storefront), 209
speed
  access providers, 31
  communication, 162
Sponsorship model, 187
Stock photos, 135
Storefronts, 207, 210-212
  CDnow, 209
  SandCastle Magic, 211
  software.net, 209
Submit It!, 121
Subscription services, 200
  MEDLINE, 205
  Florida Law Weekly, 204

T

Tables (HTML), 276
Tags (HTML), 239, 266
  Netscape, 269
TCP/IP (Transmission Control
Protocol/Internet Protocol), 8
tech support, 148
  bug fixes, 173
  design, 97
  DTP Jumplist, 92
  FAQs, 92-93
  mailing lists, 149
  newsgroups, 101, 149
  software manufacturers, 94
  WWW, 151

Technobabble, 6
Telecommuting, 164
Telephone (NetPhone), 129
Television, 313
Telnet, 72
Terabytes, 60
Text editors (HTML), 246
Text-only browsers, 237
  HTML, 275
Time Warner, 202
title (HTML), 286
Tower of Babel, 9, 315
tracking hits, 188
training, 258, 313
transparent color (GIFs), 274
TurboGopher, 62
type fonts, 237

U

URLs (Uniform Resource Locators),
40-41
  http, 41
  Zender, 5
USA Today (newspaper), 201
Usenet newsgroups, 50, 53
  FAQ archive, 93
users, 299
Uucode, 43

V

Veronica, 170
versions of HTML, 265
video
  pipeline, 67
  WWW, 256
video conferencing, 64-65, 111
  clients, 128
  software, 67
viewing WWW documents, 261
virtual malls, 212-214

virtual museums, 107
Vivid studios site, 347
VRML (Virtual Reality Modeling Language), 253

W

WAIS (Wide Area Information Servers), 63-64, 170
Wall Street Journal, 203
Weather Page (WWW), 57
WebCrawler, 120, 169
What's New lists (home pages), 123
White House site, 354
whitespace (HTML), 287
width (graphics), 286
Windows (WWW), 279
WWW (World Wide Web), 56, 238
  Adobe Acrobat, 250
  audio, 255
  bandwidth, 280
  browsers, 40, 59
    portability, 271
  CGI (Common Gateway Interface), 290
  consistency, 309
  desktop publishing, 150
  directories, 170
  dividing files, 287
  encryption, 291
  forms, 163
  graphics, 254
    antialiasing, 275
    combining, 282
    height, 286
    width, 286
  home pages, 12, 116, 119
  catalogs, 122
    links, 125
    search engines, 119
    What's New lists, 123

HTML, 59, 239, 242, 278
  Arachnid, 248
  backgrounds, 288
  conversion utilities, 246
  documents, 264
  imagemaps, 267
  layout software, 248
  links, 266
  tags, 266
  text editors, 246
  text-only browsers, 275
  title, 286
  versions, 265
  whitespace, 287
  hypertext links, 57
  Macintosh, 279
  Netscape, 59
  PDF, 250
  search engines, 169
  security, 291
  servers, 57
  tech support, 151
  URLs, 40-41
  video, 256
  viewing, 261
  VRML, 253
  Weather Page, 57
  Windows, 279
WYSIWYG (What You See Is What You Get), 249

X-Y-Z

Yahoo (catalog), 73, 170
Yale C/AIM WWW Style Manual, 333
Zender URL, 5